Probation, Parole, and Community Corrections

A Reader

Probation, Parole, and Community Corrections

A Reader

edited by

Lawrence F. Travis III

Contributors:

Harry E. Allen
Todd R. Clear
David M. Crean
Robert G. Culbertson
Francis T. Cullen
Mark C. Dean-Myrda
Rolando V. del Carmen
Thomas Ellsworth
Timothy J. Flanagan
John J. Gibbs
Edward J. Latessa
Gennaro F. Vito
George P. Wilson

Waveland Press, Inc.
Prospect Heights, Illinois

For information about this book, write or call:

Waveland Press, Inc.
P.O. Box 400
Prospect Heights, Illinois 60070
(312) 634-0081

Contents

V. Participants: Client and Staff Views

VI. Treatment Programs

VII. Effectiveness

Preface

Nearly two years ago I felt a desire to compile a book of readings on the general topic of community-based corrections. The field is so diverse and dynamic that a single author approach can not do justice to the variety of issues and topics which need to be addressed. Rather, a compendium of essays on the issues in community corrections appeared to have greater promise of providing both the depth and breadth of coverage desired.

The intervening time has been a period of both tremendous satisfaction and great frustration. It was frustrating to have to decide which of the many issues would be identified and discussed, it was difficult to accept the fact that "it" could not all be done in one volume. The reward and satisfaction have come from the opportunity I was afforded to work with the contributors to this volume.

I am very proud of the works included in this book. I am flattered that the authors devoted so much of their time and considerable expertise to this project. I am pleased to have played a role in bringing these papers to completion and circulation. For these reasons, I owe a great debt of gratitude to all of the contributors.

For support of a more substantive nature, I would also like to thank Neil Rowe of Waveland for his encouragement, understanding and insights. Karen Rohman deserves thanks for her efforts in copying manuscripts, correcting mistakes and generally doing all of those tasks that must be done to prepare a manuscript for publication. Pat Travis is to be thanked for understanding and for insuring that I see this project through to completion.

Lawrence F. Travis III
Cincinnati, Ohio

I
Introduction

Probation, Parole, and Community Corrections in Contemporary America

It seems that whenever the topics of punishment of criminal offenders or corrections arise thoughts tend to focus on such things as capital punishment or the fortress prison. Yet, the overwhelming majority of criminal offenders in the United States will serve some portion (frequently all) of their sentence in the community. At any given time it is safe to estimate that over 1.5 million offenders are under probation or parole supervision. This compares to less than a half million serving sentences in prison to yield a ratio of community corrections: prison population of 3:1.

Community correction programs serve more people and touch more lives in any given year than do prisons. If the numbers of people incarcerated in the nation's jails (local, community incarceration facilities) and those participating in the myriad of diversion programs are added to the community corrections total, this numerical superiority of the community corrections population becomes even more overwhelming. Still, the popular conception of corrections centers on imprisonment. The purpose of this book is to review and evaluate existing correctional practices which operate in a community setting.

In doing so, the complexity of the agencies, practices, philosophies, goals and people that have been pigeon-holed under the simple rubric "community corrections" becomes apparent. The readings included in this book amply illustrate the dynamic nature of community corrections. Probation and parole supervision comprise the traditional "core" of community based efforts at criminal correction. As in the past, the lion's share of the community corrections population is served through the auspices of probation and parole supervision. Contemporary community supervision practices however reflect the changes and dynamism that characterizes corrections in the community.

Despite the relatively recent origin of state-wide correctional programs emphasizing the community and the development and spread of innovative programs, current efforts represent the extension of a long-standing tradition of community involvement in the control and punishment of crim-

3

inal offenders. What is new about community corrections is more semantic and procedural than substantive. Even the label "community based corrections" is of recent vintage.

Stressing the need to attain "fit" between offenders and the community, the President's Commission on Crime and Administration of Justice Task Force on Corrections articulated the correctional goal of "reintegration." The task of corrections was to change both offenders and communities so that people could lead crime-free lives. The Task Force noted:

> The main treatment implication of reintegration concepts is the value of community-based corrections. Most of the tasks that are now carried out by correctional officials would still be required if the goal of reintegration were adopted: diagnosis and classification, counseling, application of necessary controls and sanctions.
>
> But probation and parole would have wider functions than are now usually emphasized within their casework guidance orientation...They would have to take much more responsibility....(p. 9).

In addition to an expanded role for traditional probation and parole supervision envisioned by the Task Force, a variety of new programs were developed during the late 1960s and 1970s. Diversion programs, split-sentences, restitution, community service orders, pre-trial release programs and the like proliferated. Many of these new programs were grafted on to already existing probation and parole services, some sprang into being as separate agencies and more were eventually separated from traditional community supervision caseload responsibilities. A complementary growth in private and charitable community programs for criminal and delinquent offenders also occurred.

Thus, by the 1980s there existed a set of community based correctional and diversion programs across the nation. This growth of such programs coincided with the growth of prison populations and was fed by the crisis of overcrowding. At least into the near future, the continuation of community based correctional programs seems assured in order to cope with the overflow population of our prisons.

The task of the future is to plan for the logical and rational development of community based correctional programs. It is with this goal in mind that the papers included in this book were written. Each of the contributors have examined one component of the total "community-based corrections" picture but all have done so within the context of identifying the future needs and goals of community corrections. Thus, while each of these original papers can stand alone, when taken together they provide a comprehensive overview of contemporary community corrections and provide guidance for policies for the future.

The papers are organized into six sections with each section devoted to a central theme or issue in community corrections. The six sections, in order, are History, Context, Purposes, People, Treatment, and Effectiveness.

In the first section Dean-Myrda and Cullen examine the long tradition of community corrections. They suggest that the community has always served as the basis for correctional practices and support their argument with reference to the history of American corrections. This paper places contemporary community based corrections into historical perspective and illustrates how correctional practices reflect social and intellectual developments. They conclude with the observation that community based programs appear to be the most humanitarian direction in which American corrections can move in the future.

The context of community corrections is the focus of the next section. Professor Clear examines the implications of bureaucratic structure and the public service nature of community correctional agencies for the operation of programs. He identifies five critical concerns for managers and suggests that the administrators of community corrections agencies devote their attention to these larger issues to ensure healthy organizations for the future. Professor Del Carmen next reminds us that the law is a central defining trait of all correctional practices. It is within the constraints of Constitutional and statutory limitations that community corrections agencies perform their tasks. He then reviews recent legislation and court rulings which have effected the operations of community based correctional agencies. He suggests strategies for administrators and staff and anticipates future legal developments.

In the third section the purposes of community based corrections are examined. Professor Vito identifies the traditional goals of criminal punishment and corrections and then proceeds to analyze how well community correctional programs work to meet those goals. His general conclusion is that community correctional programs can be as successful in achieving the ends of criminal punishment as any other penalties. A second major purpose of community based corrections is to serve as an efficient alternative to incarceration. Professor Latessa examines the effectiveness of different structures of community corrections practices on the costs of corrections. With a focus on intensive supervision as an alternative to incarceration, he concludes that substantial savings can be realized through a judicious use of probation in lieu of incarceration, and that such savings may be attained with no appreciable increase in the risk of new criminality by offenders.

The people involved in community corrections serve as both its greatest resource (staff) and its most important product (clients). In this section Mr. Crean, himself a probation officer, examines community corrections from the perspective of agency staff. He identifies the rewards and frustrations of "doing corrections" in the community. He suggests that community corrections staff would be well advised to enlist the support and assistance of the public in their work. The acquisition of public support and understanding would serve to reduce the frustrations, ease the workload and enhance the rewards of working in community corrections. Professor Gibbs reports the perspective of probationers. The clients of community supervision would appear to have many of the same aspirations and reservations about such programs as do staff and researchers. The views of probationers are mixed, reflecting various balances of values on individual liberty, respect, and support needs.

The fifth section is devoted to an examination of the treatment approaches commonly used in community corrections programs. Professors Ellsworth and Culbertson examine the treatment strategies and techniques of probation officers. They emphasize the need for risk and needs assessment and the matching of treatments to needs. They conclude with observations on how current treatment approaches can be better organized and applied. Professor Wilson examines treatment approaches that occur within a residential setting. Focusing on halfway house programs, he examines various counseling approaches, identifies the needs of special populations and discusses the future of residential programs for criminal offenders.

The final section tackles the question of effectiveness. Professor Flanagan analyzes the effectiveness of community supervision. By reviewing the literature on the effectiveness of parole supervision at reducing recidivism, he provides an up-to-date summary of what is known about the effectiveness of supervision. He concludes, unfortunately, that we know very little. His suggestion is that policy-makers take no drastic steps until such time as we have had the opportunity to test the effectiveness of supervision rigorously. Professor Allen then examines the effectiveness of community corrections on a more global plane. He identifies the weaknesses of current efforts and succinctly summarizes the arguments against the further expansion and development of community corrections. Nonetheless, taking the long view, Professor Allen concludes that community based corrections have proven to be worthy of continued support. He argues that such programs will be economically, ideologically and politically necessary in the future. He suggests that now is the time to take affirmative steps towards that future.

It is hoped that these eleven readings represent the state of the art in community based corrections. It is probably not possible to examine every issue and every program adequately in one volume. As a whole, these readings direct attention to the most pressing issues in community based corrections, bring to bear the most current knowledge, and provide guideposts for future actions. The reader is encouraged to go beyond these papers and conduct an independent examination of community corrections. The critical ingredient in the development of sound policies for the future is that decisions be based on the results of such investigations.

II
A History

The Panacea Pendulum
An Account of Community as a Response to Crime

Mark C. Dean-Myrda
Francis T. Cullen
University of Cincinnati

Recently, James Finckenauer revealed that American efforts aimed at controlling and preventing adolescent waywardness have been dominated by a futile search for panaceas. "One of the simultaneous causes and effects of our failures and frustrations in dealing with juvenile crime," he stated, "may be the refueling of a continuing search for the cure all" (Finckenauer, 1982:4). Notably, a similar assessment may be made of traditional approaches to thinking about the containment of adult criminality. Indeed, this "panacea phenomenon"—characterized by a cycle of unrealistic expectations, failure and dissatisfaction leading to the search for yet another foolproof elixir for the crime problem—has pervaded the entire history of American correctional policy.

Intimately connected with many of the panaceas embraced over the years has been the notion that the "community" is an integral component to a final solution of the crime problem. However, reformers of differing generations have manifested little consensus as to whether this crime-eradicating community lies within the larger society or within a specially created, institutional environment. Policymakers have also disagreed on whether such a community should be fundamentally benign or, alternatively, punitive in its orientation. Criminal justice reforms have therefore followed a pendular path, swinging between opposite extremes on these two key dimensions.

In this light, the intention here is to present an historical account of the role that the concept of community has played in the search for a cure to the ostensibly intractable problem of crime. In short, we will investigate in a beginning way how "community" has been involved in the panacea pendulum that has long prevailed within the arena of American correctional policy.

9

Community Punishment

The concept of community as a factor in American criminal justice policy can be traced back to the pre-revolution colonial period. At this time, however, the community was viewed as neither a cause of criminal behavior nor as an all-encompassing cure for it. Rather, the colonists inherited from England a religious explanation of deviance as the work of Satan (Rothman, 1971:15). Criminals were often thought to be possessed by demons or evil spirits, or to have made pacts with the Devil through such things as witchcraft, black magic, and sorcery. Punishment was therefore harsh, not so much because there was confidence that the wicked could be easily transformed into upstanding citizens but rather because it proclaimed the evil of sin and the sanctity of God's laws. As Walker (1980: 13) has remarked, "The colonists took a pessimistic view of humankind: man was a depraved creature cursed by original sin. There was no hope of 'correcting' or 'rehabilitating' the offender. An inscrutable God controlled the fate of the individual."

That the majority of these sanctions were carried out in the community itself—not behind the high walls of an institution—is also significant. Public punishments and executions provided an important opportunity for the rest of the community residents to reaffirm their commitment to one another and to reestablish bonds of mutual trust (cf. Erikson, 1963). By the community binding together to inflict a sanction that rectified the victimization of an individual citizen, social ties among the residents were strengthened. To fully understand the signficicance of this, one must bear in mind the influence of the frontier ethic on early American culture. Settlements were established at the edge of a vast and threatening wilderness. In order to survive in such a potentially hostile environment, it was functional for settlers to form closely knit communities, work together, and help each other. Undoubtedly, the early settlers were keenly aware of this interdependence, and that awareness shaped their methods of dealing with lawbreakers. The harsh, public punishments satisfied society's need to identify and single out the offender, and allowed the townspeople to reassure one another that they were different from him or her in some fundamental way. We can thus begin to appreciate the use of such "curious" practices as tarring and feathering, branding, mutilation, forcing the criminal to wear a scarlet letter, banishment, and the use of the pillory and the stocks (Earle, 1969; Newman, 1978:112-113). Rothman (1971:49) observed that in colonial times, "the offender was held up to the ridicule of his neighbors, a meaningful punishment and important deterrent where communities are closely knit." He further noted that the use of such punishments "presumed a society in which reputation was an important element in social control, where men ordered their behavior in fear of a neighbor's scorn." (p. 50)

As the colonies prospered and population centers emerged, the colonists' ideas of crime causation, and consequently of crime suppression, began to change. This change is largely attributable to the Enlightenment (or Age of Reason as it is alternatively labeled), an ideological movement that took place during the last half of the Eighteenth century. In a nutshell, Enlightenment Era philosophy said that traditional authority should be closely scrutinized and discarded whenever it seemed irrational. Such thinking led American statesmen such as Ben Franklin to criticize many aspects of British rule, including the Parliament's practice of banishing felons to the colonies (Silberman, 1978:28). The guiding power of the church was also diminishing in strength in some circles, and being replaced by the appeal of a scientific worldview.

This social climate allowed Cesare Beccaria, father of the Classical School of criminology, to interpret crime in a political fashion, rather than simply attributing it to demonic possession. In 1764, Beccaria published an attack on the legal system of the time, asserting that it was arbitrary and overly severe. He believed that criminal conduct was an expression of individual freedom, and that the only justification for curtailing such freedom was that society would be unable to function if crime was left unpunished. According to Beccaria, the purpose of punishment was deterrence, both of the offender and of potential offenders. Therefore, both the legal code and the penalties for breaking it had to be made public knowledge, and had to be universally applied to all citizens without regard for power or wealth. Only if the punishment was certain would it be an effective deterrent (Duffee et al., 1978:253-255). Rationality, not custom, should inform the construction of the justice apparatus. As Beccaria (1963:99) concluded:

> From what has thus far been demonstrated, one may deduce a general theorem of considerable utility, though hardly conformable with custom, the usual legislator of nations; it is this: In order for punishment not to be, in every instance, an act of violence of one or of many against a private citizen, it must be essentially public, prompt, necessary, the least possible in the given circumstances, proportionate to the crimes, dictated by the laws.

Institutional Treatment:
The Rise of the Therapeutic Community

The paradigm of the Classical School set the stage for the first true crime panacea in America. When crime was attributed to a person's innate sinfulness and Satan's schemes, there could be little hope for eradicating it. However, if crime was viewed as the product of free and rational choice, then a simple manipulation of punishments could be used to render such choices unfeasible, and crime could be virtually wiped out.

Following the American Revolution, policy-makers in the United States readily embraced Classical School values and turned to the task of setting differential penalties for various crimes (Barnes, 1972:121). However, many of the punishments which had previously been imposed with regularity were beginning to fall by the wayside. Banishment was eventually abandoned because the growth of cities made it impractical (Rothman, 1971:50). Corporal punishment was also denounced, partially because industrialization created a demand for human labor, thereby increasing the value of human lives and limbs. Reformers needed a new punishment to use in place of those which were being discarded.

It was the Pennsylvania Quakers, advocates of more widespread use of imprisonment, who solved the dilemma and were instrumental in establishing prisons as the primary criminal sanction in the United States. Until the late 1700s, imprisonment was rarely used as a penalty for common law violations. Instead, for all but the exceptional, offenders were institutionalized only until a court hearing could be arranged, or, if convicted, until the punishment could be meted out. As Mitford (1971:33) has commented, prisons

> were reserved for persons of quality, state prisoners, the prince, queen, statesmen who had fallen afoul of the reigning monarch, the philosopher, mathematician, religious heretic suspected of harboring dangerous or subversive ideas. Lowlier offenders were detained in prison only while awaiting trial. In colonial America as in Europe, the standard punishment for the pick-pocket, the thief, the highwayman was hanging; for lesser offenders, mutilation, the stocks, public brandings and floggings.

By contrast, the Quakers were enthusiastic supporters of incarceration as a regular reaction to crime for two major reasons. First, in the face of social forces that were rapidly precipitating the modernization of society, they felt that the very fabric of their community was coming unglued. This subsequent anxiety over the attenuation of their traditional way of life lent much legitimacy to the conclusion that society's ills—including crime—were firmly rooted in the disorder now burdening their community. In turn, this reasoning suggested that the cure for the criminally wayward lay in removing this population from the corrupting influences of a disorganized communal existence. The panacea for crime thus was manifest: place offenders in the controlled environment of an institution so as to isolate them from the moral depravity that they had not yet learned to resist. Such a therapeutic community would indoctrinate the inmate into the values of religion, hard work, and discipline, and then return the offender to society as a useful, productive, law-abiding citizen. Clearly, then, the Quakers optimistically felt that a comprehensive solution to crime was possible if only a special community based on traditional moral values were to be created and vigorously promoted.

The second factor which led the Quakers to promote prisons was their belief that offenders could not be reformed unless they came to recognize their sinfulness and repent for it (Menninger, 1966:222). The prison experience provided an opportunity to do just that; the convict was placed in solitary confinement, allowed no contaminating contact from either society or fellow prisoners, and was furnished a copy of the Bible as reading material. An initial experiment in the construction of such institutions, dubbed "penitentiaries," occurred at the Walnut Street jail in Philadelphia during the late 1700s. A more systematic reform was undertaken three decades later and achieved the opening of penitentiaries in both the eastern and western parts of the state.

The new system was not without its problems. Visiting foreign dignitaries such as Alexis de Tocqueville and his colleague Gustave de Beaumont criticized the Pennsylvania system as "conducive to depression and insanity, and endangering life" (Menninger, 1966:222). The very popularity of the system among judges was in itself a problem, as they were sentencing people to prison at a faster rate than institutions could be built and staffed. Fogel (1975:17) observed that "as the population increased, housing classification gave way to overcrowding and personal attention yielded to mass care."

The "Auburn system," originally designed as a test of the Quaker system (Menninger, 1966:222), was soon modified to provide an alternative style of prison management. Implemented in the institution located in Auburn, New York, this system aimed "to change...inmates' behavior, rather than their character—to make them, if not better, at least more obedient to the criminal law" (Silberman, 1978: 504). Maintaining physical separation of prisoners at night, the Auburn regime used rigid rules and discipline (instead of cells, as in the rival Quaker system) to achieve psychological isolation during the day. Elam Lynds, the first warden at Auburn (Silberman, 1978:504), was characterized by Fogel (1975:22) in this way:

> Lynds saw all dishonest men as cowards needing to be ruled by fear and intimidation accomplished by breaking their spirits...He saw the purpose of prison as punishment and terror, not reformation.

A major advantage to the Auburn system was that it made it possible to use congregate inmate labor. Prison industry flourished from this time until well into the Industrial Revolution, and the income it generated made the institutions less expensive to operate. Industry enjoyed the steady supply of cheap labor, and "when the new factory system began to show an excess of receipts over expenditures, the legislatures were satisfied and the (Auburn) penitentiary system was assured its place in public administration" (Fogel, 1975:28). The concept of prison as panacea seemed firmly entrenched.

Events in the succeeding years, however, did little to foster the conclusion that the penitentiary would in fact achieve the grand designs claimed for it by reformers only a few years before. As is common today, the population of offenders eligible for incarceration quickly outstripped available cell space. The resulting overcrowding undermined the capacity of prison authorities to enforce a regimen of total silence—particularly as offenders were double-celled. But this was not all. Those sent to prison proved less malleable than reformers had anticipated; indeed, the task of reformation was made difficult because only habitual criminals—not first offenders as the reformers had hoped—were being housed in the state's institutions. Further, the social characteristics of the wayward were changing. It was now evident that prisons were crammed with immigrants and other native poor. Many citizens were thus unsure that such people were reformable, and felt comfortable with the mere fact that the members of this dangerous class were being caged where they could not prey on the innocent.

In light of these considerations, it was increasingly untenable to sustain the notion that the communities prevailing within the prisons were anything approaching panaceas. Rather, it was evident that institutions were fulfilling the social function of incapacitating treacherous offenders, many of whom were seen as biologically defective. If "the promise of reform had built up the asylums," Rothman (1971:240) has observed, "the functionalism of custody perpetuated them." Indeed, the very places which had been established "to exemplify the humanitarian advances of republican government became an embarrassment and a rebuke...the evidence was incontrovertible that brutality and corruption were endemic to the institutions" (Rothman, 1980:17).

In 1870, the first Congress on the National Prison Association met in Cincinnati to discuss the crisis besetting America's prisons (Mitford, 1971: 35-36). Admitting that the system had been distorted by abuses of authority, they reaffirmed the idea that a proper prison community could effect the reform of criminals (Rothman, 1980:31). To help accomplish this task, they proposed a reclassification scheme for prisoners, based on merit, and a revolutionary sentencing policy: the indeterminate sentence. Stating that "hope is a more potent agent than fear" (Fogel, 1975:32), the *Declaration of Principles* drawn up by the Congress called for "peremptory sentences...to be replaced by those of an indeterminate duration—sentences . limited only by satisfactory proof of reformation" (Fogel, 1975:32). In theory, this took the decision of sentence length away from the keepers and placed it in the hands of the kept. Threats and harsh discipline would no longer be needed, since the convicts would enthusiastically and energetically work toward their own rehabilitation, and consequently their own release.

Seven years would see the opening of a new institutional community designed around the 1870 *Declaration of Principles*. Elmira housed only young, first-time felons whom the courts considered redeemable. Once sentenced to Elmira, a criminal could be released at any time, not to exceed the maximum penalty prescribed by law. Zebulon Brockway, superintendent at Elmira, devised a three tiered classification system for prisoners (cf. Brockway, 1969). New inmates were assigned to the middle level at entry, and stayed there until their behavior warranted demotion to the lower level or promotion to the higher one. Movement to a higher level also brought with it better quarters and privileges, as well as the possiblity of eventually winning release. Elmira claimed an eighty percent success rate, and the grumbling about dismantling the system began to subside. Elmira proved that the concept of imprisonment was not faulty; the blame for failure lay in the personnel who ran other facilities (Rothman, 1980: 35-36). However, while the idea that the prison community can be a panacea had weathered a severe challenge, little was done at this point to induce wardens to emulate Elmira. Without a mandate to reform, the penal system virtually ignored Elmira and continued to do business as usual. This condition of stagnation was to persist until the early 1900s.

The Beginnings of Community Corrections

In contrast, the three decades between the 1900s and the 1930s resulted in widespread, sweeping changes, not only in the criminal justice system but throughout American society. This was the Progressive Era—the "Age of Reform" (Hofstadter, 1955). As technology and the pressures of demand increased production, wave after wave of immigrants poured into the urban areas seeking employment. These immigrants, with their strange languages and foreign customs, tended to settle next to one another, forming little ethnic pockets in poorer sections of town. Immigrant neighborhoods soon became characterized by high crime rates (Shaw and McKay, 1932:11). This was attributed partially to conflicts between neighboring ethnic groups, but even more so to the immigrants' refusal to give up the security of their Old World beliefs. This ethnocentrism, Progressives believed, prevented the immigrants from taking advantage of the opportunities offered in America, and caused the newcomers to fall into acute poverty. Deprivation then led the immigrants to excessive drinking as an avenue of escape and to the exploration of illegitimate means of achieving prosperity.

The solution proposed by Progressive reformers was to turn the nation into a "melting pot." Through education, the immigrants would be persuaded to give up their backward ways and would be taught English. They would then be inculcated with values of honesty, hard work, thrift, and hygiene. Fully Americanized, they would finally be able to overcome their shortcomings and rise into the ranks of successful middle-class citizens. They would no longer have any reason to engage in criminal activity, and crime would be largely eradicated (Rothman, 1980:48-49).

Within the correctional system itself, Progressive designs were denoted by three key components. The first of these was a focus on treatment rather than on punishment. This view was largely an outgrowth of the Positivist School of Criminology, established by Cesare Lombroso in the late 1800s. Whereas the Classical School saw offenders as exercising considerable individual freedom and weighing the costs and benefits of crime, Lombroso's view took a much more deterministic view of human conduct. After enumerating various determinants of behavior, especially those of a biological nature, Lombroso concluded that criminals were incapable of exercising free choice and therefore it made no sense to punish them. Instead, "punishment should be replaced by scientific treatment of criminals calculated to protect society" (Duffee, et al., 1978:257).

An insistence on individualized treatment was the second hallmark of Progressive criminal justice reforms. This stance was largely a byproduct of the positivist emphasis on determinism. As Rothman (1980:53) explained:

> Reformers believed that the environmental causes of crime were so varied that no one general prescription could fit all cases. Only a one-to-one approach could uncover the slums' effects on the offender (cf. Barnes, 1972).

This concern for the individual offender dovetailed nicely with the third factor which distinguished Progressive intervention in the lives of law violators: an implicit trust in the benign power of the State to do good. As Rothman put it, "Ameliorative action had to be fitted specifically to each individual's special needs, and therefore required a maximum of flexibility and discretion" (1980:50). Consequently, Progressives were willing to give tremendous discretion and power to the state, primarily because they foresaw no reason for the state to abuse it. The government would no longer be punishing criminals. Instead, it would be responsible for reforming them into upwardly mobile citizens. The resocialization of criminals seemed to Progressives to be a win-win proposition, in which the offender was helped by the state to find his or her niche in society, and as a result was no longer driven to victimize others (Rothman, 1980:60).

Fueled by their ideological fervor and buoyed by a favorable social climate, the Progressives embarked on a campaign to renovate the criminal justice system. In notable contrast to the thinking of the Quaker and Auburn reformers of nearly a century before, the Progressives did not hold a dark vision of the prevailing social order. To be sure, certain areas of the city were seen as distinctly criminogenic and it was agreed that it was not safe to leave everyone free in society. Nonetheless, unlike the founders of the penitentiary who felt that the cure-all for the criminality rested in the re-creation of traditional orderly communities within the impenetrable confines of the penitentiary, Progressives neither looked backward for solutions nor manifested a fundamental mistrust of the principles that were now being used to organize socio-political arrangements.

It is thus instructive that attempts to construct a therapeutic prison environment took one of two paths. On the one hand, there was a complete acceptance of the new, scientific view of a "rational" response to the criminally wayward. Such deviants should not be the focus of vengeance, but rather should be placed in hospital-like settings where they would be treated just as any other sick patient would be. A community fashioned after the "medical model" would allow for the individualized treatment of the malady that drove the unfortunate beyond the confines of the law.

On the other hand, some reformers were less enthralled with the magic of medicine. But, again, they did not see past times as holding answers for the special probems of their day. Rather, they felt that the panacea for crime lay in transporting the dominant, *existing* community within the prison walls. The task was not to insulate offenders from the larger society per se, but to introduce them to the wonders of true American citizenship. It was clear to the Progressives that inmates — many of whom were not native stock — could not become contributing citizens unless they lived in a prison environment that approximated a normal community on the outside. Imposing strict silence and rigid discipline would only foster unnatural social interaction and dependence, and retard successful reintegration into society upon release from the penitentiary. A truly "progressive" solution thus involved creating a vibrant and thoroughly American social order within the institution. At its best, this meant experimenting — as did Thomas Mott Osborne — with the establishment of a fully democratic community in which convicts would learn good citizenship by engaging in the very act of participating in the governance of their own society (Rothman, 1980:117-119).

However, reformers of the day did not halt their reasoning here. Their faith in the ultimate goodness of the American order furnished them with the belief that not all offenders need remain incarcerated or even suffer this fate initially. Rather, it was asserted that with proper supervision by a state official who could be both caring and stern when necessary, many offenders might be taught to conform within the confines of their local environment. Indeed, the policies of parole and probation were trumpeted as important innovations, and won implementation across the nation. Specifically, between 1900 and the middle part of the 1920s, the number of states with parole rose from a handful to forty-four (Cavender, 1982:37), while probation was instituted in two-thirds of all states for adults and in every state for juveniles (Rothman, 1980:44). Notably, these reforms signalled the emergence of the idea that treatment *within* the community — as opposed to the artificial creation of a therapeutic prison community or, for that fact, punishment within the community as was the case in colonial times — constituted an integral part of the cure for America's crime problem.

Now the precursor of the modern parole system was developed by Alexander Maconochie, superintendant of the British penal colony at Norfolk Island, Australia. In 1840, Maconochie introduced a plan to issue "tickets of leave" to prisoners who had successfully served the majority of their sentences. They could then obtain employment and make other necessary arrangements before the actual expiration of their sentences.

Convicts who showed signs of recidivating could be returned to the penal colony to serve the remainder of their sentences (Eriksson, 1976:81-88; Cavender, 1982:13-14).

For the Progressives, parole went hand in hand with the indeterminate sentence, which they backed strongly. Indeterminate sentencing meant that they could do two things. They could adjust the length of sentence to correspond to the needs of the individual offender, and they could maintain control over an offender until they had rehabilitated the person. The alternative policy of determinate sentences and hence of mandatory release from prison was of much concern to the Progressives. Parole represented the successful completion of the prison treatment program, and it provided for additional supervision while the transition to life outside was made. Mandatory release, on the other hand, risked sending convicts back into society regardless of their condition. Having been isolated from society and lacking the prospect to earn a shorter sentence through genuine self-improvement, it was little wonder that such offenders were unable to readjust upon re-entry and eventually recidivated.

For those whose violations were not serious enough to warrant the intensive therapy of incarceration, Progressives advocated the use of probation. They believed that probation, which approximated parole without a prison sentence, would provide the guidance and supervision needed to reform those who had only begun to dabble in crime. Probation proved to be a popular reform, soon replacing suspended sentences as the normative sanction for most misdemeanants and first-time violators.

The Flourishing of Community Corrections

The reforms undertaken during the Progressive era succeeded in popularizing a blueprint for criminal justice that has informed correctional policy until recent times. To be sure, the grand hopes of the Progressives to create a system that could simultaneously regenerate and control offenders was never realized. All too often, bureaucratic interests and custodial convenience took precedence over the treatment needs of those brought within the grasp of the state's correctional apparatus. Nevertheless, until the late 1960s, there was substantial agreement that the final solution to crime in America lay in hastening the construction of the "therapeutic state" (Menninger, 1966; cf. Kittrie, 1971). Many still believed that there was nothing wrong with the theory of justice espoused by the Progressives; rather the real problem was in the failure to implement this theory—in the lack of resources allocated to carry out the task of giving offenders individualized treatment. Moreover, not all was bleak. Despite many failures progress had been made. The past century had witnessed the firm entrenchment of rehabilitative thinking and had advanced the idea that the establishment of therapeutic milieus within the prison was essential to eradicating the deviant inclinations that offenders imported into the society of captives (McKelvey, 1977:299-348).

Such optimism regarding the curative powers of the panacea offered by the Progressives was not to last. The linchpin of the design of individualized treatment was that the state could ultimately be trusted to do good for offenders. The events of the day, however, made it difficult to sustain this notion. In particular, the civil rights movement, the Vietnam conflict, and the incidents at Kent State, Jackson State and Attica caused many on the left to suspect the intentions and integrity of the government. Within the realm of criminal justice, the bloody suppression of the uprising at Attica revealed the extent to which the state would go to reinforce its order. In the face of this reality, it became common to speak of the "legitimacy crisis" confronting the state's exercise of authority (Friedrichs, 1979) and to force consideration of the "limits of benevolence" (Gaylin et al., 1978).

Yet not everyone was prepared to conclude that the search for a cure to crime was a fruitless enterprise. The mistakes of the Progressives could, in fact, shed light on where the real panacea might be found. By extending an inordinate amount of trust to the state, the Progressives had fostered the erroneous view that the most coercive instrument at the state's disposal — the prison — could be transformed into a community capable of effecting the humanistic treatment of convicts. In light of Attica, such a conception seemed utopian at best, and tragically ludicrous at worst. This reasoning thus led to a new policy agenda: if the notion — inherited from as far back as the Quakers — that the prison community was curative must be forfeited, then the solution to crime must lie outside the penitentiary's walls, in a place where the state's coercive potential is minimized. Offender rehabilitation must be undertaken not in artificially created milieus, but in the heart of society. Indeed, all logic pointed to the fact that "community corrections" was the long-awaited panacea for crime.

While the prevailing social context made this thinking plausible if not compelling, the community corrections movement drew added legitimacy from the criminological writings of the day. For one thing, research on recidivism rates revealed that prisons did little to diminish criminogenic predispositions. It was estimated that somewhere between fifty and eighty-five percent of all children committed to a reformatory eventually returned to crime after release (Jensen and Rojek, 1980:50; Horwitz and Wasserman, 1977). For adults, the return rate to prison was estimated to run as high as a third of the population (Silberman, 1978:505).

Theoretically, the appeal of community corrections was bolstered by the emergence of "labeling theory." This perspective sought to revise the traditional positivist view that the origins of crime were rooted in an abnormal psyche or in the criminogenic strains and values that confronted people located at certain points in the social structure. By contrast, the labeling theorists suggested that the real cause of illegal conduct had less to do with deviant psychological and environmental forces and much more to do with the way in which the legal system reacted to those whom it labeled as "criminals" (Becker, 1963; cf. Cullen and Cullen, 1978). In brief, they observed that a process which publicly stigmatized individuals as criminal, placed these people in a brutalizing prison environment where they only associated with other criminals, and then denied them full reintegration into society because they were, after all, "ex-offenders" could only have the consequence of deepening a commitment to a criminal career. Regardless of how benevolent one's intention might be, trying to save the wayward by placing them in institutions could only have the unanticipated consequence of making matters worse. The most rational policy was thus to start programs that would "divert" offenders from the formal legal system and into the community where they could receive the help they needed. At the extreme, authors such as Edwin Schur (1973) called for reformers to embrace the policy of "radical non-intervention." As he urged with regard to problem adolescents, "leave the kids alone whenever possible" (1973:155).

An experiment conducted by Stanford social psychologist Philip Zimbardo was perhaps most responsible for both cementing the conclusion that prisons were indeed inherently inhumane and shattering the illusion that additional funding or staffing could ever turn the penitentiary into the ideal communities the Quakers and Progressives had hoped they would be. In Zimbardo's experiment, students responding to a newspaper advertisement for paid participants in a mock prison experiment were interviewed and psychologically screened. Twenty-four normal, healthy male college students were selected to participate. Half were assigned roles as inmates by the experimenters, and these students were "arrested" by police, booked, fingerprinted, and thrown into a jail constructed in the basement of the psychology building at Stanford. There they were guarded by the other students participating in the experiment.

Guards and inmates reacted to the power structure provided by the prison setting to such a great extent that the study, which was to have lasted two weeks, had to be

> abrubtly terminated after six days because the role playing had so merged with reality that half the mock prisoners had severe emotional disturbances (uncontrollable crying, rage, disorganized thinking...) while all but a few of the guards behaved consistently in aggressive, dehumanizing ways toward their prisoners (Quoted in Wooden, 1976: 112).

If six days of experimental conditions could produce such effects in normal, intelligent college students, one shuddered to think of the effect years of time spent in actual institutions had on prisoners and custodial officers drawn from lower class backgrounds. Total institutions, concluded

Zimbardo, were inherently brutalizing:

> The potential social value of this study derives precisely from the fact
> that normal, healthy, educated young men could be so radically trans-
> formed under the institutional pressures of a "prison environment." If
> this could happen to the "cream-of-the-crop of American youth," then
> one can only shudder to imagine what society is doing both to the actual
> guards and prisoners who are at this very moment participating in that
> unnatural experiment" (Zimbardo et al., 1973:53).

Disturbingly, investigations into the actual conditions of institutions only
confirmed what Zimbardo's research had indicated (Nagel, 1973; Wooden,
1976). Prisons were now called "houses of darkness" (Orland, 1975), and
more than a few commentators advocated the "end of imprisonment"
(Sommer, 1976; Mitford, 1971). Efforts were also made to uncover the
corruption of the system which perpetuated such conditions. As juvenile
justice reformer Jerome Miller observed,

> It is just too difficult to reform these institutions because most are
> based on political patronage and the institution becomes more impor-
> tant than the child (Quoted in Wooden, 1976:168).

Miller and his colleagues eventually decided that:

> It would do no good to pump more money and more programs into the
> existing system because the system can chew up reforms faster than you
> dream up new ones. It's a sick system that destroys the best efforts of
> everyone in it, and we decided to look for alternatives (Quoted in
> Mitford, 1974:309).

The alternative that Miller settled on was the complete closing of all of
Massachusetts's reformatories. After he did so in 1972, the recidivism rate
ostensibly dropped twenty percent (Wooden, 1976:246). Community based
corrections was suddenly hailed as the cure for all the problems facing the
criminal justice system. The state would be limited to supervisory roles,
such as probation and parole. The halfway house would replace the closed
institutions of the past, and would operate under the watchful eye of the
community. Reduced program size would lend itself well to therapy techniques, and therefore would be more successful. Offenders would have an
opportunity to become resocialized with the community, rather than being
forced to adapt to the artificial environment of the institution. And all of
this would be done at a substantial savings to the taxpayer, since the
offenders would be able to partially support themselves through
employment in the community, and because resources already available in
the community (public schools, social services, recreational facilities) could
be utilized in the therapeutic enterprise. The transition from panacea to
panacea was undertaken with great hope and enthusiasm.

Legislative support came primarily through the creation of the Law
Enforcement Assistance Administration, which provided federal funding

for researching, establishing, and evaluating community based programs for both juveniles and adults. The Omnibus Crime Control and Safe Streets Act of 1968 made federal monies available to states who wished to start community-based corrections for juveniles. The Juvenile Justice and Delinquency Prevention Act of 1974, on the other hand, required state programs to deinstitutionalize all status offenders or forfeit their federal funding. Community oriented programs were established across the nation (Warner, 1977:3).

The Decline of Community Corrections

The prospects for a comprehensive community corrections movement initially seemed bright. The policy of treating offenders in the community promised to be cost effective, fundamentally humane, and a therapeutic panacea for all but the most sociopathic among us. But, remarkably, the appeal of this policy agenda was not sustained for long. Conservatives, as might be anticipated, criticized such notions as diversion and deinstitutionalization as merely more attempts by liberals to coddle offenders and rob the criminal sanction of its deterrent powers. What was unexpected, however, is that commentators on the political left also launched an attack on the concept of community corrections. Sensitized to the ways in which past reforms had been corrupted, they were quick to scrutinize community-based programs and to illuminate their shortcomings. They uncovered such problems as the lack of an emergent consensus concerning the goals of community corrections (Coates, 1981), and the local community resistance to halfway houses (Krajick, 1980). More worrisome, a number of commentators asserted that the latest panacea had, in the end, done little to facilitate the improvement of offenders and much to serve class and organizational interests (Austin and Krisberg, 1982; Lerman, 1975; Scull, 1977; Van Dusen, 1981; Rothman, 1980). These issues are touched upon below.

Many of the newly established programs suffered from a lack of clear program objectives. One of the reasons for this lack of direction was that the reformers had concentrated all their efforts on deinstitutionalizing offenders, with the assumption that getting people "out of institutions, even if the community is not geared to serve them, is all to the good" (Foster, 1973:33). As Coates (1981:88) remarked:

> For too long, we have accepted the notion that a halfway house or a group home is somehow inherently better than the institution it replaces. Little thought has been given to what factors differentiate a group home from an institution.

Community reactions to a program were also crucial in determining how well it could function. As Warner (1977:14) has stated:

> Without the support and positive involvement of good neighbors, a

group home is not a community based program at all, but simply another asylum isolated from the world which has, in the first place, alienated the child. If the task of a group home is to reintegrate children into the community, this cannot be done without the support of good neighbors.

Frequently, the newly established programs lacked such support. Nearby residents, fearing victimization and declining property values, exerted strong pressure to prevent programs from opening. Often the pressure was political in nature, involving complaints to public officials or the local zoning board. A 1974 study by the American Society of Planning Officials found that:

> The reasons cited most often why zoning boards refuse to grant permits to halfway houses were "substantial opposition from nearby landowners" and "community prejudice toward the persons to reside in the facility" (Krajick, 1980:16).

As administrator Robert Bright noted, "community corrections was officially a good idea, but if you made enough noise, you didn't have to have it in your neighborhood" (Quoted in Krajick, 1980:16). Such resistance caused some programs to close, and others to relocate in non-residential urban areas. Such sites, however, were far from ideal. "Sticking a center out between the dog pound and the peat moss factory is no answer," observed administrator Ray Messegee, adding that "It's better to get into a residential area, because that's where the inmates are returning to" (Quoted in Krajick, 1980:19).

A more fundamental attack has come from commentators arguing that the community corrections movement is merely a new and subtle means by the repressive state to expand social control over citizens. Andrew Scull set forth early insights into this issue. Scull (1977) maintained that the community corrections movement occurred not because it was more therapeutic to treat people in the community, but because it was cheaper to do so. Scull pointed to the increases in the cost of institutional care, and to the rising crime rates which increased the number of offenders to be dealt with, as factors which necessitated the rise in community-oriented alternatives. Scull noted that the extensive use of community corrections allowed the system to avoid the expense of constructing costly new facilities. In Scull's (1977:144) words:

> to the extent that the adoption of diversionary policies obviates the need for massive expansion of the physical capacity of the existing institutional system...decarceration provides a direct and immediate source of relief to the state's fiscal crisis whose importance is obvious, even while its dimensions are extraordinarily difficult to estimate with any degree of precision.

On a more general level, historian David Rothman (1980) demonstrated how the existing interest groups within the criminal justice system had historically used efforts at reform to further their own ends. While Rothman did not deal with the deinstitutionalization movement directly, he did illustrate how many of the community-oriented reforms advocated by the Progressives (e.g., parole and probation) had persisted, not because they achieved the changes that Progressives had proposed, but because they served the judges, prosecutors, and correctional officials within the system. In short, the ideals or "conscience" of the reforms had been corrupted by the pragmatics or "convenience" at the core of the legal process.

Notably, Austin and Krisberg's (1982) recent review of the effectiveness of alternatives to institutionalization in terms of reducing the use of incarceration suggests that the conscience versus convenience dichotomy is still with us today. Their analysis of existing research has led Austin and Krisberg (1982) to argue that the community corrections movement is best characterized as an "unmet promise." "In each instance," they observed of community-based programs, "the nonincarcerative options were transformed, serving criminal justice system values and goals other than reducing imprisonment" (1982:405-406). Despite expressed intentions, reform efforts thus did not result in a lessening in levels of incarceration or in government surveillance over people's lives. Instead, a close inspection of these undertakings reveals that their "conscience" has typically been corrupted and that they have ultimately been used to protect or bolster the organizational interests of the justice apparatus. As Austin and Krisberg (1982:377) have concluded:

> Alternatives to incarceration have been introduced for the espoused purpose of altering the nets of criminal justice. Organizational research, however, suggests that the reform strategies are frequently distorted, shifting their original purposes and producing unintended and undesirable consequences. The evidence indicates that alternatives have created
>
> 1. Wider Nets, in the sense that reforms have increased the proportion of persons whose behavior is regulated and controlled by the state.
> 2. Stronger Nets, in that reforms have augmented the state's capacity to control citizens through an intensification of its powers of intervention.
> 3. Different Nets, through the transfer of jurisdictional authority from one agency to another, or the creation of new social control systems (cf. Van Dusen, 1981).

Panaceas and Policy

There can be little doubt that liberal and more radical critics of community corrections, such as those discussed above, did a service in counteracting the naive conclusion that this latest reform agenda would somehow be immune to the kinds of difficulties that previous reforms have suffered. Yet, while instructive in this way, the tarnishing of the appeal of community corrections had a less attractive consequence as well: it meant that those on the political left were now bereft of any panacea for the crime problem that it could offer to policy-makers and the public. In the matter of a few years, they had reached the conclusion that not only was it foolish to imagine that crime-curing communities could be fashioned within the prison, but also it was equally misconceived to anticipate that prevailing realities would ever allow for humanistic and efficacious reforms outside the penitentiary's walls. It was manifest that "nothing works" (Martinson, 1974), and that well-intentioned criminal justice reforms unwittingly were "dangerous" undertakings (Doleschal, 1982). With hopes of curing criminality dashed, the best that could be done was to try to insure that offenders would be treated justly both before the courts and while incarcerated (Fogel, 1975; von Hirsch, 1976). Beyond this, meddling in criminal justice matters simply risked making things worse. Capturing this sentiment, Doleschal (1982:151) has remarked, "That we should leave the system alone, intervening as little as possible and only when necessary, is an idea whose time has come, and an increasing number of authors are expressing it."

To an extent, this sobering perspective was more honest than past attempts that promised unattainable achievements in the realm of crime control. But again, there is a negative side to all this. Panaceas, for all their simplicities, have one advantage: they energize correctional reform by offering the prospect that things can get better. In the absence of any easily believed panacea, those of the left have been robbed of their enthusiasm for embarking on campaigns to improve the criminal justice system. "Today," LaMar Empey (1979:10) has written, "optimism has turned to pessimism, fervent hopes to despair." In a context such as this, it is not surprising to learn that the best those on the political left have to offer are the admonitions that nothing works and to leave the system alone (Travis and Cullen, 1984).

This does not mean, however, that a new panacea has not emerged to grasp the fascination of criminal justice policy-makers. If liberal elements in society are now refraining from claiming that they have the key to solving the crime problem, their conservative counterparts have shown no such reluctance. Indeed, there is no hint of despair on the right, only answers. As Bertram Gross (1982:137) has noted with a measure of hyperbole, they advocate a forceful if "simple remedy: 'Police 'em, Jail 'em, Kill 'em.'" In real terms, this means that it has become plausible to suggest that juveniles of all sorts can be "scared straight" by letting them witness the horrors that reign within adult prisons (Finckenauer, 1982). For older offenders, there is the assumption that stringent, mandatory prison sentences have the power to enforce conformity. At the very least, lengthy stays behind bars will insure that the dangerous do not roam free in the community (Wilson, 1975; cf. Gordon, 1980). Caging the habitually wicked may create a Hobbesian state of all against all within the society of captives, but the high walls of the prison will insulate the innocent from such people. The widespread appeal of this philosophy of incapacitation is best seen in the constant escalation of the state and federal prison population—doubling in the last decade to the point where it now has surpassed the unprecedented figure of 425,000 (*Justice Assistance News*; 1983).

When these considerations are combined with our knowledge of the past, it becomes inescapably clear that the panacea pendulum is swinging steadily away from the conclusion that the cure for crime lies in either the "community" or "corrections." It would be premature to assert that this is a permanent state of affairs. For one thing, while many citizens believe we should get tough on crime, they nonetheless express the opinion that offenders should still be given an opportunity to be rehabilitated (Cullen et al., 1983). For another, the contradiction inherent in the conservatives' simultaneous call to hold the line on taxation while urging that large expenditures be allocated for the construction and operation of an enormous prison apparatus may place limitations on how far the reliance on imprisonment as a preferred response to crime can proceed. Yet it is too much to expect that underlying attitudes supporting rehabilitation or financial exigencies will, by themselves, halt the current trend in justice policy. The punitive panacea at present has no competition, and all evidence suggests that its influence in the correctional arena is growing. Unless those with more reformist impulses begin to offer policy agendas that at once reveal the inadequacies of "getting tough" and furnish answers to the crime problem, the salience of the conservatives' vision of justice thus promises to remain undiminished in the time immediately ahead (Cullen and Gilbert, 1982; Cullen and Wozniak, 1982).

In this regard, reformers would do well to reconsider whether it was a wise decision to have abandoned community corrections as their panacea when no alternative other than pessimism was at hand. Some might argue that to embrace anything as a cure-all in light of knowledge to the contrary is both disingenuous and dangerous. Perhaps so. But one must also face the reality that policymakers have shown little inclination to stop the justice process so that empirical research can instruct them on how to implement complex solutions to deal with the complex problem of crime. As such, the decision to popularize a crime panacea should transcend the issue of whether a cure-all has in fact been discovered, and consider whether the consequences of the panacea are better or worse than the policy agenda that will take its place. Such pragmatism to the noble may be unappealing, but in the end, it may prove to be the most humanistic avenue of reform to follow.

References

Austin, James and Barry Krisberg (1982) "The unmet promise of alternatives to incaraceration." *Crime and Delinquency* 28(3):374-409.

Barnes, Harry Elmer (1972) *The Story of Punishment: A Record of Man's Inhumanity to Man.* Montclair, NJ: Patterson Smith.

Beccaria, Cesare (1964) *On Crimes and Punishments.* Indianapolis: Bobbs-Merrill.

Becker, Howard (1963) *Outsiders: Studies in the Sociology of Deviance.* New York: The Free Press.

Blackmere, John (1980) "Community corrections." *Corrections Magazine* 6(5): 4-14.

Brockway, Zebulon R. (1969) *Fifty Years of Prison Service: An Autobiography.* Montclair, NJ: Patterson Smith.

Cavender, Gary (1982) *Parole: A Critical Analysis.* Port Washington, NY: Kennikat Press.

Coates, Robert (1981) "Community-based services for juvenile delinquents: Concept and implications for practice." *Journal of Social Issues* 37(3):87-101.

Conrad, John (1981) "Can juvenile justice survive?" *Crime and Delinquency* 27(4): 544-554.

Cullen, Francis T. and John B. Cullen (1978) *Toward a Paradigm of Labeling Theory.* Monograph No. 58. Lincoln: University of Nebraska Studies.

Cullen, Francis T., John B. Cullen, and John F. Wozniak (1983) "Sanctioning ideology and the prospects for reform: Is rehabilitation really dead?" Paper presented at the annual meeting of the Illinois Sociological Society.

Cullen, Francis T. and Karen E. Gilbert (1982) *Reaffirming Rehabilitation.* Cincinnati: Anderson Publishing Company.

Cullen, Francis T. and John F. Wozniak (1982) "Fighting the appeal of repression." *Crime and Social Justice* 18 (Winter):23-33.

Doleschal, Eugene (1982) "The dangers of criminal justice reform." *Criminal Justice Abstracts.* 14:133-152.

Duffee, David, Frederick Hussey, and John Kramer (1978) *Criminal Justice: Organization, Structure and Analysis.* Englewood Cliffs, NJ: Prentice Hall.

Earle, Alice Morse (1969) *Curious Punishments of Bygone Days.* Montclair, NJ: Patterson Smith.

Erikson, Kai T. (1966) *Wayward Puritans.* New York: John Wiley and Sons.

Eriksson, Torsten (1976) *The Reformers: A Historical Survey of Pioneer Experiments in the Treatment of Criminals.* New York: Elsevier.

Empey, Lamar T. (1979) "Foreword—from optimism to despair: New doctrines in juvenile justice," pp. 9-26 in Charles A. Murray and Louis A. Cox, Jr. (eds.), *Beyond Probation: Juvenile Corrections and the Chronic Delinquent. Beverly* Hills: Sage.

Finckenauer, James (1982) *Scared Straight! and the Panacea Phenomenon.* Englewood Cliffs, NJ: Prentice Hall, Inc.

Fogel, David (1975) *"We are the Living Proof...": The Justice Model for Corrections,* second edition. Cincinnati: Anderson Publishing Company.

Foster, M. (1973) "Youth service systems: New criteria," pp. 33-38 in Y. Bakal (ed.) *Closing Correctional Institutions.* Lexington: Lexington Books.

Friedrichs, David O. (1979) "The law and the legitimacy crisis: A critical issue for criminal justice." Pp. 290-311 in R.G. Iacovetta and Dae H. Chang (eds.). *Critical Issues in Criminal Justice.* Durham: Carolina Academic Press.

Gaylin, Willard, Ira Glasser, Steven Marcus, and David Rothman (1978) *Doing Good: The Limits of Benevolence*. New York: Pantheon Books.

Gordon, Diana R. (1980) *Doing Violence to the Crime Problem: A Response to the Attorney General's Task Force*. Hackensack, NJ: NCCD.

Gross, Bertram (1982) "Some anticrime proposals for progressives." *The Nation* (February 6):137-140.

Hofstadter, Richard (1955) *The Age of Reform*. New York: Alfred A. Knopf.

Horwitz, A. and M. Wasserman (1977) "A cross-sectional and longitudinal study of the labeling perspective." Paper presented at the American Society of Criminology annual meeting.

Jensen, Gary F. and Dean G. Rojeck (1980) *Delinquency: A Sociological View*. Lexington: D.C. Heath and Company.

Justice Assistance News (1983) "Prison population sets record high." 4 (September): 4.

Kittrie, Nicholas N. (1971) *The Right To Be Different: Deviance and Enforced Therapy*. Baltimore: Penguin Books.

Krajick, Kevin (1980) "Not on my block." *Corrections Magazine* 6(5):15-21.

Lerman, Paul (1975) *Community Treatment and Social Control: A Critical Analysis of Juvenile Correctional Policy*. Chicago: University of Chicago Press.

Martinson, Robert, "What works? Questions and answers about prison reform." *The Public Interest* 35 (Spring):22-54.

McKelvey, Blake (1977) *American Prisoners: A History of Good Intentions*. Montclair, NJ: Patterson Smith.

Menninger, Karl, M.D. (1966) *The Crime of Punishment*. New York: Penguin Books.

Mitford, Jessica (1971) *Kind and Usual Punishment*. New York: Random House.

Nagel, William G. (1973) *The New Red Barn: A Critical Look at the Modern American Prison*. New York: Walker and Company.

Newman, Graeme (1978) *The Punishment Response*. Philadelphia: Lippincott.

Orland, Leonard (1975) *Prisons: Houses of Darkness*. New York: The Free Press.

Rothman, David (1980) *Conscience and Convenience*. Boston: Little, Brown and Company.

———— (1971) *Discovery of the Asylum*. Boston: Little, Brown and Company.

Schur, Edwin M. (1973) *Radical Nonintervention: Rethinking the Delinquency Problem*. Englewood Cliffs, NJ: Prentice-Hall.

Scull, Andrew T. (1977) *Decarceration*. Englewood Cliffs: Prentice-Hall, Inc.

Silberman, Charles (1978) *Criminal Violence, Criminal Justice*. New York: Vintage Books.

Shaw, Clifford and Henry McKay (1931) *Social Factors in Juvenile Delinquency*, Volume II. National Commission on Law Observance and Enforcement, Report on the Causes of Crime. Washington, D.C.: U.S. Government Printing Office.

Sommer, Robert (1976) *The End of Imprisonment*. New York: Oxford University Press.

Travis, Lawrence F., III and Francis T. Cullen (1984) "Radical non-intervention: The myth of doing no harm," *Federal Probation*, 48(1):29-32.

Van Dusen, Katherine (1981) "Net widening and relabeling: Some consequences of deinstitutionalization." *American Behavioral Scientist*. 24(6):801-810.

von Hirsch, Andrew (1978) *Doing Justice: The Choice of Punishments.* New York: Hill and Wang.

Walker, Samuel (1980) *Popular Justice: A History of American Criminal Justice.* New York: Oxford University Press.

Warner, John, Jr. (1977) "Group homes: Dealing with the community." A paper presented to the Advanced Institution Development Program, West Virginia Wesleyan College Office.

Wilson, James (1975) *Thinking About Crime.* New York: Vintage Books.

Wooden, Kenneth (1976) *Weeping in the Playtime of Others: America's Incarcerated Children.* New York: McGraw-Hill.

Zimbardo, Phillip G., W. Curtis Banks, Craig Haney, and David Jaffe (1973) "A pirandellian prison: The mind is a formidable jailer." *New York Times Magazine* (April 8):38-56.

III
The Setting
Legal and Organizational Constraints

Managerial Issues in Community Corrections

Todd R. Clear
Rutgers University

Community corrections finds itself at a turning point in its history. A decade of dramatic growth from the mid-1960s to the mid-1970s was followed by a decade of decline in the public credibility of community corrections. Today, with virtually every state facing severe prison crowding, community corrections stands at the center of contemporary correctional policy, but many question the capacity of community corrections to respond to the challenge.

It would be inaccurate to portray community corrections as a strong or respected alternative to prison, for in most areas of the country, this is not the case. Citizens and political leaders alike distrust the capacity of community corrections to punish offenders or to protect the community. Despite serious lack of traditional prison space, growth in community corrections staff and resources has lagged well behind demand for its services. Perhaps this is a consequence of (and, ironically, a contributor to) lack of public confidence in community-based correctional methods.

Therefore, it is not surprising that community correction managers find themselves in something of a crisis atmosphere. Asked to name their most pressing managerial concerns, most community corrections administrators would probably mention topics such as: dealing with cutbacks in staff and budget, combating burnout, improving staff morale, dealing with the media, developing computer-based information systems and so forth. While none can question the seriousness of these contemporary problems, one is left with a sense of narrowness in managerial attention to such concerns.

An earlier version of this paper was presented to the Academy of Criminal Justice Sciences, San Antonio, Texas, March 23, 1983.

After all, this list is very temporal. A decade ago, a different set of concerns would have been expressed; presumably, in the mid 1990's the manager's immediate attention will be drawn toward other issues. Government administration seems often to be preoccupied with organizational crises and daily dilemmas, almost to the exclusion of long-range thinking.

The absence of a long range perspective has left community corrections with something of a leadership void. The failure of management to attend to the future of community corrections leaves the field vulnerable to changes that will occur in years to come. The price of crisis management is a continuation of the very instability that makes each crisis so difficult to manage. This is not meant to detract from the importance of addressing forthrightly the major problems of corrections. In the face of headlines about client recidivists and deprecatory quotations from policy makers and researchers alike, the temptation is to manage on a day-by-day basis — what some have called "muddling through." The purpose of this paper is to point out the importance of attending to more fundamental managerial issues beyond these crises.

There are underlying themes in the problems that have faced managers of correctional services over the last 20 years that will remain true for some time to come. These themes represent what might be called "larger concerns" of management in community corrections. Unlike the temporal concerns listed above, larger managerial concerns are never fully resolved in the context of crisis, but instead represent areas requiring continuing attention of correctional management.

Among these themes are broad managerial concerns that apply to most public service administrators — establishing a workable organizational structure, demonstrating productivity and so on. After all, similarities exist in the work world of public administrators, regardless of their agency. Yet, some managerial problems are especially important to correctional services agencies.

Below is a list of five major, long-term managerial concerns that have particular significance for community corrections managers. These managerial concerns were selected because they are central to the task of developing healthy community corrections organizations. Rather than short-term crises, the five concerns discussed below reflect fundamental problems of continuing importance to the effective management of community corrections. Successful attention to these five areas would form the basis for a healthy managerial practice.

Problem Area #1: Clarifying Organizational Purpose

Perhaps the most fundamental problem facing correctional services administration is to clarify the purposes served by the effort of staff. Presently, little consensus exists concerning the appropriate purposes of community corrections. This disagreement occurs on two levels. Experts differ as to what the purpose *should* be. More critically, however, within most organizations of any size, there is little agreement among staff as to the philosophy that *actually guides* their efforts. Each level of disagreement produces difficulties for managers.

Among leaders in the field, opinion about purpose runs the gamut. Most analyses attempt to separate the so-called "law enforcement" function from that of "social casework" — the former is associated with arrests, surveillance, custody and close supervision; the latter with treatment, services and counseling. In his work on parole, Glaser (1964) translated these competing purposes into scales that he used to differentiate officers on attitudes toward their work. That law enforcement and social casework roles often conflict has been a consistent theme in discussions of probation/parole work (Studt, 1978, Stanley, 1976; von Hirsch and Hanrahan, 1979; Lipsky, 1980; McCleary, 1978) and community corrections, generally (McCarrt and Mangogna, 1973; Solomon, 1976).

Apparently, the conflict has not been resolved, since most writers assume one orientation or another must be given emphasis. For example, several authors have given emphasis to the importance of the casework service-delivery function of corrections. After careful analysis of the practice and potential of supervision, Stanley (1978) argued against surveillance and in favor of voluntary services as the primary purposes of parole. Similarly, in their "modified desert" model, von Hirsch and Hanrahan (1979) established the case for non-coercive service-delivery in parole supervision. Dell'Appa and associates (1976) developed a full-scale operational model for service-delivery in community corrections called the "community resource management team." Generally, those who argue for a social caseworker model suggest that surveillance/control is either unfair, ineffectual or both, while service provision constitutes a unique role that can be played by these post-conviction functions.

In contrast, some authors have argued that service-delivery is of secondary importance in the operation of community corrections agencies, and that the forceful use of careful surveillance may help to reduce crimes by offenders. Martinson and Wilks (1977) suggest the possiblity of a one-to-one supervision model based on surveillance. A more feasible approach (Barkdull, 1978) suggests that officers' control methods ought to be developed and intensified (NY State, 1982). Under these models, services are seen as ancillary to the main functions of community corrections — law enforcement and behavior control.

Recently, a special project at University of Illinois-Chicago Circle developed an application of the idea of the "justice model" to probation supervision. From this point of view, supervision was seen as having the purpose of enforcing the orders and conditions set by the court (Fogel, 1980). This approach leads to elaborate, legalistic standards for decision-making (McAnany and Thompson, 1982).

Clear and O'Leary (1983) have argued for an integration of service/custody functions under a model called "limited risk-control." This approach promotes both services and surveillance methods, so long as they are demonstrated to be reasonably related to the correctional function of reducing offenders' potential for criminal behavior.

Each of these models, when fully elaborated, leads to quite different organizational practices, personnel and policies. That is, depending on the organization's orientation toward "purpose," a different coterie of work approaches will emerge. This has obvious import in the priorities given to competing demands for organizational performance. While virtually all supervision agencies may have to attend to a similar set of constraints in the area of organizational purpose, the weight given to the specific policy alternatives depends on the purpose. Drucker (1974) has shown how the organization's purpose determines operational priorities in his important essay on the question "who is the client?" For community corrections, the clarification of purposes will effect such managerial issues as recruitment of staff, linkage with other agencies and organization of workload. More important, purpose is relevant daily to the activities of line staff as they make choices ranging from how to approach a client interview to whether to sanction misbehavior (Robison and Takagi, 1970).

Unfortunately, very few organizations have clarified their purpose in a way that enables line workers to make these daily decisions with consistent attention to organizational purpose. The failure to clarify organizational purposes and objectives is probably a key reason why so many community corrections agencies have "failed" in their task environments (Gold, 1982). Studt (1967) recognized the problems created by ambiguous purpose when she argued that no parole agency exists in California, rather there is a conglomeration of agencies represented by the individualistic attitudes and beliefs of the officers. A consequence of this ambiguity is widespread supervision disparity (Clear, 1980).

If community corrections agencies are to improve, the effort must begin with more uniform practices by line staff. Only then can routine practices be evaluated and upgraded. However, performance uniformity has its beginnings in goal clarity (Odiorne, 1974), and this in turn requires attention to purpose. So many decisions depend on the resolution of this dilemma: what restrictions to place on residents in a work furlough program, how to handle special supervision conditions, whether to make a surprise home visit, whether to make an arrest or to allow the police to do it, etc. These policies turn on purpose, and staff can only make appropriate decisions if they clearly understand the purpose underlying their work.

Clarification of purpose involves three steps: First, the philosophical underpinnings of policy and purpose must be identified, and choices must be made by leadership as to which orientations must prevail from among competing alternatives. Second, these choices must be translated into a coherent set of organizational goals consistent with the purpose. Third, staff must be carefully and continually trained on the organization's purpose and goals.

Many administrators may believe they already do this. That is, their organizations have policy and mission statements, they provide orientations to their staff about policies, and so on. That is not the same as what is meant here: the deliberate development of policies and procedures to reflect purpose, and a system of daily practice in which all staff are aware of purpose and behave consistently with these policies. In many community corrections organizations, there is little consensus among staff concerning purpose and little support (and a tendency to ignore) some policies that implement the purpose, when those policies are inconvenient.

Without directly and effectively addressing the confusion over purpose, management of correctional services will find it difficult to improve meaningfully in other aspects of organizational functioning.

Problem Area #2: Developing Organizational "Fit"

Recently, the National Institute of Corrections designated a set of practices to be a "model management system" in probation and parole (NIC, 1981). Based on offender classification, this set of practices has been adopted by over 30 agencies across the country. Carlson and Parks (1979) have described various other approaches for structuring probation practices. For some time it has been clear that the general caseload is not a productive way to organize supervision activities—Carter and Wilkins (1970), and Banks, et al. (1970) have suggested that intensive special caseloads are preferable structural approaches, but this gives little guidance as to how to specialize. Moos (1975) has contrasted various approaches for organizing residential facilities. With so many models to choose from, how should administrators organize staff?

The answer is semantically simple but operationally complicated: the organizational structure should create "fit." The concept of fit is elusive, but is nonetheless important to human service organizations. "Fit" exists when the organization's structure and processes solidify the organization's place in its critical environment (Thompson, 1967) while also integrating the internal functions of the organization (Weisbord, 1978). For community corrections, fit means developing case management policies and practices that are consistent and reasonable in light of the organization's purpose (goals), clients, staff and other resources in the context of the organization's unique environment (Clear, et al., 1982).

For example, the classification systems recently disseminated by the National Institute of Corrections do not, in and of themselves, create fit, but may be used as a tool to do so. The relative emphasis given to the risk and needs scales will help determine whether the policy choices regarding law enforcement-social casework purposes will be operational at the line level

(Clear and Gallagher, 1983). Moreover, a heavy emphasis on service bro-
kering does not fit an offender control orientation toward correction, nor
would such an approach seem reasonable in a resource-poor environment.
Likewise, a staff well-trained in human services methods would not fit with
a surveillance-custody model, just as an underprepared staff cannot support
a casework-counseling strategy.

These are examples of how fit derives from workload practices which
organize the staff (and other resources) around clients in a way consistent
with the organization's goals. Of managerial interest in creating fit are such
issues as: How should intake operate? Should specialized caseloads be
developed? How? Which clients should be seen most often? For what
actions should our staff be accountable?

Of course, every organization has some kind of case management
process, and so it is likely that many managers feel the questions listed here
have been resolved. Yet, it may be that the existing case management
process does not lead to organizational environmental fit. In fact, most organizations maintain their approaches to case management primarily as a
result of tradition, and not because of a careful analysis of case management needs.

To establish fit, managers obviously must first have clarified the purposes
of their organization. Then it is possible to develop a structure, policies for
client assessment and assignment, and monitoring practices that flow from
the purpose but are also reasonable in light of the uniqueness of staff,
clients, and the environment. Once this process is complete, organizational
fit is attainable.

It must also be recognized that fit is not static. Rather, changes in
staffing, clients, or the environment will require managers to reassess
organizational goals and case management practices to reestablish fit. This
has been the case for much of what has been called "cutback
management," where reduced staffing levels have required adjustments in
line-level practices of the most fundamental nature.

Problem Area #3: Upgrading Technology

Probation and parole organizations operate under what Thompson
(1967) has called "technical uncertainty;" when the technologies employed
in the work have unknown reliability. Among the consequences of technical
uncertainty are accelerated staff burnout, lack of predictability of staff
decisions and conflict with the environment—the types of concerns that
managers seem to be so focused on in their crisis orientation.

Many organizations have attempted to compensate for technical uncertainty by increased reliance on "hard" technology—computers, screening
instruments, etc. There can be little question that in the area of mechanical
techniques, community corrections has remained a decade or two behind
most other organizations.

That is why there has been an increase in the use of computers as an aid to managing the supervision process (NIC, 1981), new mechanisms such as workload accounting (Bemus, 1982) instrumented classification systems (Solomon and Baird, 1981) and program-based budgeting (Nelson, et al., 1978), are attractive tools for managers in community corrections. Perhaps these methods bring with them a degree of "scientific" basis that makes them attractive to managers whose efforts so often seem to consist of experience-based guesswork about clients.

One must question, however, the potential of these managerial technologies absent the general upgrading of all technical aspects of community corrections. What good is an empirically-based classification system when staff lack expertise concerning the way to handle their clients' day-to-day behaviors or their general needs? What good is a computer-based workload system when supervisors fail to audit and control the casework decisions of their staff? The point is that the "new" technologies described above, no matter how important or helpful, are in reality ancillary technologies that can only work to their fullest when the core techniques of corrections are themselves upgraded.

This involves attention to two general classes of technologies employed directly in the work. The first is communication between staff and clients; the second is communication between staff and their supervisors. From these interactions emerge the quality of correctional work. It is precisely because the core work is so vague (communication) that the technology is so uncertain. Yet, it is possible to differentiate effective from ineffective communication (counseling, interviewing, feedback, whatever), particularly in extreme examples. That is, there is a difference between good and bad core techniques, and most people would reliably assess them in the extremes if asked to rate the quality of work they were viewing. The problem lies more in transferring the technical skills to staff, rather than deciding what constitutes the skilled communication.

This is a problem of training. Without underestimating the importance of high quality ancillary technologies, it still is reasonable to focus on the more difficult problem of developing line staff skills as interviewers, assessors, intervenors and decisionmakers. Innovative programs in this area exist; perhaps the best example is a training program called Client Management Classification (Arling and Lerner, 1981), which integrates all of these functions and provides a rational structure for doing so. Continuing emphasis on training and education of line staff may be the primary way to upgrade technical quality at that level.

The supervisor's role in technical quality is just as important. Line staff cannot learn their own roles without consultative feedback from their superiors. Too often supervisors lack either the expertise or the willingness to engage staff in the critical assessment of their casework methods. Consequently, staff exist in a feedback void and this contributes to technical

uncertainty and work ambivalence. Thus, the supervisor's role as manager
of line technologies is a critical one. Yet most supervisors are used to communicating with criminal offenders, but have little experience dealing with
professional "clients." A result is that relations at this level are often
strained, unpurposeful and overconcerned with tangible products ("paperwork") as compared to qualitative concerns ("casework").

Getting these technologies in order and working—line officers
supervising well, supervisors monitoring well—is a major task of management. Because "thing" technologies such as computers are easier to install
and keep running, they often get more attention, to the detriment of core
technical areas. Yet for technology to be truly upgraded, there must be an
equal (if not greater) emphasis given to training and educating staff and
their supervisors. Unfortunately, in times of fiscal stress, training (perhaps
because it is often of questionable quality) is one of the most vulnerable
budget items. The consequences of reduced training (or poor training) are
not as immediate, nor as tangible, as lost staff positions, and so the temptation is to absorb fiscal losses in support areas such as training.

Yet, managers must recognize that technologies do not exist in isolation
from related techniques. Poor staff supervision leads to inaccurate information on forms for input into the computer. Poor line attitudes make workload distribution methods ineffectual. The absence of readily available
ancillary technologies makes the work itself that much more difficult. The
manager's responsibility is to improve systematically all organizational
technologies.

Problem Area #4: Establishing a Community Corrections Career

Nationally the job market has been changing in virtually every career area
(Special Task Force, 1973), and corrections services is no exception. In
general, the change augers a time of greater competition for jobs, reduced
job mobility (both within and between jobs), and greater emphasis on productivity to justify continued employment (Harlow and Nelson, 1982), particularly in government positions. These changes invoke a new era for
government services, and correctional managers will be forced to bring the
career into line with the changes now occurring in other jobs.

This will not be an easy task, for community corrections agencies are
beset with a tradition of personnel problems that inhibit development of a
meaningful career. For example, in most organizations, probation is seen as
an early-career position which most people eventually leave to take other
jobs. Few people stay in community corrections work for their entire professional careers (with the exception, perhaps, of the federal system). Turnover is often high, so-called "burnout" is epidemic and work world cyni-
cism seems to pervade the office (Lipsky, 1980).

There are several reasons for this. For one thing, the lack of training for
job development make it necessary for people to continue their work

without upgrading their skills. Moreover, there is a conflict between career interests and the work itself—in order to achieve appreciable gains in income, professional staff must be promoted into managerial positions that are increasingly removed from the client-contact positions that originally attracted them to the field. Moreover, the fact that most managers come up "from the ranks" means that they are not especially well prepared or skilled to take managerial positions, a circumstance that rankles many line employees and exacerbates poor staff decision-making. Typically, even the most highly placed correctional administrators are considered lower-prestige employees by comparably-placed government workers. All conditions militate against accepting a long term career in the field.

At the center of this web of disincentives is a normally self-defeating personnel system. As for most government workers, hiring, promotions and salary increments for corrections staff normally are based either on a civil service model or a patronage alternative, each of which is deficient for the profession (Tobin, 1979). Patronage often leads to favoritism, cronyism and arbitrariness in staffing decisions. On the other hand, civil service, which is intended to serve as a cure for these ills, too often substitutes a paper-pencil testing irrationality for what should be a personnel development process. While the need for predictability and visibility in the appointment/promotion practices of government cannot be denied, it is equally true that no profit-making enterprise would be satisfied with the personnel policies commonly used in the field of corrections (Gold, 1982).

The most paralyzing characteristic of these practices is that good performance remains virtually unrewarded, and the greatest available reward—promotion—is sometimes given to those whose work is perceived by colleagues as wanting in quality. Under civil service models, the annual raise is normally unrelated to performance; instead, access to major increments is tied to written tests and seniority, not performance. Under patronage, its "who you know." What better way to make it clear that "working hard and well doesn't count?" Even more ominous is the fact that workers who do not perform even adequately are often retained under both systems, making a mockery of those who take their positions seriously.

The responsibility for developing a career in the field lies with the manager, and changes must be made to produce a career potential for those who would enter the profession.

The most fundamental step is to make the work of supervising offenders meaningful, respectable and lucrative. Those who do their jobs well should expect recognition of their achievements in the form of money (salary) prestige (title) and honor (awards). Because the work of the line employee is the essential productive labor of the community corrections organization, outstanding performance in the job should not result in removal from office (promotion to supervisor); rather a career line must be developed in which "super-workers" make good salaries (comparable to administrators) and enjoy satisfying prestige (office, vacations, etc.) commensurate with the significance of their achievement. In practice, this may require a "dual-track," in which professionals may choose a career of direct-service without suffering financial or personal restrictions as a result.

The same kind of job development needs to be applied to the managerial functions of community corrections. Too often, the supervisor's role is ambiguous, with many paper responsibilities but few areas of delegated authority. Instead, as line supervisors demonstrate their effectiveness, they should expect to be given wider authority over their units and greater autonomy in managing unit workload. Moreover, emphasis should be given to management development and training for line supervisors. Finally, tangible and symbolic rewards available to staff should be made similarly open to supervisors.

Four prerequisites exist to ideal personnel practice. First, the job responsibilities of the line worker must be sufficiently specified so that performance (output) indicators for staff positions may be defined (Tobin, 1979). Obviously this is difficult to do for a job requiring the kinds of subjective judgements common to community corrections. Moreover, the focus should be on results, not activities, since placing emphasis on the latter too often defeats the purpose of a productivity-grounded approach by rewarding "busy-ness" rather than results (Balk, 1978).

Second, routine and acceptable performance evaluation must be conducted for all staff, using standard, objective performance criteria. This will enable relative and absolute performance to be assessed at various levels of the organization.

Third, to a meaningful degree, rewards must be linked to performance. This can occur in at least two ways. One option is to link some portion of annual salary increments to performance on a "range" basis, so that all staff receive increments, but high performers receive a greater share of rewards. In addition, lateral promotions (promotions within rank and job responsibility) can be based on relative (competitive) performance.

Fourth, vertical promotions can be partly based on "readiness" for new positions rather than simply performance in prior assignments. In this way, job changes to positions that contain very different job behaviors (such as line to-supervisor moves) can be given to those who are more capable of doing the job. This requires testing procedures that more directly assess job skills (as do assessment centers) rather than simply measuring knowledge (as in a paper-pencil test approach).

Of course, creating meaningful careers presupposes two conditions: one, that management has an orientation toward building and developing staff careers through a systematic process; and two, that long range planning and personnel practices are consistent with organizational aims. Increasingly, the administrator will find there is little choice in this regard—with a tightening job market, staff movement is much less rapid within or between organizations. Personnel policies that resist the tendency toward stagnation will be a critical tool in the maintenance of viable, professional work.

Problem Area #5: Making Evaluation Systematic

The difficulty with writing about the need for evaluation is that it has already been discussed virtually to death. Yet evaluation still remains a low priority in most organizations. Nonetheless, without creating "learning systems" in community corrections agencies (Duffee, 1975), the other four problem areas will probably remain unresolved for they are deeply affected by evaluation issues: Which utilitarian purposes are achievable? How? What interventions produce which results? Therefore, which techniques should be emphasized? And what staff behaviors lead to better organization performance, and are therefore deserving of rewards? Evaluation, understood, in its proper way, is essential to organizational growth.

What is not meant by the term "evaluation" is the usual "special project research" model so commonly suggested, with experimental and control groups. Instead, the idea of evaluation advanced here includes continuing, systematic, routine practices of analyzing information to reduce organizational uncertainties (Glaser, 1974).

Staff should be given data about the results of their work. Supervisors should give staff feedback about the quality of their efforts. Supervision units should regularly monitor their practices for consistency with purpose and applicability to the client workload. Agencies should be demonstrating their accountability by evaluating their outputs, while holding critical support organizations equally accountable for the impact of their policies on clients and staff.

Implicit in this discussion is the idea of data—about staff, clients, processes, results—and these data should promote comparative and descriptive findings about the organization (Twain, 1983). Technologies oriented toward useful data need to be in place (information systems, concise case records, follow-up reports, etc.), but even more important is a managerially-created climate in support of data-based decision-making. This is encouraged by developing an inquisitive climate in which the leadership is free to question current assumptions and traditional practices: Why do supervision conditions require full-time jobs? What has been achieved by allowing urine-sample monitoring? What happens to those who are required to attend A.A. programs? Do technical revocations for non-authorized, out-of-state travel help to control crime? What offenders are most likely to succeed? These are but a sampling of the questions that might evolve from an inquisitive managerial approach toward community corrections. Each question assumes evaluation as a routine of the organization and an administration that is both interested in the answers and, perhaps more to the point, capable of asking the questions.

It would be laudable if organizations undertook the responsibility to be evaluative on their own, but experience suggests this will not happen. There is a more sure way toward this end—the budget process—and managers will probably have no choice in the matter, eventually. Those who effectively evaluate their practices will be better equipped to make the case for resources; the others will continue to languish. The evaluators will survive.

Discussion

This has been a presentation of the problem areas that community corrections managers must address if their organizations will remain healthy through the 1980's and into the 1990's. The areas presented here were based on the belief that contemporary crises have their genesis and solutions in larger, more fundamental managerial issues in correctional services.

It was not the intention to suggest that resolving the issues listed here will be easy or will automatically change the nature of community corrections. The tasks facing administrators of these agencies are difficult and will require a long-range commitment. Indeed, these are areas of managerial attention that are probably never fully resolved; instead they require constant attention.

But the potential payoffs for correctional services should not be underestimated. There is a great need for healthy field services organizations, and the future of the field lies in continuing attention to the issues described here.

References

Arling, Gary and Kenneth Lerner, (1981) *Client management classification,* Washington, D.C.: National Institute of Corrections.
Balk, Walter, (1978) Toward a government productivity ethic, *Public Administration Review,* January-February.
Banks, Jerry, et al., (1976) *Special intensive probation: phase I evaluation,* Washington, D.C.: National Institute of Justice.
Barkdull, Eugene, (1978) Probation: call it "control," and mean it, *Federal Probation* 42:2.
Bemus, Brian, (1982) *Workload accounting in probation/parole,* Washington, D.C.: National Institute of Corrections.
Carlson, Eric W. and Evelyn C. Parks, (1979) *Critical issues in adult probation,* Washington, D.C.: National Institute of Justice.
Carter, Robert M. and Leslie T. Wilkins, (1970) *Probation and parole: selected readings,* N.Y.: John Wiley & Sons.
Clear, Todd R., (1980) Disparity in probation supervision, paper presented to the American Society of Criminology, San Francisco, November.
Clear, Todd R. and Kenneth Gallagher, (1983) Management issues in screening devices in probation and parole, *Evaluation Review,* (Vol. 7, No. 2).
Clear, Todd R., P. Kevin Benoit and Stephen Morris, (1982) Objectives-based case management, *Criminal Justice Journal* (Fall).

Clear, Todd R. and Vincent O'Leary, (1983) *Controlling the offender in the community,* Lexington, MA: Lexington.

Dell'Appa, Frank, et al, (1976) Advocacy, brokerage, community: The ABC's of probation and parole, *Federal probation* 40:4, 3-8.

Drucker, Peter F., (1974) *Management: tasks-responsibilities-practices,* NY: Harper & Row.

Duffee, David, (1975) *Correctional policy and prison organization,* Beverly Hills: Sage.

Fogel, David, (1980) *The mission of probation: a model statement,* Chicago: University of Illinois—Chicago.

Glaser, Daniel, (1964) *The effectiveness of a prison parole system,* Indianapolis: Bobbs-Merrill.

Glaser, Daniel, (1974) *Routinizing evaluation,* Washington, D.C.: National Institute of Mental Health.

Gold, Kenneth A., (1982) Managing for success: a comparison of the private and public sectors, *Public administration review,* November-December, 568-575.

Harlow, Nora and E. Kim Nelson, (1982) *Cutback management in probation parole,* Washington, D.C.: National Institute of Corrections.

Lipsky, Michael, (1980) *Street-level bureaucracy,* NY: Russell Sage.

Martinson, Robert and Judith Wilks, (1977) Save parole supervision, *Federal Probation* 41:3, 23-26.

McAnany, Patrick and Doug Thompson, (1982) *Revocation practices: a guide for probation managers,* Chicago: University of Illinois — Chicago.

McCarrt, John and Thomas Mangogna, (1973) *Guidelines and standards for halfway houses and community treatment centers,* Washington: U.S. Dept. of Justice—LEAA.

McCleary, Richard, (1978) *Dangerous men: the sociology of parole,* Beverly Hills, CA: Sage.

Moos, Rudolph H., (1975) *Evaluating correctional and community settings,* NY: John Wiley & Sons.

National Institute of Corrections, (1981) *Model probation and parole management system,* Washington, D.C.: National Institute of Corrections.

Nelson, E. Kim, Howard Ohmart and Nora Harlow, *Promising strategies in probation and parole,* Washington, D.C.: Department of Justice.

New York State Division of Probation, (1980) *Evaluation of intensive supervision program,* Albany: NY Division of Probation (Mimeo).

Odiorne, George, (1974) *Management and the activity trap,* NY: Harper & Row.

Robison, James and Paul Takagi, (1970) The parole violator as organizational reject, in Robert M. Carter and Leslie T. Wilkins, eds., *Probation and Parole: selected readings,* NY: John Wiley & Sons.

Solomon, Hassim M., (1976) *Community Corrections,* Boston: Holbrook Press.

Solomon, Larry and S. Christopher Baird, (1981) Classification: past failures future potential, *Corrections Today,* (May/June), pp. 4-6.

Special Task Force, (1973) *Work in America,* Cambridge, MA: MIT Press.

Stanley, David T., (1976) *Prisoners among us, Washington, D.C.: Brookings.*

Studt, Elliot, (1967) *The reentry of the offender into the community,* Washington, D.C.: U.S. Department of Health, Education and Welfare.

Studt, Elliott, (1978) *Surveillance and service in parole,* Washington, D.C.: National Institute of Corrections.

Thompson, James D., (1967) *Organizations in action,* NY: McGraw-Hill.

Tobin, Robert, (1979) *Personnel management,* Washington, D.C.: Department of Justice.

Twain, David, (1983) *Creating change in social settings,* NY: Prager.

von Hirsch, Andrew and Kathleen J. Hanrahan, (1979) *The question of parole,* Cambridge, MA: Ballinger.

Legal Issues and Liabilities in Community Corrections

Rolando V. del Carmen
Sam Houston State University

Introduction

It is axiomatic that criminal justice is influenced heavily by law. Procedures and practices among various components of the criminal justice system are oftentimes mandated or shaped by legislation or court decisions. Community corrections is no exception. Its limits and liability consequences are defined by law and court decisions. A working knowledge of the legal environment of community corrections is therefore essential for students and professionals in community corrections.

For purposes of this article, the term "community corrections" is defined broadly as referring to correctional strategies for maintaining the offender in the community, as opposed to incarceration. Probation and parole fall under that definition and in fact constitute the predominant segment of community corrections as above defined. There is justification for focusing attention on probation and parole in considering legal issues in community corrections. Statistics show that in 1981, probation and parole constituted 74% of all adults under correctional supervision.[1] Moreover, an overwhelming majority of decided and pending cases in community corrections are in probation and parole. Very few cases have been litigated thus far in non-probation/parole programs, hence jurisprudence on that topic is scant and uninformative.

This article discusses legal issues under three general headings. Part I looks at the legal limits of probation and parole; Part II takes a brief glance at the legal limits in other community corrections programs; and Part III probes into the legal liabilities of probation, parole, and community corrections officers—a topic which has generated widespread concern in recent years because of the big increase in the number of cases against probation and parole officers. The conclusion assesses briefly the impact of judicial

47

intervention in community corrections.

To avoid confusion and misunderstanding, a few considerations must be stressed before discussing substantive legal issues. The first is that the law in this field is complex and confusing, partly because of the varied sources of rights and limitations. Legal rights and limits are set by such diverse sources as: the United States Constitution, federal law, state constitution, state law, administrative rules and practices adopted by the agency, and court decisions on the federal and state levels. What is not guaranteed by the Constitution may in fact be given by state law or administrative policy. Conversely, state law or administrative policy may specifically deny certain rights if these rights are not constitutionally guaranteed. Secondly, community corrections laws and practices may differ markedly among states and even among judges in a state. The federal system of government tolerates discrepant practices among states as long as they are not violative of basic constitutional rights. The same is true on the state level where state court judges often enjoy immense discretion in setting terms of probation and in the imposition of sentence. Creativity and innovative approaches are countenanced unless they infringe basic constitutional or statutory rights. Thirdly, a strong presumption of validity accompanies community corrections rules and practices, as long as they are "rehabilitative" of the offender or "protective of the community," whatever those terms mean. This helps legitimize the vast amount of authority and discretion vested on judges, parole boards, and community corrections personnel. Fourthly, many practices, procedures, or conditions in community corrections persist despite their dubious validity because the process of challenge carries high risks for the client. Revocation leading to incarceration is just a step away and often depends upon personal decisions of the probation or parole officer. Challenging conditions and practices can hasten revocation, hence submission becomes the wiser option. Finally, only a few cases thus far have been decided by the United States Supreme Court in community corrections. Thousands have been litigated in state and lower federal courts, but only a few have been decided by the United States Supreme Court for authoritative nation-wide guidance. The result is sometimes inconsistent decisions among state and federal courts. What is valid practice in one state may be invalid in another; what is deemed constitutional by one federal court in a state may be adjudged unconstitutional by another federal court in the same state, hence the confusion.

Given the above realities, it is important for criminal justice personnel to know the law in their particular jurisdiction and not simply rely on what may be applicable in most jurisdictions in the country. The discussion in this article proceeds along generic rules and does not refer to rules in specific jurisdictions, unless the issue has been settled by a United States Supreme Court decision. It affords the reader a view of the law and practice in most states, but not necessarily the law and practice in a particular

state. There is no substitute for knowing the specifics in a particular jurisdiction if the dangers that come with misinformation are to be avoided.

I. The Legal Limits of Probation and Parole

A. The Nature of Probation/Parole

Probation/parole is a privilege and not a right.[2] Consequently, it may be
withheld by the judge or board, unless there is a reasonable expectation of
release created by state law. Some jurisdictions have decided, however, that
if the legislature has provided for probation as a possible sentence, it ought
to be considered by the judge, otherwise there is possible abuse of discretion.[3] Once given, probation/parole ceases to be a privilege and instead
becomes an entitlement. This means that revocation cannot take place
unless the procedures prescribed in *Morrissey v. Brewer*[4] are followed,
giving probationer/parolee certain basic due process rights.

Since parole is a privilege, there is no constitutional right to a hearing
prior to the release process; neither is there a constitutional right to counsel — although some states do provide for a hearing and counsel by law or
administrative practice. Closely akin to the questions of hearing and
counsel is the matter of release guidelines. Courts have consistently held
that inmates have no constitutional right to release guidelines, although
such are used in many states. In the *Greenholtz*[5] case, the United States
Supreme Court said:

> Unlike the revocation decision, there is no set of facts which, if shown,
> mandates a decision favorable to the individual. The parole determina-
> tion, like a prisoner transfer decision, may be made for a variety of
> reasons and often invokes no more than informed predictions as to what
> would best serve correctional purposes or the safety and welfare of the
> inmate.[6]

In practice, many states use parole guidelines as a matter of state law or
administrative policy. This has the effect of limiting discretion and structuring inmate behavior expectation as conditions for parole. Where guidelines are set, there are expectations, sometimes amounting to an actionable
claim, that the guidelines will be followed. Despite the absence of guidelines, however, there are limits to what parole boards can do, such
limits being of constitutional nature. For example, despite wide discretion,
parole release cannot be refused on the basis of race, religion, national
origin, or the exercise of the right to court access, since these are established
constitutional rights which cannot be negated by discretion.[7]

If parole guidelines are used, retroactivity of application of unfavorable
provisions becomes a constitutional issue. Should the new unfavorable
guidelines be applied to inmates who are already serving sentence, or should
they apply only to those sentenced after the new guidelines take effect?

Courts are divided on the issue, some saying that retroactive application of unfavorable guidelines does not violate the constitutional prohibition against *ex post facto*; while others have ruled the practice unconstitutional. Whatever be the ruling on unfavorable guidelines, the converse rule is that guidelines favorable to inmates may be applied to everybody immediately — at the discretion of the board or legislature (if guidelines are set by law).

B. Parole Release Proceedings

In *Greenholtz v. Inmates of the Nebraska Penal and Correctional Complex,*[8] the United States Supreme Court held that no due process right applies unless state law creates a reasonable expectation, amounting to a liberty or property interest under the Fourteenth Amendment, that the prisoner will be paroled. Such reasonable expectation can be inferred from the wording of the state statute when the term used is "shall release" instead of "may release." In the *Greenholtz* case, the Nebraska law provided that the parole board "shall order an inmate's release unless in the final hearing, the board concludes that inmate's release should be deferred for at least one of four specified reasons."[9] The Court then held that the law as worded created the necessary reasonable expectation of parole that entitled inmates to due process. Such is not the case in most states where no state-law-created liberty interest exists that would entitle inmates to expectation of release. In most states, therefore, no due process applies.

The *Greenholtz* case is also significant in that it articulates several principles which clarify the legal status of parole. In summary, the Court said that[10]:

1. There is no constitutional or inherent right of a convicted person to be conditionally released before the expiration of a valid sentence.

2. The state may, as Nebraska did, establish a parole system, but it has no duty to do so.

3. Parole release and parole revocation are not the same in that there is a crucial distinction between being deprived of a liberty one has, as in parole, and being denied conditional liberty that one desires.

Despite the specific wording in *Greenholtz,* the Court failed to clarify what due process rights are to be given inmates prior to release in states, such as Nebraska, where the law creates liberty or property interests. This issue needs Court clarification in subsequent cases.

In *Connecticut Board of Pardons v. Dumchat,*[11] prisoners seeking parole relied on the frequency with which the Connecticut Board of Pardons had in the past commuted and paroled life sentences, arguing that the consistency of the board's actions in the past had created an unwritten common law of sentence commutation and parole acceleration and had given rise to an unspoken understanding between the board and the inmates. The Court rejected this contention, saying that "no matter how frequently a particular form of clemency has been granted, the statistical probabilities standing alone generate no constitutional protections."[12] Agency practice does not rise to the level of a constitutional right.

Another frequently litigated question is whether inmates have a right to see their parole file. The *Greenholtz* case implied that there is no constitutional right of access to file, but here again state law and agency rules must be considered. The inmate may be entitled to access if state law or agency rules establish a due process right and if such right includes the right of access to file. Most courts, however, rule that even if due process is established, such right does not include access to file, hence real legal impediments exist if a prisoner wants to see his parole file.

Parole Boards are not constitutionally required to state reasons for denial of parole, but such may in fact be required through the state's Administrative Procedure Act, the state constitution, or by board policy.[13] Despite the absence of a constitutional mandate, an overwhelming majority of states do give reasons for parole denial, although the procedure and form by which that information is given to the inmate vary. Some states go into specifics for the denial of parole; others use standardized pre-printed forms which do not convey much information other than a general reason for parole rejection.

C. Parole Board Liability for Release of Inmate

Parole board liability for the release of an inmate on parole who subsequently commits an offense is an important legal issue which has drawn the attention of the courts and will continue to be litigated in the immediate future. The question centers on possible liability of parole board members to victims or their families for crimes, particularly of a violent and predatory nature, committed by inmates released on parole.

Most courts grant absolute immunity to parole officials for damage or injury emanating from the decision to release an inmate on parole. This is based on the rationale that such decision is "judge like" in nature and therefore entitled to the same type of absolute immunite enjoyed by judges.[14] A few courts, however, reject the absolute immunity defense and impose liability in cases where parole officials acted in a certain manner in releasing a potentially dangerous prisoner. In one case, the Arizona Supreme Court imposed civil liability on parole board members for releasing a prisoner who later robbed a tavern, murdered one man, and injured another critically.[15] Liability was based on the finding that the release decision was *reckless* or *grossly or clearly negligent.* In jurisdictions that reject the absolute immunity rule and therefore allow liabilty, the central issue becomes — when is a parole board reckless or grossly or clearly negligent in granting a parole release? There is no definitive answer; however, courts tend to use the standards of duty and foreseeability—meaning whether there is a legal duty of care imposed on the parole board and whether, given a set of circumstances, the danger could have been foreseen.[16] There are obviously subjective terms whose meaning can vary from state to state or from one judge to another.

D. Conditions

The imposition of conditions is not a major concern of probation/parole officers because conditions are imposed either by the judge or board and usually in standardized fashion. Most states by law suggest conditions to be imposed, but the judge or board has absolute discretion and authority to accept, modify, or reject these conditions.

In general, conditions are valid if they are: (1) constitutional, (2) reasonable, (3) clear, and (4) contribute to the rehabilitation of the offender and/or the protection of society.[17] These terms are difficult to operationally define and therefore leave the judge or board vast discretion in imposing conditions.

Of special interest is the validity of conditions requiring certain types of treatment as a condition for probation/parole. The treatment prescribed may be in the form of counseling, psychotherapy, medical treatment, or surgery. The validity of these conditions, particularly of the experimental type, hinges on whether or not the treatment prescribed is so harsh as to violate the prohibition against cruel and unusual punishment, and whether a relationship exists between the offense and the treatment prescribed. A subsidiary issue is whether probation/parole can be revoked for failure to undergo treatment because of indigency. The *Bearden* case, discussed below probably answers this question in the negative.

The imposition of special conditions and the delegation of power to impose conditions create special problems. The general rule is that the imposition of conditions is a responsibility of the judge or board which cannot be delegated to an officer in the absence of specific legislation. In practice, judges or boards do authorize the setting of "such other conditions as the probation officer may deem proper to impose"; or may leave the mode of implementation of a condition (such as the method of mental treatment) to the discretion of the officer. This is fraught with risks because should the condition imposed or the method of implementation prescribed turn out to be unlawful, the officer faces possible liability. To minimize possible exposure, officers should avoid the imposition of special conditions and refrain from accepting delegated authority to impose conditions. If such be unavoidable because of judicial or board insistence, the officer is best protected if an agreement to the condition is secured in writing from the probationer/parolee and a copy of the signed document is furnished the judge or board.

Conditions imposed should not be changed or modified unilaterally by the officer. Unauthorized changes or modifications carry a high risk of liability. It must be realized that while judges enjoy absolute immunity for judicial acts and therefore are not liable even if the condition imposed turns out to be unconstitutional, such protection is not available to a probation/parole officer who is immune only if the act was done in good faith. The officer bears personal responsibility for changing a condition which change turns out to be unconstitutional.

E. Supervision

The area of supervision raises a host of potential liability pitfalls for probation/parole officers. The first concerns possible liability to the client for disclosing information to prospective or current employers which leads to job rejection or dismissal. There are no cases addressing this issue, but chances are that no liability ensues as long as such disclosure was made by the officer without malice. This is because there are strong justifications for disclosure, foremost being public protection and the high probability that the record revealed is a public record.

A second concern stems from disclosure of information given by the client to the officer in confidence. Chances of liability in these cases are minimal because of the nature of the role of a probation/parole officer. In *Fare v. Michael C,* [18] the United States Supreme Court said:

> A probation officer is not in the same posture (as a lawyer) with regard to either the accused or the system of justice as a whole. . . . He does not assume the power to act on behalf of his client by virtue of his status as adviser, nor are the communications of the accused to the probation officer shielded by the lawyer-client privilege. . . . In most cases, the probation officer is duty bound to report wrongdoing by the juvenile when it comes to his attention, even if by communication from the juvenile himself. [19]

The situation is different and liability may arise if disclosure of confidential information is prohibited by state law or agency policy.

Perhaps the most-widely litigated issue in the area of supervision is officer liability for failure to disclose a probationer/parolee's background to a third party, resulting in subsequent death or serious injury. In these cases, the general rule is: The duty to warn arises when, based on probationer's/parolee's criminal background and past conduct, the officer can "reasonably foresee" a prospect of harm (physical or non-physical) to a third party." [20] The key terms are "reasonably foresee" and "specific third party." Reasonably foresee means that the circumstances of the relationship between the client and the client's employer suggests that the client may engage in a criminal or anti-social conduct similar, or related to, his previous offense. [21] An example would be a rapist-parolee working as a security guard in an apartment complex, or an embezzler working as an accountant in a bank. Here the officer has an obligation, given the foreseeability of the harm, to warn the employer of the probationer's/parolee's background. Conversely, there is no duty to warn if an embezzler-parolee obtains a job as a construction worker because here foreseeability does not exist since the opportunity to embezzle in a job where the parolee is not entrusted with money is remote, if not non-existent.

Other liability concerns in supervision are search and seizure and self-incrimination waivers. Are probation/parole conditions allowing home visits and/or search and seizure at unspecified hours valid? Court decisions are mixed, but even in those jurisdictions which uphold these conditions, there is insistence that the terms of the condition be narrowly drawn to obviate abuse, and that the condition be reasonably interpreted, meaning that the time and manner of execution be reasonable. In essence, blanket authorization for the officer to conduct visits or searches at any time is most probably not valid, unless there be a compelling justification for imposing such condition. An example would be allowing unannounced home visits for probation stemming from conviction for drug use or possession. Even here, the condition must be implemented reasonably so that it does not become a vehicle for harassment.

Are conditions requiring probationers/parolees to in effect waive their right against self-incrimination and answer all questions asked by the officer valid? The courts are split on this issue; some upholding the condition as valid, while others maintain that this is an invalid waiver of rights because the alternative, in case of refusal to waive, is denial of parole or probation. The United States Supreme Court has yet to resolve this issue.

A Minnesota case,[22] decided in 1984 by the United States Supreme Court, raises the following question: Should the Miranda warnings be given in cases of noncustodial interrogation of a probationer by a probation officer wherein incriminating admissions were obtained? In that case, the probationer was required by probation conditions to meet with the probation officer as directed and to be truthful. The questioning took place without the Miranda warnings even though the officer suspected that the probationer was involved in prior criminal activity. The Minnesota Supreme Court ruled that the Miranda warning ought to have been given, hence excluded the admission from the criminal trial. The United States Supreme Court reversed that decision saying that such admission was validly obtained and therefore admissable as evidence in a criminal trial.

Note that the Minnesota case involves *noncustodial* interrogation where the officer suspected that probationer was involved in criminal activity and evidence obtained was to be introduced in a criminal trial. Custodial interrogation of probationers/parolees by officers without the Miranda warnings have generally been held inadmissible in criminal trials. Most states admit evidence obtained without Miranda in revocation proceedings even though the same states exclude it in criminal trials.

Another issue often litigated under self-incrimination concerns conditions compelling clients to submit to urine or blood tests for drugs. These conditions have generally been upheld as valid as long as they are rehabili-tative and reasonably related to the offense committed. Physical self-incrimination, such as is involved in blood or drug tests, does not come under the protective umbrella of the Fifth Amendment which protects only against testimonial self-incrimination.[23]

Is there need for a warrant in search and seizure cases? Despite judicial preference for warrants, courts have rejected the warrant requirement in cases of probationers/parolees on the ground that their status affords them diminished privacy or Fourth Amendment protection. The degree of cer-tainty needed before warrantless search or seizure can take place varies from one state to another, some requiring probable cause while others are satisfied with "reasonable suspicion."

F. Revocation

Perhaps the most important case decided by the United States Supreme Court thus far in probation/parole is *Morrissey v. Brewer.*[24] That case held that parolees are entitled to a two-step procedure for revocation and that certain due process rights must be afforded the parolee prior to revocation. A year later, the same rights were extended by the Court to probationers in *Gagnon v. Scarpelli.*[25] Though enlightening, these cases left a number of important issues unaddressed, giving lower courts no authoritative guidance.

A troublesome issue is whether or not the Exclusionary Rule (which pro-hibits the admission in court of illegally-seized evidence) applies in proba-tion/parole cases. Most states admit evidence obtained illegally in revoca-tion proceedings; others reject it. Regardless of state rule in revocation cases, evidence illegally obtained by probation/parole officers cannot be used in a criminal trial.

The most recent case decided by the United States Supreme Court in probation/parole settles an issue in which lower courts were divided. The issue concerns revocation of probation/parole for failure to pay fines, costs, fees, or restitution. In *Bearden v. Georgia,*[26] decided in 1983, the Court held that a judge cannot properly revoke a defendant's probation for failure to pay a fine and make restitution—in the absence of evidence and finding that the probationer was somehow responsible for the failure, or that alternative forms of punishment were inadequate to meet the state's interest in punishment and deterrence. In that case, the defendant pleaded guilty in a Georgia trial court to burglary and theft, but the trial court did enter a judgment of guilt. Instead, it sentenced the defendant to probation on condition that he pay a $500 fine and $250 in restitution, payment to be made in installments. Defendant paid the first $200, but a month later was laid off from his job and, despite repeated efforts, was unable to find other work. Probation was revoked by the trial court, conviction was entered, and defendant was sent to prison. On appeal, the Court said that if a state determined a fine or restitution to be the appropriate and adequate penalty for the crime, it may not thereafter imprison a person solely because he lacked the resources to pay it since this would be a violation of probationer's right to equal protection. It is important to note that a distinction must be made between inability to pay (due to indigency or temporary lack of resources) and refusal to pay despite the availability of resources. Inability to pay cannot lead to revocation, whereas refusal to pay can be the valid basis of a motion to revoke.

II. The Legal Limits in Other Community Corrections Programs

As stated in the introduction, probation and parole constitute the biggest segment of community corrections, hence the major portion of this article is devoted to a discussion of their legal limits. There are, however, programs other than probation or parole which keep the offender out of jail or prison. Hussey and Duffey cite the following as examples of such community programs: The Highfields Experiment, Synanon, The Community Treatment Project, the Probation Subsidy, the Des Moines, Iowa Programs, the Massachusetts Program, and Halfway Houses.[27] Despite their wide variety, the common characteristics among these programs are that they are community based without being under probation or parole and are aimed at rehabilitation of the offender or the protection of the public.

Only a few cases have been decided by the courts in community corrections outside probation and parole, but several issues deserve attention. Foremost is whether or not proprietor or personnel of private programs can be held liable in a civil rights (Section 1983) lawsuit. The issue arises because one of the essential elements of a civil rights case is that the person or agency sued must have been "acting under color of law." Public officials are presumably "acting under color of law," but private individuals generally do not fall under this category. Most courts have decided that the relationship can be such that private agencies or individuals can in fact be considered to have acted under color of law under these circumstances,[28] hence may be held liable in a civil rights lawsuit by virtue of a contractual relationship. The rationale is that there is sufficient governmental involvement in these cases to justify the exposure of private individuals.

A subsidiary issue is whether or not a private agency can compel a client to do what government officials otherwise cannot compel him to do because of limitations in the Bill of Rights. An example is a halfway house, owned and managed by a private agency, requiring all its residents to attend religious instruction and services as part of its rehabilitative program. The Constitution prohibits required religious instruction if imposed by government officials, but private individuals ordinarily do not come under the constraints of the Bill of Rights. Courts have indicated, however, that there may be sufficient government involvement in these instances to justify bringing private persons or agencies under constitutional prohibitions.[29]

Another important issue goes into the liability of a governmental agency for what a private person or agency, with whom it has a contractual relationship, does. Will the governmental agency be subsidiarily liable if the proprietor or personnel of a private halfway house grossly violates the rights of a client? There are no clear laws or court decisions on this issue, however, a prediction would be that governmental agencies can be held liable if there is sufficient governmental involvement by the private agency in the form of financial support and regulation such that the act committed loses its purely private nature.

A final issue concerns the use by private agencies of volunteers. This is an even bigger problem in probation and parole where agencies have used volunteers extensively to implement or supplement programs. The potential for liability comes from two fronts—liability for damage done to clients by volunteers and liability to third parties from clients supervised by volunteers. Despite the litigation potential of this issue, the courts have not adequately addressed it. A prediction, based on cases raising similar concerns, would be that the use of volunteers will probably not exempt the agency from liability if there is sufficient involvement by the government in what the volunteer does and if negligence in agency supervision exists.

III. Legal Liabilities of Probation, Parole, and Community Corrections Officers

A. Federal and State Liabilities: An Overview

The sources of legal liabilities to which probation/parole officers may be exposed are many and varied. They range from state to federal law and from civil to criminal. For purpose of an overview, legal liabilities may be classified as follows:

Potential Sources of Personal Liability for Individual Probation/Parole Officers

	I. Federal	II. State Law
A. Civil Liabilities	• Title 42 of U.S. Code, Section 1983-Civil Action for Deprivation of Civil Rights	• State Tort Law
	• Title 42 of U.S. Code, Section 1985-Civil Action for Conspiracy	• State Civil Rights Law
	• Title 42 of U.S. Code, Section 1981-Equal rights Under the Law	

B. Criminal Liabilities • Title 19 of U.S. Code, • State Penal Code Pro-
                           Section 242-Criminal   visions   specially
                           Liability for Depriva-   aimed at Public Offi-
                           tion of Civil Rights   cers for such crimes
                         • Title 18 of U.S. Code,   as official oppression.
                           Section 241-Criminal
                           Liability for Conspir- • Regular Penal Code
                           acy to Deprive a Per-   Provisions Punishing
                           son of Rights   Criminal Acts
                         • Title 18 of U.S. Code,
                           Section 245-Violation
                           of Federally-Protect-
                           ed Activities

Despite the availability of several legal remedies as indicated above, pro-
bationers/parolees prefer to use one of two remedies which are: civil liability under state tort law and civil liability under 42 U.S. Code, Section 1983.

A state tort may be defined as a wrong, in which the action of one person
causes injury to the person or property of another, in violation of a legal
duty imposed by law.[30] Torts may involve a wrongdoing against a person,
such as assault, battery, false arrest, false imprisonment, invasion of privacy, libel, slander, wrongful death, and malicious prosecution; or against
property, such as trespass. A tort may be intentional (acts based on the
intent of the actor to cause a certain event or harm), or caused by negligence. Probation/parole officers may therefore be held liable for a tortious
act that causes damage to person or property of another. Note that Section
1983 actions are sometimes referred to as tort cases, but the reference is to
federal instead of state tort.

B. Civil Liability Under 42 U.S. Code, Section 1983: Civil Rights Cases

This is by far the most widely-used provision of law in the whole array of
legal liability statutes on the state and federal levels. From all indications, it
continues to be the main source of legal redress, hence it deserves extensive
consideration.

Title 42, U.S. Code, Section 1983 reads as follows:

> Civil action for deprivation of rights: Every Person who, under color of
> any statute, ordinance, regulation, custom, or usage, of any State or
> Territory, subjects, or causes to be subjected, any citizen of the United
> States or other persons within the jurisdiction thereof to the deprivation
> of any rights, privileges, or immunities secured by the Constitution and
> laws, shall be liable to the party injured in an action at law, suit in
> equity, or other proper proceeding for redress.

In 1960 there were only 247 civil rights cases filed in federal district courts
throughout the United States. In 1970, there were 3,985 such suits, an

increase of 1,614% and in 1976, the figure had grown to 12,329, an increase of 4,991% over 1960. These suits involve claims against almost every type of government official, from the President of the United States, the Attorney General, high White House and FBI officials, and Cabinet Officers to sheriffs, police officers, school administrators, IRS agents, hospital superintendents, governors, state military officials, building inspectors, prison officials, and other correctional officers. They also cover a variety of alleged civil rights violations ranging from assaults, illegal searches, illegal arrests or break-ins, inadequate medical attention, tax investigation, illegal wiretaps, and a range of improper actions taken by just about every type of public officer.[31]

Only a small percentage of these cases actually, however, go to trial. For example, in 1979, 9,943 out of 10,301 civil rights cases filed by prisoners (96.5%) in federal court were dismissed or otherwise concluded prior to trial. Only 358, or 3.5% of state prisoner civil rights cases, went to trial.[32] Nonetheless, a tremendous amount of effort and anxiety is invested by both parties even if the case never gets to the trial stage.

1. Basic Elements of a Section 1983 Suit:

There are four basic elements of a 1983 suit as interpreted by the courts. These are:

- The defendant must be a natural person or a local government;
- The defendant must be acting under "color of law";
- The violation must be of a constitutional or a federally-protected right; and
- The violation must reach constitutional level.

a. *The Defendant Must be a Natural Person or a Local Government:* Until recently, only natural persons could be held liable in 1983 suits. State and local governments were exempt because of the doctrine of sovereign immunity. In 1978, however, the United States Supreme Court, in *Monnell v. Department of Social Services of the City of New York,* held that local units of government may now be held liable if the allegedly unconstitutional action was taken by the officer as a part of an official policy or custom. What "policy or custom" means has not been made clear and is subject to varying interpretations. State immunity is still alive despite *Monnell* because that decision applies to local governments only. This is not of much consolation to state probation/parole officers, however, because the suit can be filed against the state officer himself (although not against the state) who then become personally liable. While the *Monnell* case involved Department of Social Services officers, there is reason to believe that this ruling will apply to probation/parole officers. It has already been applied by lower courts to many local agencies.

b. *The Defendant Must be Acting Under "Color of State Law":* This means the misuse of power possessed by virtue of state law and made possible only because the wrongdoer is clothed with authority of state law. The problem is that while it is easy to identify acts which are wholly within the term "color of state law" (as when a probation officer conducts a presentence investigation upon court order), there are gray areas which defy easy categorization (as when a probation officer who moonlights as a private security guard illegally arrests a person whom he knows to be a probationer). As a general rule, anything a probation/parole officer does in the performance of his regular duties and during the usual hours is considered under color of state law. Conversely, what he does as a private citizen during his off-hours falls outside the color of state law. There are, however, cases in the above continuum which are difficult to classify. In these instances, the court makes a case by case determination based on the facts presented in court.

The term color of state law has been interpreted by the courts broadly to include local laws or regulations. Therefore, a probation officer who acts in accordance with a county or city ordinance is acting under color of state law. Moreover, the phrase does not mean that the act was in fact authorized by law. It is sufficient if the act appeared to be lawful even if it was not in fact authorized;[34] hence, if the probation/parole officer exceeded his lawful authority, he is still deemed to have acted under color of law. An example is a probation officer who searches a probationer's residence without legal authorization. The officer is nonetheless considered to have acted under color of law and therefore may be sued under section 1983.

c. *The Violation of a Constitutionally or Federally Protected Right:* Under this prerequisite, the right violated must be one guaranteed by the United States Constitution or that given by federal law. Rights given by state law are not protected under section 1983. For example, the right to a lawyer during a parole release hearing is not given by the federal Constitution or by federal law. If this right is given an inmate by state law, such violation does not give rise to a 1983 suit. The violation may be punishable, however, under state law or administrative regulation.

The difficulty is that while certain acts of probation/parole officers may be blatantly violative of a constitutional right (as when probation officer searches a probationer's house without any authorization whatsoever), others are difficult to determine. This is particularly troublesome in probation/parole where the courts have just started to define specific rights to which probationers and parolees are constitutionally entitled. There have been only a handful of cases decided thus far by the United States Supreme Court defining the rights of probationers and parolees, although many have been decided by federal district courts and courts of appeals. Some of these decisions may also be inconsistent with each other. For example, some courts say that probable cause is necessary for search and seizure, while others consider searches and seizures valid on less than probable cause.[35] It is therefore important for the probation/parole officer to be familiar with the current law in his/her jurisdiction. This is the law which must be followed regardless of other decisions to the contrary in other states.

d. *The Violation Must Reach Constitutional Level:* This means that not all violations of rights lead to liability under section 1983. The violation must be of constitutional proportion. What this means is not exactly clear except that generally serious violations are actionable whereas non-serious ones are not. In the words of the 8th Circuit Court of Appeals:

> "Courts cannot prohibit a given condition or type of treatment unless it reaches a level of constitutional abuse. Courts encounter numerous cases in which the acts or conditions under attack are clearly undesirable...but the courts are powerless to act because the practices are not so abusive as to violate a constitutional right."[36]

Mere words, threats, a push, a shove, temporary inconvenience, or even a single punch in the face do not necessarily constitute a civil rights violation.[37] Neither does section 1983 apply to such cases as the officer giving a false testimony, simple negligence, or name-calling.[38] On the other hand, the denial of the right to a parole revocation hearing as mandated in *Morrissey v. Brewer,* constitutes a clear violation of constitutional rights.

A probation/parole officer is liable if all of the above four elements are present. Absence of any of these means that there is no liability under section 1983. The officer may be liable, however under some other provisions of law, such as under state tort or the Penal Code, but not under section 1983. For example, a probation officer who beats up a probationer in a downtown bar for something unrelated to his probation may be liable under the regular Penal Code provisions for assault and battery, but not under section 1983. It must be stressed that the absence of any of the above elements may not prevent the filing of a 1983 suit. Suits may be filed by anybody at any time; whether the suit will succeed or fail is a different matter which goes into the merits of the case.

2. Defenses in Section 1983 Suits:

Various legal defenses are available in civil rights cases. Some of these are the usual defenses available under state tort actions, while others are such defenses as probable cause, collateral estoppel, res judicata, laches, justiciability, obstruction, and the Younger doctrine. The defenses which are most-often invoked by defendants, however, are official immunity and good faith.

a. *The Official Immunity Defense:* There are classes of defendants for whom the law, for reasons of policy, has conferred immunity or exemption from civil liability. Official immunity may be classified into three categories; namely: (1) absolute; (2) qualified; (3) quasi-judicial.

(1) Absolute immunity: The need to encourage decision making has led to the recognition of an absolute immunity for some offi-

cials. This privilege protects the official from liability for his official acts even if they were done with malice, and allows the courts to dismiss actions for damages immediately without going into the merits of plaintiff's claim.[39] Federal and state legislators, judges, and prosecutors enjoy absolute immunity. Probation/parole officers do no.

(2) Qualified immunity: The courts have been less willing to find absolute immunity for other public employees who are not involved in the legislative or judicial process. These officials, most of whom are from the executive department of government, enjoy only qualified immunity. The qualified immunity doctrine is used in two different but related concepts. According to the first concept, the immunity defense applies to an official's *discretionary* acts, meaning those that require personal deliberation and judgment. The immunity defense is not available, however, for *ministerial* acts, meaning those which amount only to the performance of a duty in which the officer is left with no choice of his own.[40] For example, a parole hearing officer's recommendation to revoke or not to revoke parole is a *discretionary* act, but the duty to give parolee a hearing before revocation is *ministerial* in that the parole hearing officer is mandated to do so by the United States Supreme Court. A major difficulty with the discretionary-ministerial dichotomy is that there is no standard method of distinguishing discretionary from ministerial duties. The distinction is subjective and can vary with specific judges and jurisdictions and is thus difficult to predict. Generally, however, officials in policy-making positions (such as probation/parole board members) are more likely to make discretionary decisions, and thus are better able to invoke the immunity defense for their actions. Field officers usually perform only ministerial acts and are therefore advised to consider their functions as merely ministerial, unless declared otherwise by the court.

A second and better known way of interpreting qualified immunity is by relating it to the "good faith" defense. Under this concept, a public officer (other than those who enjoy absolute immunity) is exempt from liability but only if he can demonstrate that his actions were reasonable and performed in good faith in the scope of his employment.[41]

(3) Quasi-judicial immunity: Absolute immunity generally applies to officials in the judicial and legislative branches of government while qualified immunity applies to those in the executive branch. Some officials, however, have both judicial and executive responsibility, such officials as court personnel, parole

board members, and some probation officers. These officials are given some protection, referred to as "quasi-judicial immunity." Under this type of immunity, the official enjoys absolute immunity if performing judicial-type functions, but only qualified immunity if performing other functions. The emphasis therefore is on the function performed instead of the agency for whom the officer works.

Probation/parole officers enjoy qualified immunity, with some exceptions. Probation officers, although employees of the court who work under court supervision in most jurisdictions, do not enjoy the absolute immunity of judges, but they have been given absolute immunity for some acts. For example, the 5th Circuit Court of Appeals has held that a probation officer is entitled to absolute immunity when preparing and submitting a presentence report.[42] Another case, decided by the California Court of Appeals in 1978, held that in preparing and submitting a probation report on the defendant, the probation officer was performing a "quasi-judicial" function and was therefore absolutely immune from liability under section 1983. Most of the actuations of such court-supervised probation officers, however, are considered executive in nature and hence are likely to be categorized under qualified immunity. This means that probation officers are liable unless the act is discretionary or done in good faith. Parole officers are usually employees of the executive department of the state and as such enjoy only qualified immunity.

Most federal courts of appeals have ruled that higher officials of the executive branch who must make judge-like decisions are performing a judicial function which deserves absolute immunity. This has particular relevance to parole boards when performing such functions as considering applications for parole, recommending that a parole date be rescinded, or conducting a parole revocation hearing.[44]

  b. *The Good Faith Defense:* Good faith is by far the most-often invoked defense in civil rights cases. It has been made available since 1967 in actions seeking damages under section 1983. Good faith basically means that the probation or parole officer is acting with honest intentions, under the law, and in the absence of fraud, deceit, collusion, or gross negligence.[45] The opposite of good faith in legal language is bad faith. For good faith to succeed as a defense, the defendant must prove two elements, namely:

  (1) The officer must be acting sincerely and with a belief that what he is doing is lawful, and;

  (2) The judge or jury must be convinced that such belief was reasonable.[46]

General Guide to Types of Official Immunity in Damage Suits

	Absolute*	Quasi Judicial**	Qualified***
Judges	X		
Legislators	X		
Prosecutors	X		
Parole Board Members		X (If performing a judge-like function, such as the decision to parole)	X (If performing other functions)
Supervisors (all criminal justice agencies)			X
Probation Officers		X (If performing functions under order of judge)	X (If performing other functions)
Parole Officers			X
Prison Guards			X
Police Officers			X
State Agencies	X (Unless waived by law or court decision)		
Local Agencies	No Immunity		No Immunity

* Absolute immunity means that a civil liability suit, if brought, is dismissed by the court without going into the merits of plaintiff's claim. No liability.

** Quasi-judicial immunity means that officers are immune if performing judicial type functions and liable if performing other functions.

*** Qualified immunity means that the officer's act is immune from liability if discretionary, but not if ministerial. It also means that an officer may not be liable even if the act is ministerial if it was done in good faith.

The first element probes into the officer's state of mind at the time of the commission of the act, something which is obviously difficult to ascertain. In most cases, this is a matter of testimony by the probation/parole officer as to his state of mind at the time the action was taken. The second element somehow diffuses this subjectivity by interjecting a third-party standard — that of the reasonableness of the act based on the conclusion of the judge or jury before whom the case is tried. Even if the defendant proves that he sincerely believed that his act was lawful, he is still liable if he cannot prove that his belief was reasonable.

The good faith defense is strongly enhanced by a number of acts which tend to establish that the officer did not in fact act in bad faith. This includes such acts as: following agency manual and guideline, acting on advice of legal counsel, following the order of a supervisor, or acting in accordance with law or court decision.

C. Legal Representation and Indemnification:

A probation or parole officer facing a liability suit under federal or state law has two immediate concerns: One is legal representation and the other is monetary indemnification, if held liable.[47]

There are various guidelines states use in deciding the kind of acts of public officers states will defend. In general, states are more willing to provide legal assistance to state employees sued in civil cases than they are to those accused of criminal wrongdoing. All states provide representation in civil actions, at least some of the time, for both probation and parole officers. A substantial percentage, however, will not defend in all civil suits.

a. Civil liability cases: Most of the states have a fairly liberal criteria for defending civil suits requiring only that the officer's act or omission occur during the scope of employment. Some states require, however, in addition that the officer be acting in "good faith." The term "good faith" varies in meaning from state to state, some defining it as instances where the officer was "not grossly negligent," while other states' primary concern is that the officer has not violated a state rule or law.

If an act comes within the guidelines, the attorney general usually serves as the officer's legal representative in the suit. Eighteen states allow outside lawyers to be hired at state expense to defend a state employee. Some states allow reimbursement by the state for lawyers' fees and court costs if the employee wins the suit *after* the state's attorney general office has refused to defend the officer.

b. Criminal cases: The picture is less promising if the probation or parole officer is involved in a criminal action. In about one-half of the states, the state will not undertake a defense of an officer. Since the state is an interested party in criminal proceedings, a conflict of interest might prevent the state from representing the probation/parole officer. The responses from several of the states in the survey indicated that state legal representation in these cases is at the discretion of the Attorney General's office. Others stated that the situation had never arisen and that the policies were unclear. Very few states indicated unequivocally that the state would undertake the defense of an officer charged with a criminal offense.

2. Indemnification in Case of Liability

If probation/parole officer is held liable in a lawsuit, who pays for damages assessed against him by the court? A majority of the states provide for indemnification for public employees. The amount states are willing to pay varies considerably. Some states set no limits, but the majority do. If the court awards the plaintiff an amount larger than the maximum allowed by the state, the employee would pay the difference.

Although most states provide some form of indemnification for officers who are sued, it does not follow that the state will automatically indemnify. The majority of states will help pay the judgment only if the errant act on which the finding of liability is based was "within the scope of employment." Again, this phrase is susceptible to different interpretations in different states. Moreover, most states also require that the employee performed the act in good faith.

D. Insurance:

Since probation/parole officers in many states may be unable to obtain legal representation or indemnification if sued, professional liability insurance would be a reasonable alternative. Some states have purchased insurance for probation and parole officers. In cases where the employing agency does not pay for the premium, the officer may have to pay for it himself if he wants liability protection. Aside from paying for any damage award, the insurance company will most likely undertake the officer's defense for obvious reasons. A number of correctional organizations have made arrangements for liability insurance for their members at a reasonable rate. The American Correctional Association now has professional liability insurance available to its members at reasonable cost.[48]

Insurance for public employees is sometimes discouraged on the ground that it serves to encourage the filing of lawsuits against public officers. It is also feared that the amount of damages awarded would increase if the judge or jury became aware that the costs would be borne by insurance company, rather than by an individual or governmental unit. In many jurisdictions, however, insurance ownership or governmental indemnification cannot be mentioned at the trial or hearing, hence negating this adverse effect.

E. General Legal Advice

In 1980, a project sponsored by the National Institute of Corrections on the "Legal Responsibilities of Probation and Parole Officers" sent a questionnaire to attorneys general of all the fifty states which asked, among others, this question:

> What three most important bits of legal advice would you give probation and parole officers to help them avoid or lessen possible legal liability in connection with their work?[49]

Responses were received from 49 states. Ranked in the order of response frequency, the top five answers to this open-ended question were as follows:

1. Document your activities. Keep good records. (40%)

2. Know and follow department rules and regulations and your state statutes. (35%)
3. Arrange for legal counsel and seek legal advice whenever questions arise. (27%)
4. Act within the scope of your duties and in good faith. (20%)
5. Get approval from your supervisor if you have questions about what you are doing. (18%)

It behooves community corrections officers to heed these words of advice from the legal professionals in the field in the face of mounting civil rights and state tort liability cases. On the other hand, a word of caution is in order. Knowledge of legal responsibilities and awareness of possible legal liabilities can lead to needless paranoia and paralysis of action. This should be avoided because in many cases, reluctance or failure to perform duties can be more harmful to the client than acting incorrectly.

Conclusion

It is imperative that community corrections officers take into careful consideration the limits set by law, otherwise serious consequences ensue. The erstwhile "hands off" attitude of the courts has given way to an "open door" era in judicial litigation. Consequently, the vast amount of discretion hitherto enjoyed by community corrections personnel has diminished, primarily in response to constitutional mandate as perceived by the courts. This has raised serious concerns among criminal justice practitioners who feel that community corrections deal with human problems needing individualized solutions which court judges are not in a position to understand, much less solve through judicial edict.

Judicial intervention, either in the form of an injunction or holding officers monetarily liable for violations of constitutional rights, has had a significant impact in community corrections, particularly in probation and parole where most cases thus far have been litigated. It has judicialized the corrections arena and fostered an antagonistic relationship between officer and client where none is desirable or desired by either party. Officers are aware that the courts are looking over their shoulders and are in a position to second-guess decisions with the benefit of hindsight. This has had the effect, in some cases, of stifling innovation in a field where innovative ideas are badly needed. Understandably, judicial intervention has created paranoia and generated antagonism for the judiciary.

On the positive side, judicial intervention has resulted in less arbitrariness and a standardization of decision-making in community corrections. Fear of possible liability and the perceived need for clearer guidelines have led to the adoption of manuals by community corrections agencies. Manuals tend to curb discretion, but when followed constitute a good defense in liability lawsuits. The fear of legal liability has led to greater emphasis on training programs and enhanced competency and professionalism among officers. Community corrections agencies have become proactive and anticipative of problems, rather than being merely reactive, as they tended to be in the past. Crisis management has given way to careful planning. The fear of liability lawsuits and court injunction has spurred community corrections chiefs to become more assertive lobbyists and informed supervisors; managerial virtues which community corrections badly needs. It has also forced political decisionmakers to give community corrections the funding and attention it deserves.

There used to be a time, not long ago, when community corrections escaped judicial scrutiny and when legal problems merited the concern only of government lawyers who gave disinterested attention to what they were doing. That time is gone. The advent of judicial intervention demands basic knowledge on the part of community corrections officers concerning law and legal liabilities. Judicial intervention in community corrections is here to stay, although its intensity may abate in the future after basic constitutional questions are addressed and settled. That may take a while. In the meantime, it is a reality which community corrections officers will have to learn to live with and cope.

References

[1] "Probation and Parole 1981," *Bureau of Justice Statistics Bulletin,* Bureau of Justice Statistics, U.S. Department of Justice.

[2] For cases holding that probation is not a constitutional right, see *U.S. v. Savage,* 440 F2d 1237 (5th Cir. 1971); and *U.S. v. Birnbaum,* 421 F2d 993 (2nd Cir), *cert denied,* 397 U.S. 1044 (1970). For cases holding that parole is not a constitutional right, see *Greenholtz v. Inmates of the Nebraska Penal & Correctional Complex,* 442 U.S. 1 (1979).

[3] See *U.S. v. Hayward,* 471 F2d 388 (7th Cir. 1972).

[4] 408 U.S. 471 (1972).

[5] *Greenholtz v. Inmates of the Nebraska Penal & Correctional Complex,* 442 U.S. 1 (1979).

[6] *Ibid.* at 10.

[7] See *Block v. Potter,* 631 F2d 233(3d Cir. 1980), also *Texas Supporters of Workers World Party Presidential Candidates v. Strake,* 511 F. Supp. 149 (S.D. Tex. 1981); *Candelaria v. Griffin,* 641 F2d 868 (10th Cir. 1980); *Farris v. U.S. Board of Parole,* 384 F2d 948 (7th Cir. 1973).

[8] 442 U.S. 1 (1979).

[9] *Ibid.* at 1.

[10] *Ibid.* at 1-16.

[11] 452 U.S. 458 (1981).

[12] *Ibid.* at 465.

[13] As a practical matter, this issue had been resolved in favor of the giving of reasons when as of 1976 47 jurisdictions routinely gave written explanations. See V. O'Leary and K. Hanrahan, *Parole Systems in the United States* 44 (3d ed. 1976).

14See *Keeton v. Procunier,* 468 F2d 810 (9th Cir. 1972); *Bennett v. People,* 406 F2d 36 (9th Cir. 1969).

15*Grimm v. Arizona Board of Pardons & Paroles,* 115 Ariz. 260 (1977).

16See *Thompson v. Alameda County,* 152 Cal. Rptr. 226 (1979).

17See *U.S. v. Consuelo-Gonzales,* 521 F2d 259 (9th Cir. 1975); *Porth v. Templar,* 453 F2d 330 (10th Cir. 1971).

18442 U.S. 707 (1979).

19*Ibid.* at 719-720.

20See *Johnson v. State,* 69 Cal. 2d 782 (1968); *Georgen v. State,* 196 N.Y.S. 2d 455 (Ct. Cl. 1959); and *Rieser v. District of Columbia,* 563 F2d 462 (D.C. Cir. 1977).

21Unpublished copy of the remarks of Judd D. Kutcher, Federal Probation Service legal adviser, to the American Probation and Parole Association (Oct. 29, 1980).

22*Minnesota v. Murphy,* 34 CrL 3057 (1984).

23*Gilbert v. California,* 388 U.S. 263 (1967).

24408 U.S. 471 (1972).

25411 U.S. 778 (1973).

2633 CrL 3103 (1983).

27F. Hussey & D. Duffee, *Probation, Parole, and Community Field Services: Policy, Structure, and Process,* at 280-286 (1980).

28See *U.S. v. Price,* 383 U.S. 787 (1966); *Williams v. U.S.* 341 U.S. 97 (1951).

29See *Owens v. Kelley,* 681 F2d 1362 (11th Cir. 1982).

30Intergovernmental Report, *Handbook of the Law of Personal Tort Liability of Texas Public Employees and Officials,* No. VI-3, Texas Advisory Commission on Intergovernmental Relations, Sept., 1978, at 1.

31See L. Friedman, *The Good Faith Defense in Constitutional Litigation,* 5 HOFSTRA L.R. 501, at 501-503 (1977).

32The Federal Center, *Recommended Procedures for Handling Prisoner Civil Rights Cases in the Federal Courts,* at 9 & 10 (1980).

33436 U.S. 658 (1978).

34*Williams v. U.S.,* 341 U.S. 97 (1951); *Monroe v. Pape,* 365 U.S. 167 (1961).

35Decisions on this issue vary from one jurisdiction to another. The Fourth Circuit view is that Fourth Amendment rights are fully applicable, meaning that probable cause is required, particularly in new criminal proceedings. At the opposite end is the view held in *People v. Hernandez,* 229 Cal. App. 2d 143 (1965), wherein a California parolee was told that his status deprived him of the right to insist on Fourth Amendment guarantees with respect to personal and automobile searches initiated by correctional authorities. The Ninth Circuit has held that a test of reasonable necessity, relative to the enforcement of the probation and parole systems, was justified. A final view holds that a warrantless search is legitimate whenever an officer has reasonable cause to believe that the client is violating, or is about to violate a condition.

36M. Weisz and R. Crane, *Defenses to Civil Rights Actions Against Correctional Employees,* (March, 1977) at 9.

36See *Burszka v. Johnson,* 351 F. Supp. 771 (E.D.Pa. 1972); *Sheffy v. Greer,* 391 F. Supp. 1044 (E.D. Ill. 1975); *Fisher v. Turner,* 335 F. Supp. 577 (D. Utah, 1972).

38See *Smith v. Sinclair,* 424 I. Supp. 1108 (W.D. Okla. 1976); *Johnson V. Hackett,* 284 F. Supp. 933 (E.D. Pa. 1968).

39See Texas Advisory Commission on Intergovernmental Relations, *Personal Tort Liability of Texas Public Employees and Officials: A Legal Guide,* 12 (1979).

[40]W. Prosser, *Handbook of the Law of Torts,* 4th Edition (1971), at 988-989.

[41]See in general *Pierson v. Ray,* 386 U.S. 547 (1967).

[42]*Spaulding v. Nielsen,* 599 F2d 728 (5th Cir. 1979).

[43]*Burkes v. Callion,* 433 P. 2d 318 (9th Cir. 1970); *cert. denied* 403 U.S. 908 (1970).

[44]See generally *Johnson V. Wells,* 566 F2d 1016 (5th Cir. 1978); *Keeton v. Procunier,* 468 F2d 810 (9th Cir. 1972); *Bennett v. People,* 406 F2d 36 (9th Cir. 1969).

[45]*Black's Law Dictionary* 822 (1968).

[46]See *Scheuer v. Rhodes,* 416 U.S. 232 (1974).

[47]The materials used in this section on Legal Representation and Indemnification are taken from R. del Carmen, *Legal Responsibilities of Probation and Parole Officers: A Manual,* at pp. 246-271 (1981), as submitted to the National Institute of Corrections, NIC Grant Award #BZ-5.

[48]For further information, see American Correctional Association, *On The Line,* Vol. 6, No. 4 (June 1983), at 1-2.

[49]See *supra,* note 47, at 278.

IV
Purposes and Goals

Probation as Punishment

New Directions and Suggestions

Gennaro F. Vito
University of Louisville

In recent years, the aims and goals of American corrections have shifted away from rehabilitation to retribution, deterrence, and incapacitation (see von Hirsh, 1976; van den Haag 1975). Some theorists have argued that such a move, accomplished largely through a shift toward determinate or mandatory sentencing, would also serve the interests of justice in that persons convicted of the same crime would receive the same or very comparable sentences (see Fogel, 1979). Traditionally, probation has not been included in this movement toward stiffer sentencing. Yet, probation can and should be a part of this process and new programs and added sanctions have been developed which emphasize the nature of probation as a sanction.

The Lenient Image of Probation

Probation is typically defined as a conditional sentence which avoids the incarceration of the offender. Although it results from the conviction of the offender, probation substitutes supervision by a probation officer for confinement in an institution. Of course, rehabiltation has long been promoted as a legitimate goal of probation. John Augustus, generally acknowledged as the "father of probation," clearly stated that his primary motivation for originating this process was his belief that "the object of the law is to reform criminals and to prevent crime and not to punish maliciously or from a spirit of revenge" (Dressler, 1962:17).

Yet public and, in some cases, official opinion have condemned probation as a lenient measure which allows offenders to escape their just punishment. For example, a Justice Department memo from 1925 contained the following argument against the establishment of probation at the Federal level: "It (probation) is all a part of a wave of maudlin rot of misplaced sympathy for criminals that is going over the country. It would be a crime, however, if a probation system is established in the federal courts." (Evjen, 1975:5). To date, probation suffers from this "soft on criminals" image. As Thomas (1983:3) has noted:

> Probation lacks the forceful imagery which other occupations in crim-
> inal justice can claim. Police catch criminals, prosecutors try to get them
> locked up, judges put them in prison, guards and wardens keep them
> there but, probation, in the public view, offers crime and the criminal
> a second chance.

There are several examples of how the surveillance/punishment component of probation have been elevated over the helping/treatment function (see Marshall and Vito, 1982). Some current examples of new conditions of probation reveal the manner in which probation can be enhanced to serve the basic aims of punishment: retribution, deterrence and incapacitation.

Retribution and Probation
Sentencing to Community Service

Clear and O'Leary (1983:14) have written that certain conditions of probation have the potential to serve retributive ends: "To the degree that community supervision involves coerced compliance with legally mandated restrictions on liberty, it is clearly retribution for the offense." Similarly, Singer (as cited by Harris, 1980:16) outlined the manner in which probation would play an important role within a just deserts model:

1. Under a desert model, these sentences of non-incarceration must not be, and must not be viewed as, nonpunishment. Both in theory and in practice nonincarcerative sanctions must be punitive.
2. Probationers should be put into community service, or required to live in a halfway house, make restitution to their victims, or accept other similar conditions on their liberty.
3. The conditions of a desert model probation would require the probationer to perform some affirmative act, perhaps utilitarian, but in any event arduous and punitive.

One of the best examples of using a probation term to serve these ends has been community service sentencing.

Since the late 1970's, community service as a condition of probation has been recognized as a way to punish offenders whose incarceration would not otherwise perform a demonstrable service to society. Typically, the kinds of work completed by offenders under this type of program have been "non-essential stuff that a community would never pay to have done" — i.e., maintenance of vacant lots and services provided to non-profit organizations such as hospitals (Krajick, 1983:8-9). Community service sentencing is usually a condition of probation. Offenders are required to perform a certain duty for a specified number of hours during their probationary term. The probation officer then monitors the number of hours worked and the quality of work performed by the offender. If the offender fails to comply with the conditions of community service, the offender will be a candidate for probation revocation.

Community service sentencing has the potential to serve several utilitarian purposes for the offender and society. First, the services performed by the probationers and the fruits of their labor are visible to society. This attribute may generate community support for such programs. Second, community service sentencing permits the offender to demonstrate expiation/atonement for their misdeeds. Third, it provides an opportunity for offenders who do not have either the financial means to benefit from other sanctions (particularly victim restitution) or the specialized skills to perform work in the community. In this fashion, both white collar and "street" criminals can be accommodated by community service sentencing. Fourth, although current evidence on this point is mixed, community service sentencing has the potential to reduce institutional populations. One New York city-based program (PACT) estimated that, if the program were abolished, half of their clients would have gone on to prison. Fifth, this program provides the opportunity to punish offenders who would otherwise go unpunished, such as persons who commit "victimless" crimes. Sixth, community service sentencing can serve as a vehicle to involve outside organizations seeking offenders to work in their businesses and programs, in the justice process. This expansion of service can also have the added benefit of enabling probation departments to deal with funding cutbacks through increased community involvement in such agencies (see Cocks, 1982).

Finally, the attitudes of the probationers themselves provide an argument for the program. As one client of PACT stated (Krajick, 1982:18), "I don't care how bad this is, it's like a reward. This is work, but it's freedom. This community sentencing program, this used to be for the Kennedy kids, when they got in trouble, not for blacks."

This statement may represent the most utilitarian rationale of all. Community service sentencing can visibly demonstrate that equal punishment under the law can be a reality. In turn, this example could foster a respect for law and administration of justice among the public—an attitude which could go a long way in promoting crime prevention.

Deterrence and Probation:
Occupational Disqualification of Corporate Executives as a Condition of Probation

A review of the basic elements of deterrence theory reveals exactly how probation relates to this theory of punishment. According to theorists from the Classical School of Criminology, such as Beccaria and Bentham (see Vold, 1979), deterrence theory makes a number of assumptions about criminal behavior. First and foremost is the assumption that man is rational and will freely choose that course of action which will maximize his pleasure and minimize pain. The criminal, therefore, will consciously calculate the cost and benefits of committing a crime before he takes action. Subsequently, the aim of punishment is prevention. If the punishment is known, certain and severe enough to prevent the rational criminal from committing the crime, deterrence can be achieved.

Probation supervision can be viewed as a deterrence mechanism largely through the manner in which conditions of probation are determined. Clear and O'Leary (1983:16) have noted that "the restrictions on liberty associated with the status of offenders in the community may well be sufficiently undesirable to deter a substantial portion of would-be offenders."

A recent example of a potentially deterrent condition of probation is the occupational disqualification of corporate executives. As defined by McDermott (1982:604-605), disqualification is typically imposed as a condition of probation for a limited period of time and under stated circumstances in order to bar or prohibit persons from the post-conviction exercise of managerial functions which bear a reasonably direct relationship to the conduct which constituted the offense.

In fact, there are several ways in which corporate disqualification as a condition of probation represents a more severe punishment than a prison sentence. First of all, it promotes deterrence by individualizing the punishment. Here, the punishment can truly "fit the crime." McDermott (1982:628) gives examples of union officials, medical doctors, security dealers, and policemen who abused their position and authority for their own personal gain and who were then forbidden to hold their former position. Since offenders of this type are less likely to be incarcerated, this probation sanction may be the most severe punishment available. As a result, the offender suffers the financial costs of lost work opportunities without eliminating, as imprisonment does, the ability to make a living elsewhere (McDermott, 1982:633).

Perhaps, the main deterrent effect is the stigma associated with the conviction and the loss of status. If a corporate executive is disqualified from office and he/she is forced to assume a position of decreased authority in the organization, the punishment of this person becomes not only a lesson for the individual (specific deterrence) but an example to other persons who may contemplate such crimes (general deterrence).

In this fashion, conditions of probation can be "tailor-made" (see Marshall and Vito, 1982) to truly fit the deterrent aims of punishment and actually represent a stricter sanction than incarceration for a specific type of offender who may truly fit the model of the rational criminal.

Incapacitation and Probation
The FADAS Program

Generally, incapacitation involves the imprisonment of the offender for the purposes of societal protection. In probation, incapacitation is tied to the surveillance responsibilities of the probation officer (Clear and O'Leary, 1983:16). Put simply, incapacitation with probation involves a close monitoring of the offender's behavior by the officer.

A current example of the use of incapacitation with probation is the Fulton County Diagnostic Socialization Program (FADAS). As described by Carnes (1982), the FADAS program is aimed at offenders who have a drug problem which is ultimately responsible for their crime—i.e., the addict burglar. The offender is required to submit to a number of psychological and physiological tests in order to determine the extent of his/her problem. However, the most incapacitating condition of probation which is utilized in the program is that:

> the probationer shall submit to a search of his person, house, papers and or effects, as these terms of the Fourth Amendment of the United States Constitution are defined by the Courts, any time of the day or the night, with or without a search warrant, whenever requested to do so by a probation supervisor or any law enforcement officer, and specific consent is given for the use of anything seized as evidence in a proceeding for revocation (Carnes, 1982:73).

Also, FADAS probationers could be given urinalysis, breath, spittle and blood tests for drug usage at anytime. In short, these probationers sign away their Fourth and Fifth Amendment rights and are constantly threatened with the possibility of probation revocation.

The effectiveness of this program has not yet been determined. Yet, the incapacitative aspects of FADAS have been clearly stated. Conditions of such strength have seldom been seen in the area of probation.[1]

Conclusion

The preceeding examples demonstrate that probation can be viewed as a punitive sanction. In fact, probation supervision, regardless of the type of conditions developed, does meet the characteristics of punishment developed by Packer (1968:21):

1. It involves pain or other consequences normally considered unpleasant.
2. It is invoked for an offense against legal rules.
3. It is imposed on an actual offender for his/her offense.
4. It is intentionally administered by human beings other than the offender.

5. It is imposed and administered by an authority constituted by the legal system against which the offense is committed.

By this definition, probation does constitute punishment.

Yet, in order for probation to take its place within a Justice Model perspective, McAnany, Thompson and Fogel (1981:11) have offered the following suggestions concerning its continued use:

1. Probation is a penal sanction whose main characteristic is punitive.
2. Probation should be a sentence, not a substitute for a real sentence that is threatened after future violation — it should not be subject to reduction or addition.
3. Probation should be part of a single graduated range of penal sanctions and should be available as the sentence for all levels of crime, except the *most* serious felonies.
4. The gravity of the probation sentence should be determined by both the length of term and the quality and quantity of the conditions.
5. Conditions should be justified in terms of the seriousness of the offense, though other purposes may be served by such conditions, such as incapacitation.

These suggestions, taken with our examples, outline the current movement to strengthen or better identify the punitive aspects of probation. They may also serve to clarify the purpose of probation, a sanction which is used in place of incarceration for a certain category of offenders for whom imprisonment would not serve a functional purpose. Since it replaces the penal sanction, probation conditions should and do reflect the seriousness of the crime committed.

Endnotes

[1] It is not at all certain that such restrictive conditions of probation would withstand a court test. Judge Carnes (1982:74), however, does not appear to be overly concerned about any potential legal problems. "We want to have constitutional programs [i.e., constitutionally acceptable]; but by the time it gets into the Supreme Court, we may have caught a lot of drug pushers, even if it's not."

References

Barkdull, W.L. (1976) "Probation: Call it control — and mean it." *Federal Probation,* 40:3-8.

Carnes, C. (1982) "Judicial and sentencing view," pp. 70-76 in *Final Report: 1982 UPR/NRP Seminar: National Reporting in the 1980's,* San Francisco, CA: National Council on Crime and Delinquency.

Clear, T.R. and V. O'Leary (1983) *Controlling the Offender in the Community,* Lexington, Mass: Lexington Publishing.

Cocks, J. (1982) "The use of 'third sector' organizations as vehicles for community service under a condition of probation." *Federal Probation,* 46(4): 29-36.

Dressler, D. (1982) *Practice and Theory of Probation and Parole,* New York: Columbia University Press.

Evjen, V.H. (1975) "The Federal Probation System: The struggle to achieve it and its first 25 years." *Federal Probation,* 39:3-15.

Fogel, D. (1979) *We are the Living Proof,* Cincinnati: Anderson.

Harris, M.K. (1980) "Rethinking the probation sanction." Paper prepared for the Probation Mission Project, Center for Research in Criminal Justice, University of Illinois at Chicago Circle.

Krajick, K. (October 1982) "Community service: The work ethic approach to punishment." *Corrections Magazine,* 7:6-19.

Marshall, F.H. and G.F. Vito (1982) "Not without the tools: the task of probation in the eighties." *Federal Probation,* 46(4):37-39.

McAnany, P., D. Thompson and D. Fogel (1981) "Probation mission: Practice in search of principle." Paper presented at the National Forum on Criminal Justice, Cherry Hill, N.J.

McDermott, M.F. (1982) "Occupational disqualification of corporate executives: An innovative condition of probation." *Journal of Criminal Law and Criminology,* 73: 604-641.

Packer, H. (1968) *The Limits of the Criminal Sanction,* Stanford: Stanford University Press.

Thomas, R.L. (1983) "Professionalism in Federal Probation: Illusion or reality?" *Federal Probation,* 47(1):3-9.

Van Den Haag, E. (1975) *Punishing Criminals,* New York: Basic Books.

Vold, G.B. (1979) *Theoretical Criminology,* New York: Oxford University Press.

Von Hirsh, A. (1976) *Doing Justice,* New York: Hill and Wang.

Community Corrections as Diversion
Saving Money and Reducing State Commitments

Edward J. Latessa
University of Cincinnati

Introduction

Recent figures released by the Federal government indicate that the prison population of the United States stands at 412,303; an all time high. Ohio, which ranks sixth in total prison population in the nation, has reported a 15.7 percent increase over a twelve-month period (Bureau of Justice Statistics, 1983). Ohio's prison population currently stands at approximately 6,000 over capacity, and the projections are for a 20,000+ inmate population by 1985.[1]

While the public has demanded tougher sentences, it has become increasingly apparent that the costs associated with increased incarceration and prison construction are astronomical. Estimates place the cost of constructing a maximum security prison at approximately $70,000 per bed, with the cost of maintenance and housing inmates ranging between $10,000-$15,000 per year (Allen and Latessa, 1983a:8). The acute shortage of prison space has made the prison cell a scarce resource. Many states are faced with severe budget deficits, and legislators and the public are reluctant to vote for new prison construction. There is also ample evidence that once prisons are built, they are filled. In addition, many states and jurisdictions are under court orders to reduce or limit their prison population.

In an attempt to offset or at least alleviate the rising prison population problem and high costs of incarceration, many jurisdictions have turned to alternatives to incarcerating offenders, including halfway houses, furlough programs, shock probation and parole, contract probation and probation subsidy programs (Allen and Latessa, 1983b). Traditional arguments for community-based correctional programming include the contention that they are effective alternatives to incarceration, and that a large percentage

81

of offenders can be diverted into the community without substantially increasing the risk to community safety. A major traditional rationale for community corrections is that such programs are much less expensive than incarceration in terms of dollar costs. Indeed, while prison populations are increasing, so are the number of offenders being supervised in the community. During 1981, the probation population increased by more than 100,000 persons, a 9 percent increase, and the parole population rose by 2 percent (Bureau of Justice Statistics, 1982).

The question of effectiveness has generally been addressed through "risk control," which has historically been achieved through a screening process of selecting the "most deserving" or the "lower risk" clients. Unfortunately, we have never been able to "predict" success or failure with much reliability. As the correctional system expands, the decision-making process becomes even more complex and inaccurate. As more and more offenders are released to the community, the "threshold" of risk taking will invariably increase. Simply stated, "worse" offenders would be returned to the community. Whether or not legislators, judges or the public will support increased usage of community corrections still depends in large part on the effectiveness of these programs in terms of risk control.

Given the new demands on the correctional system, it stands to reason that supervision practices will need to change in order to address increased workloads and changes in the community supervised population. In a general sense, these changes can be considered innovations. It is also reasonable to argue that the primary purpose of most innovations has been to maximize the efficiency with which community services are delivered and to improve the rate of success for individuals under supervision. To meet these ends, innovations can involve changes in the structure of supervision, emphasis on various supervision activities, and delivery of community services and treatment.

The literature suggests that innovations in community supervision over the past quarter-century have tended to be of two fairly distinct types: 1) broad, policy-level innovations, and 2) program-level innovations. Innovations at the policy level are those changes which affect the character or process of community supervision itself. Ordinarily, policy innovations tend to be implemented at the highest appropriate level, which may be the state or federal level. Occasionally, however, a policy innovation may also be made at the local level. Innovations at the *program* level are changes which introduce a new management or treatment technique aimed primarily at improving a local agency's capability for providing needed services to its clients.

Program-level innovations can be seen as representing varying degrees of control exercised by the local supervising agency over its clients, i.e., residential treatment centers, hostels, day training centers, and outreach programs. These also include specialized programs aimed at a particular group of clients or their common problems, i.e., the unemployed, drug addicted, uneducated, minority, etc.

Innovations in service delivery systems, in management techniques, and in strategies for change all have as their basic intent the management of offenders and protection of public safety. It must be remembered that community supervision is both supervised freedom *and* a mechanism for controlling further criminal behavior by such treatment philosophies as rehabilitation, reintegration, etc.

One such innovative and unique program is the Incarceration Diversion Unit (IDU) operating out of the Lucas County Adult Probation Department (Toledo, Ohio.) This program involves the use of intensive supervision to a select group of offenders. The assumption underlying intensive supervision is that decreased caseload size will lead to increased contact between the client and supervising officers, resulting in improved service-delivery and more effective treatment, which in turn will affect a reduction in recidivism (Banks et al., 1977). While the idea of differentiated levels of supervision is not new, this program differs from most previous efforts in that it was designed to deal with a select group of offenders rather than a general population.[2]

This article examines the effects the IDU program has had on reducing the prison commitment rate, and subsequent cost savings. Furthermore, through extrapolation a retrospective analysis of potential statewide impacts are addressed and discussed, thereby providing a "case study" of community treatment as an alternative to incarceration.

Incarceration Diversion Unit

The Incarceration Diversion Unit was an offspring of the theory of intensive supervision, incorporating both reduced caseload size, and intensive service provision. However, unlike previous examples of intensive probation supervision programs, only those that had been given a state prison term were eligible for inclusion. This unit, funded as a subsidy program by the State of Ohio, has been in operation since January of 1978. The primary program objectives were to reduce county commitments to state penal institutions, provide increased service and contacts, reduce the costs of traditional incarceration, and maintain community safety.

In December of 1977, Toledo entered into a probation subsidy grant agreement with the Ohio Department of Rehabilitation and Correction. Funds for the probation pilot program totaled $109,545 for the period of January 1978 to June 1979. Since that time, the State has refunded the Program through 1983.[3] The unit currently consists of four probation officers and a unit supervisor. Each officer is assigned a maximum of 25 cases with the exception of the unit supervisor, who is assigned 15 cases. The program officers are responsible for assessing the needs of their clients;

negotiating a contract; providing or arranging for the needed services, and making four contacts per month (of which two must be face-to-face).

Program clientele are unique because they are diverted after conviction and recommendation for commitment to state prisons.[4] Screening and intake procedures excluded cases that would normally qualify for regular probation; non-probatable cases, transfer cases from other counties; extremely dangerous offenders;[5] and offenders who would qualify for other community programs that contain residential treatment modalities.

The IDU operates within the larger adult probation department serving a metropolitan area of over 400,000 population. The IDU is an ongoing program with referrals made on a continuous basis. Program evaluation has occurred on four separate occasions (Latessa, 1979, 1980, 1981, 1982), and the overall results from these studies have been generally positive on a number of parameters.

Research Methods

A quasi-experimental design was used to evaluate the effectiveness of the IDU program. A comparison group of matched probationers was drawn from the balance of the agency caseload, and cases were matched on three parameters: race, gender and risk.[6] Outcome data were collected at regular intervals over the five year period of program operation, and analysis included both in-program and outcome performance measures.

Among these measures examined were: services and contact provided, needs assessed, positive adjustment, criminal behavior severity,[7] arrests, convictions, incarcerations, technical violations, employment, commitment rates and costs. This article addressed the latter two outcome indicators.

In order to determine the commitment rate reduction brought about by the program, commitment figures were collected from the records of the Lucas County Common Pleas Court for a five-year period.[8] The actual number of diverted cases were provided by the program staff on a monthly basis for the entire period of program operation (February 1978 to January 1983).

The savings generated by the program were determined by comparing IDU costs with those of incarcerating an offender in the Ohio penal system. The cost figures for this program were based on the *direct* costs borne by the state ($630,502). Costing did not include in-kind services provided by the parent agency since the program was housed in an ongoing probation department. The rationale for excluding this category of charges was that a program of this type would generally be added to an existing department, and thus only incremental costs should be considered. The cost savings of this program were determined from the commitment rate reduction brought about by the program. Each offender diverted by the IDU program led to an incarceration cost savings of $6,098 per year of incarceration time

(Annual Report, 1981). Assuming an average incarceration time of 17 months in the Ohio penal system, this results in a saving of $9,456 per offender diverted.

Certain other cost savings were calculated, including the amount of monies collected toward court costs and restitution. These monies would not have been available had the offender been incarcerated, and thus were included in the analysis. Obviously, these were not all the costs and benefits which accrue through the program. Incarcerated offenders do not pay taxes (income lost by the state), and their families frequently receive welfare benefits. On the other hand, they do not receive unemployment compensation, should they otherwise be eligible, and there are the unknown costs associated with continued criminal behavior.[9] A host of such costs and benefits could be included in these analysis calculations; however, the assumption was made that second-level costs and benefits would "zero-out" and that the major consideration should be direct cost to the state.

Results

Table 1

Commitment Data for Lucas County and the IDU February 1978 to January 1983

Year	Time Period	Total Sentenced to IDU	Probable Offender Sentenced to State From Lucas County	Percent Diverted
1	February 1978 to February 1979	54	216	20.0%
2	February 1979 to February 1980	48	176	21.4%
3	February 1980 to February 1981	55	228	19.4%
4	February 1981 to February 1982	32	243	11.6%
5	February 1982 to January 1983*	51	307	14.2%
	Total	240	1,170	17.0%

*This is an eleven month period.

Commitment Data

One objective of the IDU program was to reduce state commitments from Lucas County. Table 1 provides both a yearly breakdown of commitment data for Lucas County and number of offenders diverted into the IDU. A total of 240 offenders were diverted into the program as of January 1983, and 1,170 were sentenced to state commitments from Lucas County during the same time period. The commitment rate reduction varied from a high of 21.4 percent in the second year to a low of 11.6 percent in the fourth year. Overall, the program has resulted in a 17 percent reduction in the number of offenders sentenced to State prisons from Lucas County for the period February 1978 through December 1982. Offenders diverted after January 1983 were not included in the total, inasmuch as commitment data were not yet available from the court.

Cost Data

As mentioned previously, the savings generated by this program were based upon the *direct* costs to the state of Ohio for the subsidy program, minus the alternative costs of incarcerating an offender in the Ohio penal system. The total cost of the program to the state was $630,502, through January 1983. Each offender diverted led to an incarceration cost savings of $9,147 for the estimated 17-month period. An adjusted figure of $2,152 was derived for each "shock" case diverted, due to the reduced time served for these cases.[10]

A total of 244 offenders were diverted into the IDU through January 1983. Of these, 58 were shock cases. A total of 36 regular IDU cases and four shock cases were incarcerated on felonies or committed on other charges, as of August 1982.[11] These cases were subtracted from the total number of diverted cases for each category. Resulting cost figures were based on the remaining 204 IDU cases, of whom 54 were shock probationers. Table 2 presents the cost data for the IDU program through January of 1983. Subtracting the failure cases from the total and calculating the 54 shock cases separately, a total of $1,488,258 was obtained. Subtracting the costs of the program to the state indicates a total of $887,756 saved. When the court costs and restitution paid were added to this figure, a total savings of $901,409 was generated by the program.

Obviously, these were not all the savings and costs of the program. The assumption was that the second-level costs and benefits would zero-out, and that the major consideration was direct costs and savings to the state. By using the State-provided figure of $6,456 per year of incarceration costs and calculating the number of offenders diverted, a substantial cost savings can be documented to-date.

Table 2

Total Cost Savings of IDU Program
From February 1978 through January 1983

$ 9,147	Cost of Incarceration for 17 Months
× 150	Offenders Diverted
$1,372,050	"Full" Savings
$ 2,152	Cost of Incarcerating "Shock" Cases
× 54	"Shock" Cases Diverted
$ 116,208	"Shock" Savings
$1,372,050	"Full" Savings
116,208	"Shock" Savings
$1,488,258	Savings
− 630,502	Direct Program Costs
$ 887,756	Direct Savings to State
$ 43,653	Court Costs and Restitution Paid
$ 901,409	Total Savings of IDU Program

Retrospective Analysis

It is difficult if not impossible to predict the future, especially in the area of corrections. Therefore, instead of looking forward, a retrospective analysis was conducted over a similar time span for the five largest counties in Ohio.[12] These five counties include: Cuyahoga (Cleveland), Franklin (Columbus), Hamilton (Cincinnati), Montgomery (Dayton), and Summit (Akron). Collectively, they represent over 55 percent of Ohio's current incarceration total and rate.

This analysis was relatively"straight line." Data on the number of offenders incarcerated from these five counties by type of offense were provided by the State for the period June 30, 1978 through December 31, 1982.[13] Those offenders that would not normally qualify for the IDU program were excluded from the totals.[14] Based on the remaining totals for the five counties, a projection was made of the number of offenders that could have been diverted into a similar type program had it been available in these counties. A similar procedure was used to estimate the possible savings that could have resulted from such a five-county program.

Table 3

The Number of Offenders Eligible and the Projected Number
of Possible Offenders Diverted from Five Counties

County	Total Number of Eligible* Offenders Sentenced from 7-1-78 to 12-31-82	Projected Number of Offenders Diverted**
Cuyahoga (Cleveland)	4,623	786
Franklin (Columbus)	3,114	529
Hamilton (Cincinnati)	3,832	651
Montgomery (Dayton)	1,330	226
Summit (Akron)	1,640	279
Total	14,541	2,471

*This is the actual number of offenders incarcerated that would be eligible for the IDU program under current eligibility criteria. Approximately 73.43% of the cases sentenced would be elibible.

**Based upon the 17% reduction rates obtained in Lucas County for the same time period.

Projected Commitment Data

Data in Table 3 illustrate the projected number of offenders that could have been diverted from state incarceration had a similar program been in operation in these five counties in Ohio. A total of 19,805 offenders were sentenced from these five counties during this fifty-four month period. Of this number, 14,541 offenders would have been eligible for the IDU program under current criteria. Applying the 17 percent reduction rate from Lucas County for approximately the same time period, an estimated 2,471 offenders could have been diverted from state commitment.

Obviously, this is straight line and hence a rough estimate of the number of possible offenders who could have been diverted. However, given the five-year success of the Lucas County program and the rate of penal commitment of the State, it is reasonable to assume that these gains were at least possible if not probable.

Projected Cost Savings

The estimated savings of an IDU program in five counties were derived, based on estimates of costs and savings extrapolated from the existing program's estimates. Data in Table 4 provide an estimate approximation of the savings that could have been generated from this type of program. The projected number of program offenders was based on an estimate of 2,471 diverted offenders, minus the projected number of failures.[15] It was assumed that the number of shock probationers diverted would be similar to the percentage diverted into the IDU program.

Once again, using the State provided figure of $9,147 for 17 months of incarceration, a total of 1,527 projected offenders diverted could have resulted in a savings of nearly 14 million dollars. Combined with the estimated "shock" savings, over 15 million dollars was projected. The estimated program costs of $6,385,124 were based on a figure of $2,584 per offender diverted.[16] Subtracting the estimated *direct* costs to the state, a total of $8,758,429 was obtained. Estimating court costs and restitution paid, the total estimated savings could have exceeded 9.2 million dollars.

Table 4

Projected Cost Savings for the State
Based on a Five County Program

$	9,147	Cost of Incarceration for 17 Months
×	1,527	Projected Offenders Diverted
$13,967,469		Estimated "Full" Savings
$	2,154	Cost of Incarcerating "Shock" Cases
×	546	Projected "Shock" Cases Diverted
$ 1,176,084		Estimated "Shock" Savings
$13,967,469		Estimated "Full" Savings
$ 1,176,084		Estimated "Shock" Savings
$15,143,553		Estimated Savings
$ 6,385,124		Estimated Direct Program Costs
$ 8,758,429		Estimated Direct Savings to the State
$ 443,580		Estimated Court Costs and Restitution Paid
$ 9,202,009		Total Estimated Savings

Summary and Conclusions

The Incarceration Diversion Unit has been operating within the Lucas County Adult Probation Department for over five years. This unique and innovative program offers a form of intensive supervision to diverted offenders. Primary among the objectives of the program were to reduce the state commitment from the county, and maintain community safety at a cost less than traditional incarceration. The commitment rate reduction and the cost savings were the primary focus of this article. In addition to the actual program gains, a retrospective analysis was conducted to determine the impact this type of program could have had, *if* it were in operation in five additional large counties in the state.

The commitment data for the program indicated that by diverting 240 offenders through January 1983, the IDU was able to reduce state commitments from Lucas County by 17 percent over a five year period. The diversion of these offenders permitted the program to offset the costs and to show a savings of $901,409, including court costs and restitution paid. These figures were derived from the most conservative estimates of state incarceration costs.

These results shed further light on the success of the IDU program. Indeed, the previous research conducted on community safety indicated that the program maintained a relatively high degree of community safety when IDU clients were compared with regular probationers. The prior research has also demonstrated that the IDU sample, in contrast to regular probationers, was "worse" on almost all criminal history measures, and that they would not qualify for regular probation under normal sentencing criteria. It is of interest to note that the IDU program has existed within the regular probation department with minimum agency disruption or morale problems, and it has been independently evaluated four times without major inconvenience to the program's operation.

These data and their implications suggest the policy potential for replication of a similar program to other counties within the state. There is no evidence at this time that this type of program could not have similar results throughout the larger counties in Ohio. Indeed, there is considerable evidence that such an expansion could significantly reduce the state commitment rate and could save the State and taxpayers considerable money. This preliminary analysis suggests that over 2,471 offenders could have been diverted from prison and that an estimated 9.2 million saved had this type of program existed in the larger five counties over a five-year period.

A friend of the author, recently released from federal prison, once commented: "Forty percent don't belong there, forty percent got too much time, and fifteen percent can't get enough." Researchers have long maintained that there are many offenders in prison that do not belong there and that incarceration is counterproductive to the intended aim of rehabilitation.[17] Research has also strongly indicated that the community, not the prison, is where rehabilitation must occur;[18] the bottom line is that we cannot afford to continue incarcerating offenders at current levels. Prison capacity must be viewed as a scarce resource and as such, used wisely and more sparingly.

This article has focused on monetary costs of intensive diversion as opposed to incarceration for a select group of convicted offenders. In doing so, many other types of costs were not examined. The traditional "cost-effectiveness" argument in support of community corrections as an alternative to incarceration, like this article, stresses the dollar costs of correctional supervision. Nonetheless, it is quite possible that the social and psychological cost savings realized through the use of community corrections are far more important than the dollars saved.

The IDU is an example of community corrections fulfilling the promise of probation. It was carefully planned, implemented, and evaluated over a five year period. While it has undergone staff and programmatic changes, it has maintained its consistency and routinization throughout. This program has demonstrated that through careful correctional programming, considerable gains can be achieved with regard to commitment reduction and cost savings.

While the IDU represents an innovation at the program level, the implication for policy level changes are clear. Indeed, several states, most notably Georgia, Texas, New York and New Jersey have already initiated statewide intensive supervision programs designed specifically to reduce overcrowding.[19] The concept has also been expanded and applied to parolees. The State of Washington has been using intensive parole supervision with low-risk felons on parole. Their research has indicated very favorable results, both in terms of community safety and cost savings (Fallen, et al., 1981). The need to expand and improve our correctional capacities are self-evident. Community correctional programming as represented by these programs, provides an opportunity to apply an old concept in a new and expanded form. Unlike previous experiments with intensive supervision, they are demonstrating success with selected offenders and proving to be as cost-effective alternatives to prison.

Endnotes

[1]According to Ohio's Department of Rehabilitation and Correction, the total prison population in Ohio as of February 28, 1983 was 17,527. See: Smith, F., "Prison Bill Confusing," *Cincinnati Enquirer,* March 6, 1983, pg. C-4.

[2]Many of the previous experiments with differentiated levels of supervision involved random or non-random assignment from the regular probation or parole populations. See for example: Sunbil B. Nath, et al., "Parole and Probation Caseload Size Variation: The Florida Intensive Supervision Project," *Criminal Justice Review,* Vol. 1 (Fall, 1976): Human Systems Institute. *The Intensive Services Unit: Refunding Report,* Philadelphia, Pennsylvania: Philadelphia Adult Probation Department, Court of Common Pleas, (1975); Joseph D. Lohman et al., *The "Intensive" Supervision Caseload A Preliminary Evaluation, The San Francisco Project Services, Report #11* (Berkeley, California: University of California at Berkeley, School of Criminology, 1967).

[3]The additional funding for the program has totalled $587,359.

[4]Following the first year of operation, the IDU began admitting shock probationers. Under Ohio Law, an offender is eligible for shock probation after a short period of incarceration (30 to 130 days). All shock cases were matched with similar shock cases released to regular probation. The rationale for accepting shock probation-

ers, and for categorizing them as diverted cases, is based on the assumption that these offenders would *not* have granted shock if this program were not available. See for example: Gennaro Vito and Harry Allen, "Shock Probation in Ohio: A Cost-Effectiveness Analysis." *Chitty's Law Journal,* Vol. 27, (December, 1979); 347-355; Gennaro Vito, "Shock Probation in Ohio: A Re-Examination of the Factors Influencing the Use of an Early Release Program," *Offender Rehabilitation,* Vol. 3 (Winter, 1978): 123-133.

[5]The Program primarily selected repeat property offenders. Personal offenders were usually excluded from the Program.

[6]Classification levels included: high, medium, and low risk, and were determined by a base expectancy scale. Twenty-six percent of the cases for each group were high risk; 70 percent were medium risk; and 4 percent were low risk.

[7]The positive adjustment and criminal behavior severity measures were based upon an index developed by the Program for the Study of Crime and Delinquency, Ohio State University. This index includes a continuous measure of criminal behavior based upon severity of offenses as prescribed by the Ohio Revised Code, and a positive adjustment scale which includes factors relating to employment, education, residential situation, financial situations, and progress on probation. This index has been tested and validated in a number of criminal justice settings.

[8]Excluded from these figures were non-probatable offenders and parole violators, who were not otherwise eligible for the program.

[9]These include the costs of law enforcement, courts and the property, physical and emotional losses of the victims and their families.

[10]This figure is based on an estimated four months incarceration for shock probationers.

[11]These are the most recent "failure" figures available on incarceration for the program. The "failure" rate is 14.8 percent.

[12]This analysis was undertaken to estimate the number of offenders and the amount of money that could have been saved had similar programs been in operation in these counties. The analysis of future projections are based on similar assumptions.

[13]The IDU program began in February, 1978. Data on State commitments from these five counties were based on fiscal year figures (July 1, through June 30), and monthly breakdowns were not available.

[14]These figures were based on the percentages obtained in Lucas County.

[15]These figures were estimated from the failure rate for the IDU program over a five-year period.

[16]This figure was obtained by dividing the total number of offenders diverted into the IDU program into the total program costs.

[17]See: Harry Allen and Clifford Simonsen, *Corrections in America: An Introduction* (New York: Macmillan, 1981), pg. 66. Allen and Simonsen write: "Most offenders — perhaps as many as 85 percent — do not need to be incarcerated and could function better back in the community under supervision,"; and, Board of Directors, National Council on Crime and Delinquency, "The Nondangerous Offender Should Not Be Imprisoned," *Crime and Delinquency,* 19 (October 1973): pp. 449-456.

[18]See: Gresham Sykes, "The Pains of Imprisonment," in *Crime and Justice, Volume III: The Criminal Under Restraint,* L. Radzinowicz and M. Wolfgang (eds.) (New York: Basic Books, 1977), pp. 213-214: The President's Commission on Law

Enforcement and Administration of Justice, *Task Force Report: Corrections* (Washington, D.C.: U.S. Government Printing Office, 1967).

[19]For an excellent discussion of intensive supervision in these states, see: Stephen Gettinger, "Intensive Supervision: Can It Rehabilitate Probation?" *Corrections Magazine* (April 1983), pp. 6-17.

References

Allen, H., and Latessa, E. "The Conservative Coup in Crime-Policy and Corrections," paper presented at the annual meeting of the Academy of Criminal Justice Sciences, San Antonio, Texas (March 1983a).

Allen, H., and Latessa, E. "Options for Improving Offender Control in the Community," paper presented at the annual meeting of the Western Society of Criminology, Las Vegas, Nevada (February 1983b).

Annual Report 1981, Ohio Department of Rehabilitation and Correction.

Banks, J., Porter, A., Rardin, R., Siler, T., and Unger, V. *Summary Phase I Evaluation of Intensive Special Probation Projects,* (National Institute of Law Enforcement and Criminal Justice, Law Enforcement Assistance Administration, U.S. Department of Justice), September 1977.

Bureau of Justice Statistics Bulletin, "Prisoners in 1982," U.S. Department of Justice, (April 1983).

Bureau of Justice Statistics Bulletin, "Probation and Parole 1981," U.S. Department of Justice, (August 1982).

Fallen, D., Apperson, C., Hall-Milligan, J., Aoe, J. *Intensive Parole Supervision* (Department of Social and Health Services, Analysis and Information Services Division, Office of Research, Olympia, Washington) October 1981.

Latessa, E., "Intensive Probation: An Evaluation of the Effectiveness of an Intensive Diversion Unit." Doctoral Dissertation, The Ohio State University, 1979.

_____, A Follow-Up Evaluation of the Lucas County Adult Probation Department's "Incarceration Diversion Unit," Criminal Justice Program, University of Cincinnati, 1980.

_____, The Third Evaluation of the Lucas County Adult Probation Department's "Incarceration Diversion Unit." Criminal Justice Program, University of Cincinnati, 1981.

_____, The Fourth Evaluation of the Lucas County Adult Probation Department's "Incarceration Diversion Unit." Criminal Justice Program, University of Cincinnati, 1982.

V
Participants
Client and Staff Views

Clients' Views of
Community Corrections

John J. Gibbs
Rutgers University

Introduction

Communinty supervision differs from other criminal sanctions, most notably confinement, in that it is based almost exclusively on the relationship between two people—the client and his supervisor or agent. For the most part, community corrections can be defined as the interactions between these two people, and in order to understand and control these interactions, we must know something about these people. Their perceptions, attitudes, and preferences shape the interactions that take place between them.

The purpose of this chapter is to provide information about one side of this human equation—the client. The objective is to explore the world of the client. In this chapter, we will step into the client's shoes. We will try to see the world as he sees it.

The portrait of the world of the client presented in this chapter is based on tape recorded interviews with over 50 men and women sentenced to probation.[1] The interview was designed to elicit information on the client's perception about various aspects of probation, for example, the probation officer, rules, and the purpose of probation.

The Major Concerns of Probationers

The dimensions described in this section are the most salient concerns expressed by a group of probationers when they were interviewed about their thoughts and feelings about probation. The themes are defined below in the order of their prevalence as a dominant or primary concern among probationers.

Support was the most common need expressed by the probationers interviewed. It was the dominant concern for about 30 percent of the interview

97

group. The support dimension reflects a need for understanding, empathy, and warmth. It is a desire for emotional support and help with personal problems. Probationers who had strong support needs wanted a probation officer who was interested in their problems and would listen to them. They wanted their probation officer to combine the characteristics of a clinical psychologist and best friend.

The second most common concern expressed was autonomy. Over one-fourth of the probationers interviewed indicated that autonomy was their major, probation-related concern. Autonomy is a need to be in control of one's life. It is a desire for minimum restraint and maximum freedom. It is a concern about being treated with deference and respect when one's perceived perogatives are involved.

Those who were concerned with autonomy wanted a probation officer who would maintain what they considered the proper distance from them. Unlike those who expressed strong support needs, those with substantial autonomy needs did not want their probation officers to try to "get close to them" or "get to know them." Those who expressed primary autonomy needs in their interviews preferred an officer who would "mind his own business." The ideal officer was one who interfered in their lives as little as possible.

Flexibility was expressed as the major concern by about one-fifth of the probationers who were interviewed. Flexibility is a theme that represents a need for adaptability, a concern about pliable regulations and requirements, or a desire for controller discretion when there is a perceived necessity for lenient or merciful adjustments.

Probationers who desired flexibility wanted a probation officer who was willing "to give them a break" under special circumstances. They preferred an officer who was willing "to bend the rules a little" when necessary. Their ideal officer was aware that probation was only one part of the probationer's life, and that sometimes other business should take precedence over a scheduled meeting with a probation officer.

The need for flexibility was expressed in relation to all aspects of probation including conditions, fines, and time and place of meetings. Those who expressed strong flexibility concerns felt that their particular life circumstances, which included their life style and personal schedule, should be considered by the probationer officer when he makes conditions and revocation decisions. Officers who did not incorporate these factors into their decisions were considered rigid and dangerous.

Thirteen percent of those interviewed indicated that assistance was a major concern. Assistance is defined as a need for aid in dealing with concrete problems, a desire for help in planning or achieving tangible goals, or a concern about help in solving practical problems or completing necessary tasks.

Those with strong assistance needs wanted a probation officer who could help them in areas like employment, housing, education, finances, and health. In many cases, those probationers who expressed a primary assistance concern wanted their probation officer to function as a social worker. They wanted help in dealing with social service agencies and other government bureaucracies.

The concern that was least often expressed as primary was control (11 percent). The control dimension is defined as a need for external regulation to avoid troublesome situations, a desire to delegate responsibility for one's behavior to the controller, or a concern for external restraint which is seen as necessary. Those with strong control concerns wanted a probation officer who was willing to make clear rules and enforce them if necessary. They felt that the probatin officer should act as an external agent to keep them from getting into trouble, which they stipulated they could not avoid on their own. As they saw it, the probation officer's job was not only to show them the way to crime-free life but also to keep them on it.

The percentage distribution of the primary concerns which emerged from the interviews with probationers indicates that most probationers were interested primarily either in warm supportive relationships with their officers or freedom, minimal restrictions, and personal respect. We will return to the needs of probationers and how they can be measured and incorporated into a classification scheme later in this chapter, after a discussion of some of the attitudes and opinions probationers provided in response to a series of questions.

Nature of Contact

One question the probationers were asked in the interview was "Typically, what goes on at these meetings? What do you usually talk about?" The responses to this question were coded into two categories—reporting and counseling. A response was coded as reporting when, as the probationer saw it, the purpose of the meeting was for the probationer's officer to gather information on the client's activities and progress. Almost 90 percent of the probationers interviewed reported that their meetings with their probation officers were mainly for reporting. They indicated that the atmosphere of these meetings was more conversational than clinical, and typical questions centered on employment and finances. In most cases, it appeared that the probation officer was trying to determine if there were any concrete problems.

Only a little over 10 percent of the probationers indicated that their meetings with their officers primarily involved counseling. They described these meetings as clinical, problem-centered encounters, which centered less on activity and more on the probationer as a person with a unique set of problems.

Extent of Concern About Probation

Probationers were asked, "Do you think about the fact that you're on probation very often? Is it something that's on your mind?" The responses were coded into the categories of constantly, frequently, occasionally, and never.

The best way to describe these response categories is in relation to each other. Responses coded in the constantly category reflected a concern with probation that was foremost in the probationer's mind. For these clients, probation represented a major dimension of life, and influenced many aspects of their lives. Approximately 14 percent of the probationers reported that probation was constantly on their minds.

Twenty-one percent of the probationers reported that they thought of probation frequently. Those whose responses were classified in the frequently category expressed a substantial concern with probation. However, these probationers were not preoccupied with thoughts of probation as reflected in the constantly category.

The most common response (45 percent) was that probation was thought about occasionally. Probationers who responded in this fashion did not consider probation a major concern in their lives and did not think of probation very often.

The meaning of the last response category, never, is self-evident. Almost one-fifth of the probationer's reported that thoughts of probation never crossed their minds.

The responses to the question about extent of concern about probation suggest that most probationers were not bombarded with or tormented by continual thoughts of probation. For the majority of clients, images of probation did not intrude into everyday thoughts.

Nature of Concern

Another way that responses to the questions "Do you think about the fact that you're on probation very often? Is it something that's on your mind?" and related probes were classified was into nature of concern categories. These included the following content categories: (1) prior to contact with the probation officer, (2) situational—occasions of sin, (3) meaning to self and significant others, and (4) opportunity—restrictions. These response categories and others presented in the remainder of this chapter are not mutually exclusive; for example, a probationer could think of probation prior to contact with his probation officers and in situations he considered occasions of sin. For this reason, if one sums the percentage of probationers whose responses are represented in each category, it will total more than 100 percent.

Those whose responses were classified as prior to contact with the probation officer thought of probation as the time for their scheduled appointment with their officer approached. The situational—occasions of sin category contained content representing a concern with probation that emerged when the probationer was faced with temptations or situations that could have resulted in "trouble." The meaning to self and significant others category reflected the concerns of those who thought about probation in terms of the consequences for their relationships with significant others, sense of adequacy, or feelings of worth. Thoughts about probation that arose when clients considered the limits on employment opportunities and mobility and other restrictions related to probation were represented in the opportunity—restrictions category.

Almost half of the probationers who reported that they thought about probation considered probation an impediment to travel, employment, and other activities (opportunity—restrictions). For approximately one-third of the probationers, thoughts of probation came to mind around reporting time (prior to contact with the probation officer). Approximately one-fourth of the clients associated thoughts of probation with illicit temptation (situational—occasions of sin), and about the same percentage of clients thought about probation in terms of its effect on personal and public image (meaning to self and significant others).

Desirable Features of Probation

Probationers were asked, "Is there anything that you especially like about your probation?" The responses to this question were classified into the categories of (1) alternative to confinement, (2) relationship with probation officer, (3) external control, (4) concrete assistance, and (4) relative leniency. Since probationers could furnish more than one response to this question, each probationer could be represented in more than one category.

Those who considered themselves fortunate because probation was less harsh than other sentences they could have received were represented in the alternative to confinement category. A wide variety of content ranging from descriptions of officers who were pleasant conversationalists to portraits of officers who were helpful clinicians was represented in the relationship with probation officer response category. The external control category contained responses that reflected an appreciation of the assistance probation conditions and probation officers provided in keeping the client out of "trouble." Responses classified in the concrete assistance category represented a recognition of the tangible aid offered or provided by the agent to the client in the areas of housing, employment, programs, or solid advice. Those who mentioned desirable features of probation that were coded in the relative leniency category perceived their probation conditions and officer as less restrictive than expected or stated in the law as they understood it. These clients felt that their probation officers were reasonable in their demands, and that their probation conditions were tolerable.

Most of the respondents, about three-fifths, perceived probation as having desirable features, whereas approximately four-tenths did not feel that probation possessed any redeeming features. The relationship with probation officer category accounted for about three-fourths of the subjects who responded positively to the question "Is there anything that you especially like about your probation?" Each of the other response categories represented less than one-fifth of the respondents.

Undesirable Features of Probation

Probationers were asked, "Is there anything that you especially dislike about your probation?" Responses were classified into the following categories: (1) relationship with officer, (2) lack of concrete assistance, (3) restrictions, (4) inconvenience and associated costs, and (5) implications for other areas of life.

Those who considered their relationships with their officer as an undesirable feature viewed their officer as cold, unfriendly, and uninterested. Such officers were seen as persons without feelings and without clinical talent. The lack of concrete assistance category contained responses that reflected an individual or organizational failure to provide the client with what he considered desirable or necessary services. Responses that were coded in the restrictions category represented specific complaints about probation conditions and the practices of officers, and more general complaints regarding feelings of impotence and lack of control over one's life. Probationers whose responses were classified in the inconvenience and associated costs category felt that visits to the probation officers were a burden and a waste of time. They suggested that their time could be spent more productively and more comfortably in settings other than the probation office. The implications for other areas of life category contained responses that demonstrated, from the subject's perspective, ways in which probation affected employment, public image, and the probability of contact with criminal justice agents.

As was expected, more respondents described features of probation that were considred undesirable than the number of subjects who described desirable features. Over 70 percent of the probationers interviewed reported that probation had at least one undesirable feature. About two-fifths of the probationers who described an undesirable feature considered the inconvenience and lost time associated with meetings at the probation office as the major drawback of probation. Approximately one-third of the respondents mentioned that probation translated into social and economic costs (implications for other areas of life). One-fifth of those who mentioned an undesirable feature of probation considred the restrictions on mobility and autonomy imposed by probation burdensome. Less than 15 percent of the respondents considered their relationship with their probation officer as a liability. This, however, would be expected because, as we saw in the last section, three-fourths of those who reported desirable features of probation mentioned the client-officer relationship as a positive feature of their probation. The complaint that was mentioned least often was lack of concrete assistance. Only a little over one-tenth of those who reported undesirable features of probation offered complaints that were coded in this category.

Satisfaction

A measure of satisfaction with probation was gathered by administering a modified version of the Self-Anchoring Striving scale, which was developed by Cantril (1965) and modified by Toch (1977) for use in prison settings. In the version of the scale we used, probationers were asked to describe the "best possible" and "worst possible" probation situation for them. After the self-generated anchors of the scale (the best and the worst) were described by the probationer, he was asked, "Here's a picture of a ladder with 10 rungs. Suppose that the top of the ladder represents the best possible probation situation as you have described it, and the bottom of the ladder represents the worst possible probation situation for you. Where would you place your current probation?"

If the scale was a valid measure of satisfaction, the probationers interviewed were a satisfied group. The average (mean) score was 8, and almost 30 percent of the probationers rated their probation a 10. None of the probationers rated their probation lower than a score of 3.

Purpose of Probation

The probationers were asked, "What do you think the purpose of probation is?" Their responses were classified into five categories, the definitions of which are fairly self-evident. The categories included punishment, rehabilitation, deterrence, control, and mercy/alternative disposition.

Rehabilitation was the most popular response category (41 percent), closely followed by control (37 percent). The mercy/alternative disposition category was used in coding the responses of about 30 percent of the probationers, and punishment and deterrence were each mentioned as an objective of probation by less than 20 percent of those interviewed.

It should be noted that there is considerable unreliability built into the reduction of the question "What do you think the purpose of probation is?" into response categories because many probationers responded in terms of what they thought ought to be the purpose of probation.

Comparative Severity

The probationers who were interviewed were asked to estimate the amount of time in jail and prison that they would consider the equivalent of the amount of time they had served on their current probation sentence, and

they were requested to provide a money fine that they considered the equivalent of the amount of time they had spent on probation supervision. In
order to obtain a relative measure for each probationer, the dollars, jail
time, and prison time that they considered the equivalent of the time they
had served on probation was divided by the number of days they reported
that they had served on probation.

Over two-fifths of the respondents felt that there was not any amount of
jail time that would be the equivalent of probation. Many of these subjects
poignantly rejected the notion of serving time in jail in lieu of probation.
Over one-third of the probationers interviewed reported that they would
spend one percent to 10 percent of the amount of time they had served on
probation in jail as a substitute for probation. About one-fifth of the subjects were willing to spend more than 10 percent of the time they had served
on probation in jail as an alternative sentence.

The average jail time equivalent of probation time was 7.8 percent. If
respondents were thinking in 24 hour days, this would mean that for every
day spent on probation, the average respondent would be willing to spend
approximately two hours in jail or almost a month in jail for every year on
probation. It is unlikely, however, that respondents were thinking in terms
of hours or even days. In most cases, respondents were making more global
judgements, and not using standard units of time as their frame of
reference. Future researchers should consider transforming the
respondent's global judgement into hours and days, and asking him if he
wants to change his response in light of this information.

The majority of the probationers interviewed (55 percent) reported that they
were not willing to spend any time in prison as a substitute for probation.
Approximately one-third of the respondents reported that spending
between one-percent and 10 percent of the time they had served on probation in prison would be the equivalent to their probation. About one-tenth
of the probationers were willing to spend over 10 percent of their probation
time in prison as a substitute disposition.

It is surprising that the probationers were willing to spend so little money
as a probation equivalent; 37.5 percent of the respondents were not willing
to spend any money, and another 12.5 percent felt that one dollar or less
equaled one day on probation. This adds up to fully one-half of those interviewed were willing to pay only a dollar or less as a substitute for each day
they spent on probation.

The average substitute fine was $2.10 per day, and the most any proba-
tioner was willing to pay in lieu of probation was $13.88 per day. Here, as
with the jail and prison equivalent time, the amount of money that the probationers considered equal to the amount of time they had spent on probation may seem low because the money-time frame in which the subjects were
responding may differ from the money-time frame used for analysis. Also,
it is likely that as the amount of time spent on probation increases, the

ratio between probation time and dollars, prison time, or jail time will decrease. For example, there may be some absolute limit to the money a person is willing to spend as the equivalent of his time on probation independent of the amount of time he has served on probation. A fine of $1,000 may appear to be a huge sum to some clients. However, if a person has served a year on probation, $1000 is only $2.74 per day on probation.

Conclusion

The picture of the average probationer that emerges from their responses to the questions described in this chapter is someone who is primarily concerned either with a warm, understanding, and supportive probation officer or a probation officer who does not interfere and allows the probationer a considerable amount of autonomy. The majority of probationers do not think of probation very often, and the undesirable feature that was mentioned most often, was that it was an inconvenience. The probationers interviewed seemed to be satisfied with their probation situation, and they comparatively rated probation as a mild penalty. As a substitute for the amount of time they served on probation, 40 percent would not spend any time in jail, 55 percent would not spend any time in prison, and 37.5 percent would not spend any money.

Some of the kinds of data we have collected on probationers may be useful for improving probation and other community corrections programs. The concerns or needs that were extracted from the interviews constitute one useful source of information. If we know which needs are important to a client, and we know which officers best satisfy those needs, we can match clients with officers. For example, if we interview a client and find that he has a strong need for support, we can assign him to an officer who considers himself a clinician. Or, if a client indicates a strong desire for someone to "keep him on the straight and narrow" (control), he may be well matched with an officer who sees his job as social control of those with little self-control.

The simple formula of matching demand (the self-specified needs of the probationer) with supply (a probation officer who can satisfy those needs) is not without problems. It presupposes, for example, that matching is desirable. We can all think of situations in which giving a person what he wants does not benefit the person or society. For example, providing someone with strong autonomy needs with complete freedom — no restrictions or guidance — could be disastrous. This is why matching can only be done within the framework provided by the objectives of probation. If one objective of probation was control, for example, the purpose of matching would be to accomodate the person with strong autonomy needs without losing sight of the need to control him. In this situation, consideration for his need for autonomy would take the form of assigning him to an officer who was aware that people with strong autonomy needs are concerned about issues of respect. We would not want to place this probationer with an officer who was insensitive to respect issues or an officer who occasionally bullied his charges for, what he considered, their own good.

Matching a probationer with strong autonomy needs with an officer who knows how to handle probationers who want to be treated with respect and who want to exercise as much control as possible over their lives can serve the objective of control — or any other utilitarian objective that is related to the goal of reducing the chances that the individual will be involved in crime or other behavior that could result in the revocation of probation — because it reduces the probability of friction between the officer and the probationer that could lead to behavior which would result in revocation.

Discussing the probationer's needs profile with him is one way to demonstrate that you are sensitive to his needs, and you are willing to try to accomodate them within the limits set by the objectives of supervision. In this way, the probationer is provided with the information needed to develop a realistic set of expectations about probation. These expectations should help to avoid resentment and other problems that can arise when expectations are not grounded in reality. It may be beneficial, for instance, that a client who expresses an unusually strong need for emotional sustenance is told at the outset that his probation officer can not satisfy that need. In such a case, the probation officer should guide the client to the appropriate psychological services.

The ability to make the most beneficial matches or to avoid the most harmful mismatches requires that we know something about individual probation officers. There are a number of ways this information could be gathered. We could, for example, ask probationers to describe their officers and content analyze their descriptions using the categories flexibility, assistance, control, support, and autonomy; or we could see, by examining probationer need profiles in conjunction with a measure of satisfaction (the Self-Anchoring Striving scale), if probationers with certain needs who were assigned to certain probation officers were relatively satisfied with their probation, and those with different needs patterns who were assigned to the same officer were not satisfied.

One potentially productive way to gather information on the needs that individual probation officers satisfy is to invite them to participate in self-study. This method is not only valuable for collecting data but also it can provide an opportunity for the officers to see how vital they are in shaping the climate in which the clients serve their time on probation. It is a vehicle for demonstrating to the officers that clients vary in their needs and officers vary in their ability to satisfy needs, and this variation can be used to make probation more effective.

Self-study of this kind may result in job enrichment for some officers. Some officers may acquire a broader view of their jobs when they see the variety of needs that they can satisfy for the probationer. In some cases, officers may begin to redefine their jobs from simply social control or the implementation of a sentence for a crime to providing human services.

It would be naive, of course, to think that as soon as probation officers realize what many of them already know, we can expect them to become flesh and blood examples of the human services perspective in action. The rewards structure for probation officers must in some way be tied to this perspective if we expect them to adopt it. It would also be naive to think that those in charge of probation departments would implement demand-supply matching programs of the kind suggested in this chapter without some evidence that they would serve, or at least not undermine, the goals of the department. Such evidence would require the implementation and evaluation of experimental matching programs.

Probation is not the only form of community corrections in which the needs of the clients and the characteristics of the supervisor or the qualities of the environment in which the client will serve his sentence should be taken into consideration. It may be possible to develop effective matching programs for parole, halfway houses, community service programs, and other forms of community corrections.

Endnotes

[1]This project was supported by Grant No. 78-NI-AX-0152 awarded to the Research Center of the Graduate School of Criminal Justice, Rutgers, The State University, Newark, New Jersey. The funding was provided by the National Institute of Law Enforcement, and Criminal Justice, Law Enforcement Assistance Administration, U.S. Department of Justice. Points of view or opinions stated in this document are those of the author and do not necessarily represent the official position or policies of the U.S. Department of Justice.

A random sample of 57 persons sentenced to probation in two counties in New Jersey was interviewed. In County A, the Chief Probation Officer contacted members of his staff he felt would be interested in the project. Although we were aware that a sample of officers biased in this way could influence both the type of probationers we interviewed and their impressions and concerns, it was the most reasonable procedure in light of real world constraints. Each of the selected staff members provided a list of their current cases (n = 206). A total of 50 probationers was randomly selected from these lists as interview candidates.

In County B, we randomly selected two Probation Officers from the two most urban areas in the county; and selected a random sample (n = 60) from their caseloads (n = 322). We concentrated on the urban areas in County B because we unsystematically observed that in County A most of the clients we interviewed were white, educated, and sentenced to probation for minor offenses. We felt that capturing a broader range of concerns required a sample from areas which contained more ethnic and economic diversity.

We interviewed about half the people in our sample, attrition was a substantial 53 cases. In some respects, the attrition can be considered artificially inflated because we did not attempt to contact 18 members of the sample. After conducting and transcribing a small number of interviews, we realized that about 30 interviews from each site was a more realistic goal considering the resources available. The other major source of attrition was termination of probation ($n = 11$). For these cases, we found that the subjects had completed their probation sentences by the time we attempted to contact them.

Six of the probationers contacted declined the invitation to participate in the project.

References

Cantril, H. (1965). *The Patterns of Human Concerns* New Brunswick, New Jersey: Rutgers University Press.
Toch, H. (1977). *Living in Prison: The Ecology of Survival.* New York: Free Press.

Community Corrections

On the Line

David M. Crean
U.S. Probation Officer

Community Convicts

Most of us at some point or other in our lives break one or more of our community's rules. The most common consequence of this is that no one notices; for example: the highway patrolman is not around when you exceed the speed limit, your neighbor doesn't complain when you burn your pile of fall leaves or the Internal Revenue Service's computer chooses to ignore your income tax return. Transgressions that we may occasionally knowingly or unwittingly commit, however, do have the potential of bringing us into contact with the criminal justice system. When this happens, and we have the misfortune of losing our pleading, we end up adjudged guilty of a criminal offense. This can come about by our own admission of the offense (pleading guilty), by the unanimous decision of a group of our neighbors (the jury) or in some circumstances by the verdict of the court (the judge). Once declared guilty of committing a crime, we then legally stand convicted and are thus "convicts." In today's society, a great many of us achieve this sad distinction.

Here we are a newly designated convict; someone suddenly distinct and somehow separated from the rest of our community. Now what happens? Depending on the severity of the violation of the community code (legal norms), a wide variety of options stand available for our fate. These range from the simple admonition — go and violate no more; to the more ominous — Marshall, take him away! Between those two extremes the sentencing official has a wide latitude in deciding what punishment we should receive to "correct" our behavior, protect society and insure that future transgressions will not occur. This "treatment" can be applied to us while we live in our own community or while we reside in a community of convicts where our liberty is restricted. If the latter is the case, we are most likely eventually to be released back to our community prior to the end of our sentence.

The first instance is usually known as probation. This alternative, "by far the most widely used form of correctional supervision, has traditionally been granted by the courts as an alternative to a prison or jail term."[1] The second instance is normally known as parole. This is "the second major form of community supervision (always follows release from jail). Although some prisoners are released to the community unconditionally, approximately 75 percent are released to parole supervision."[2] Thus, once you become a convict, you are one way or another, *eventually* going to be living in the community under a community corrections program. As a matter of fact, "seventy-two percent of all adult offenders under correctional supervision in the United States are supervised in the community through probation and parole agencies; twenty-eight percent are incarcerated in prison or jail. Supervised probationers and parolees are granted conditional liberty—they may live in the community as long as their behavior meets certain conditions. They are required to maintain some degree of contact with the supervising agency, ranging from mail or phone contact only to frequent direct contact with the parole or probation officer. Restrictions may be imposed on various aspects of daily life, including drinking, companions, employment, residence and travel. Violation of the law or violation of probation and parole conditions can result in a prison or jail term—with or without a new sentence."[3]

After joining this outlaw class, convicts, if you luck out and are like the majority of your fellow travelers, you "get probation." What is supposed to happen now? "The basic idea underlying a sentence to probation is very simple. Sentencing is in large part concerned with avoiding future crimes by helping the defendant learn to live productively in the community which he has offended against. Probation proceeds on the theory that the best way to pursue this goal is to orient the criminal sanction toward the community setting in those cases where it is compatible with the other objectives of sentencing. Other things being equal, the odds are that a given defendant will learn how to live successfully in the general community if he is dealt with in that community rather than shipped off to the artificial and atypical environment of an institution of confinement. Banishment from society, in a word, is not the way to integrate someone to society. Yet imprisonment involves just such banishment, albeit for a temporary sojourn in most cases ...probation is an affirmative correctional tool, a tool which is used not because it is of maximum benefit to the defendant (though, of course, this is an important side product), but because it is of maximum benefit to the society which is sought to be served by the sentencing of criminals."[4]

However, if you are not so lucky, you go to jail. The vast majority of convicts, who are incarcerated in prison or jail, are granted the conditional release to the community to become community convicts prior to having fully completed their jail sentence. They are paroled. Thus, community corrections must deal at one point or another with almost everyone who graduates into the "convict" class.

"During 1982, the adult probation population rose by more than 100,000 persons to 1,335,359 (a nine percent increase); the adult parole population rose by about 18,000 to 243,880 (an eight percent increase). Both parole and probation populations have been steadily increasing for several years. Since 1979 the probation population has grown by more than 265,000 — a twenty-five percent increase, while the parole population has risen by more than 26,000 — a twelve percent increase."[5]

Studies indicate prison populations are increasing in every state; and, in state after state, programs to house these institutional convicts are falling behind the pace. Buildings needed for this purpose are very expensive and what can be built is limited by the available funding money which is being strongly competed for by community corrections and other societal needs. Much debate is under way over what is to be done. Several methods have been adopted to try and keep the prison population in line with the physical capacity. Solutions such as "sentencing guidelines that use available prison capacity as a consideration in setting the length of terms (such as those in Minnesota); . . . mechanisms for accelerating good time; and . . . direct release of certain prisoners — usually those already close to their release date under administrative provisions (such as emergency crowding law in Michigan, the use of commutation in Georgia, and the early release program in Illinois)."[6]

Innovative approaches are being debated and/or implemented, but in all cases, the end result is that the responsibility for dealing with the problem is falling back, in ever increasing measure, on the community correction system; and the bottom line there is the line officer.

Ah, but here's the rub! Just as community probation and parole programs are being called upon to deal with ever increasing numbers of unique individuals with their own special set of values, experiences, needs and problems, the line officers are also being called upon to be more professional in the performance of their duties. The emphasis on accountability is constantly growing, public awareness and public scrutiny are increasing and proven performance is being demanded. All the while, the process on which these evaluations are being made is one of person to person contact, communication, understanding of human foibles and motivation, reeducating, or educating in the first instance — all in a very inexact science and in truth, a very delicate art form.

Finally, probation and parole faced with this constantly increasing workload, along with the enlarged expectations for improved performance and proved results, also has to contend with the current financial reality of diminishing resources. On all levels (county, state and federal), probation and parole practitioners are having to argue long and hard for an increase in qualified personnel, adequate training to keep up with the new obligations and requirements, maintenance of appropriate work environments, and incentives to lure from the private sector competent individuals to provide this human service. Also being fought for is the ability to obtain state of the art office equipment to enable the handling of the immense volume of documentation mandated by the nature of the services performed.

In late 1983 all across the North American continent, probation and parole systems are being severely tested. Can they meet the challenge? Can they provide the services expected in the professional manner required? The burden of the answer to these questions falls on the line officer. The one who is the "in the flesh" service provider; the one who is being asked to do more, in a better way and with less assistance and back up. As Don Quixote's Pancho Sanchez states, "Whether the rock hits the pitcher, or the pitcher hits the rock, it's going to be hard on the pitcher."

The Service Providers

The "pitcher" or vehicle through which society's expectations (protection from further law transgressions and a just performance return on monies expended) are to be met is the line or field officer. While in a small percentage of cases, courts and/or parole authorities do order convicts into community correction programs conducted by private or community volunteer organizations, the overwhelming majority of offenders are directed into publicly run probation and parole services. Here their contact is with "my PO," a line officer, and here is where success or failure is achieved.

Thus, it naturally follows that the most common corrections staff person is the line probation or parole officer. Obviously, within their own systems, they are the base line on which the managerial and support triangle is erected. It is to these people that society turns for prevention of new crime and new victimization; while at the same time, the past perpetrators of crime are demanding that their own very real needs be met by receiving through the officer mental and emotional support, financial assistance, vocational or educational training, physical care and an ever expanding universe of treatment support.

Line staff thus find themselves confronted with increasingly complex and often contradictory demands. In an attempt to manage, and efficiently turn to their advantage, the expanding tide of expectation, field probation and parole practitioners are counting on the hoped for "professionalization" of their livelihood. Literature abounds with statements concerning the struggling to achieve a professional status.

David Fogel, in his 1981 paper, *Probation in Search of an Advocate,* states that probation is "afflicted with problems of lack of direction, low status and lack of public confidence." Probation is a little over a hundred years old, and even though it claims to be extremely successful, the general public perception is that a probation sentence is one of leniency (a non-sentence if you will). Various segments of the system are "subject to local pressures which negatively affect its venturesomeness," it has neither an obvious local or national constituency or spokesman." Associations representing the profession are in their infancy; there are no local reference groups such as other professions have. Due to this state of affairs, probation/parole is "even more vulnerable in times of diminishing resources," it lacks an appealing image even in relation to other criminal justice occupations, it "lacks a professional identity" in that "there is no widely recognized professional school to prepare leaders for probation," nor are there any "nationally recognized scholars, practitioners or administrators who can be called eminent leaders...Probation is uneasy about what it actually produces in the way of measurable results."[7]

What John Agustus started in Massachusetts in 1878 with his volunteer community service to wayward juveniles has come a long way to the present situation where we find independent local, state and federal systems operating under a diverse and ever increasing set of statutory mandates. There is still a long way to go.

As can be seen from Fogel's extensive shortcomings listing, achieving professionalism is a matter of the long term development of public recognition that in this field the practitioners have a viable image and identity, they possess a unique body of knowledge, acquired through recognized schools noted for preparing such individuals and there exist nationally identified individuals who have achieved eminence in the field through scholarship, practice or administration. Once it is accepted that probation/parole possesses a body of proven results, its image as an effective and useful service worthy of public confidence will follow.

Current literature reflects a situation where all the essential elements expressed above are in existence, developing and moving toward the goal of professional recognition. There is a growing number of institutions offering specialized education in the field; there is an ever increasing body of knowledge being developed by and available to practitioners in the field. The service providers themselves are becoming more conscious of the need to educate the public with respect to the services they perform, the effectiveness with which they do it and the benefits derived from its being done. An increasing number are seeking and achieving higher educational levels. A national association, the American Probation and Parole Association is working to be the catalyst around which professionalism crystallizes.

This quest does not lay solely at the feet of the line officer but also must involve the efforts of the organization employing him. The process has to "involve the whole organization in an effort to reset its directions, orientations, strategies as well as tactics. Professional as well as bureaucratic incrustations have to be overcome. We will have to be reeducating practitioners as well as retraining them, reorganizing and remolding agencies as well as adding new services to them."[8]

Current research indicates line officers themselves are much in favor of this process and are seeking the improved education, techniques and expertise required. However, literature also indicates that the structure of the system itself, especially since it lies in the public domain, can in some instances be a hindrance rather than a major force behind the drive to achieve professionalization. This fact is summed up in a paper on professionalism by Robert L. Thomas when he states that probation/parole "is an emerging profession that is in the process of being professionalized. A majority of the incumbents have achieved a degree of professionalism beyond that of the parent organization; the latter can catch up and then perhaps the efficiency, effectiveness, and humanity of the overall system will benefit; otherwise, our framework for professionalism is incomplete."[9] Thomas was speaking of the Federal Probation System, but what is said applies to the field as a whole.

A negative perception long held by the general public characterized probation and parole officers as individuals who are into second careers as a result of being failures at their first career choice. This line of thought supports the idea that the field is primarily composed of individuals who are former social workers, former religious, former policemen and former failures of other more worthy occupations. This image does not jibe with reality. Today's probation and parole officers are on the average relatively young, trained in institutions which for the past 20 years have been developing appropriate curricula and are working in their first career choice field. They are motivated not so much by a desire to receive recognition but rather by a desire to make a positive contribution to others; being instrumental in bringing about positive change which allows "convicts" a life of greater happiness and less self-inflicted suffering and pain. They are quietly enthused by the idealistic goal of being able to personally contribute to the making of a better community around us all. PO's must be able to relate well with others, enjoy working with people and have a firm belief that offenders can modify and change their behavior.

What PO's Do

The actual probation and parole service provider has many masters to serve.

"Although probation and parole evolved independently and occur at different points in the criminal justice process, probationers and parolees are supervised in a similar way. In 30 states, a single agency administers both probation and parole, the staff may supervise combined caseloads, and probationers and parolees are required to follow similar conditions. As probation supervision increasingly follows a period of incarceration, the main difference between the two is in the proceeding for entering supervision. Probation is granted by the court, while the executive branch controls parole release (discretionary parole is granted by parole boards and mandatory parole is administered by corrections departments).''[10] What a typical probation or parole officer's caseload may be is governed by the nature of the employing agency and by its basic philosophy. However, leaving the juvenile system aside, ''the average parole/probation officer will have a caseload made diverse by age, past record, attitude, and individual needs of his clients.''[11]

Since the supervising officer is a public employee, what is expected of him is usually codified in law and that code is then greatly expanded by managerial interpretation and direction. An example of the whole spectrum combined into one is the United States Probation system which states the duties of its officers are as follows:

> Rule 32(c) of the Federal Rules of the Criminal Procedure require the probation system to conduct presentence investigations. Title 18 U.S.C. 3655 provides that the probation officer ''shall keep informed concerning the conduct and condition of each probationer under his supervision and shall report thereon to the court placing such person on probation. He shall use all suitable methods, not inconsistent with the conditions imposed by the court, to aid probationers and to bring about improvements in their conduct and condition.

> In addition, ''each probation officer shall perform such duties with respect to persons on parole as the Parole Commission shall request.'' Probation officers at the request of the Bureau of Prisons and the United States Parole Commission, conduct investigations relative to persons in prison or on parole (18 U.S.C. 4205(e).) The probation officer also assists the U.S. Attorney in diversion matters and the U.S. Air Force, U.S. Army, and U.S. Navy in their parole programs. Maintaining a close cooperative working relationship with other agencies is an essential function of the probation officer.

> ...probation and parole are systematic and constructive methods of correctional treatment which through counseling, guidance, assistance, surveillance, and restraint facilitate the offender's reintegration into society as a law abiding and productive member. The end result is a safer and better community. Probation officers should seek out the assistance of the community in the rehabilitation effort and as time allows and the court permits, interpret to the community the role of the probation officer and the purposes of probation and parole.[12]

In general the first responsibility of the line officer is to the authority who placed the individual offender under his supervision. With respect to the Court, this responsibility usually begins with the preparation of a presentence report. Here the officer performs a complete background investigation beginning with the offender's birth up to the time he appears before the Court for sentencing. This report is prepared to assist the sentencing Court in the selection of an appropriate sentence, given the nature of the offense committed and the status of the individual who committed it.

Typically, a presentence investigation report breaks down into the following catetories:

    I. Information concerning the offense. Here the exact nature of the offense to which the individual stands convicted is set forth followed by a narrative account of his and others actions leading up to the commission of the offense. A section is provided wherein the individual reports his version of what happened and this is usually followed by any statements made by codefendants, witnesses and/or victims.

   II. Individual's prior record. Here juvenile adjudications as well as adult arrests are listed. Not only is the nature of the arrest, the time, place and disposition given, but also background detail is provided along with verification of the nature of the judicial process which led to disposition.

  III. Personal background. A narrative usually verifies defendant's birth date, identifies his parents and siblings and the nature of their relationship. It covers his upbringing, marital situation, educational background, employment, physical, mental, emotional health, military service and the financial situation.

  IV. Prosecution comments. The prosecution is given a formal opportunity to enter into the report its beliefs in regard to the offense and what the appropriate disposition should be.

   V. Overall summarization and evaluation. Here a concise review of the foregoing information is drawn together and presented along with the possible sentencing alternatives available to the Court. More and more frequently also appearing here is statistical data indicating the type and length of sentences given to previous similar cases.

  VI. Recommendation. Here the probation officer submits to the Court what he believes to be the most appropriate sentence based upon the information in the report. The recommendation should logically follow from all the information compiled as "the probation officer has the responsibility to offer a sound recommendation with supporting rationale which will assist the Court in achieving its sentencing goals."[13]

Once sentence is pronounced, the officer then becomes involved in supervision: immediately through probation; or on a delayed basis through parole following incarceration.

In either situation whether the convict is on probation or on parole, the general conditions of supervision are usually the same. In exchange for being allowed to live in the community rather than in an institution, an individual is required to obey all laws and failing that, to notify his line officer immediately upon any law enforcement contact or arrest. He is restricted from associating with people known to him as former or current law breakers and he is expected to conduct his affairs at reasonable times and places. Further, he must make a good faith effort to maintain full-time lawful employment, support people dependent upon him and if unable to work, keep his probation officer informed of his current status. In addition, the probationer/parolee cannot travel outside a limited area without prior approval, must keep the probation officer informed of his place of residence, must follow his instructions and report to him as directed.

Added to these general conditions can be special conditions unique to the individual and his or her situation. Such conditions as payment of fines, restitution, attendance at counseling, community service, job training involvement and an almost unlimited universe of other specific requirements suited to meet individual needs and situations can be ordered.

The "conditions of supervision provide a framework within which the offender and the probation officer attempt reintegration of the offender into law-abiding society. Conditions of supervision are used to set forth objectives and methods to assist in improving the offender's conduct and life circumstances. Conditions are legal tools with which to build a successful probation or parole experience.... at the onset of probation and parole supervision, the probation officer thoroughly reviews the conditions of supervision with the offender and each specific condition is discussed to insure that the offender understands the basis for the condition and how it is to be fulfilled. The officer supplies a copy of the conditions which the offender signs indicating receipt. Certain conditions require continuous participation and commitment on the part of the offender as, for example, in the treatment of substance abuse. Periodic classification of the purpose of such conditions reinforces the spirit of cooperation."[14]

It is the probation officer's job to keep accurately informed of where a person under his supervision is living, under what conditions and with whom; how leisure time is spent and with whom; where the employment is, what it involves and what compensation is being received; when and where the individual travels, with whom and for what purpose; what other sources of income are, and what the person's general financial status is; and of course, whether or not the individual is involved in any further law violations.

To do this, it is necessary not only for the person under supervision to truthfully and accurately convey the above information to the field officer; but also, it is equally as necessary for the field officer to get out from behind the desk, away from the mail and the phone, and into the individual's environment by visiting the home, the job and other such places and situations that the offender is involved in. Doing this brings the field officer in contact with family, friends, spouses, employers, fellow employees, and community law enforcement officers familiar with that individual's behavior. Getting out and becoming a real and present entity in the life of the individual under supervision not only increases the line officer's knowledge and understanding of the person he is trying to assist, but it also serves to verify the data received either from the individual himself or from some other collateral source.

The line officer then, thus informed by these activities, can adequately assess the needs of the individual under supervision, develop or improve strategies for dealing with these needs, provide whatever services are directly available through his agency, make appropriate referrals to cover other needs and then monitor progress being made. This is not a static process but it is an active one where the plans and goals can be and usually are in constant flux as the person under supervision responds to the attention being provided and eliminates some needs while developing others.

In addition, the line officer is then in the correct position to report to the appropriate authority on the progress being made. These occasional behavioral updates are usually motivated by the necessity for the Court or paroling agency to intervene in one manner or another. If the supervised individual over a significant period of time responds well to the conditions and supervision plan, shows an ability to function as a law-abiding, self-supporting, positively contributing citizen, then authority is usually requested to grant an early termination of supervision. This is a reduction in sentence, allowing the community convict to finish his sentence prior to the original date set by the court.

On the other hand, if the probation officer's report contains bad news, due to failure or inability to properly respond and adjust to the community; then the request is for an appropriate change in the conditions of supervision or a cessation of the privilege of serving the sentence in the community. In the former instance, the release conditions of supervision can be altered so as to more adequately address the problems currently being faced with the desire that it will lead to correction of poor adjustment. Such things as alcohol, drug and counseling requirements could be added. If greater support is needed, the individual can be required to enter a half-way house. Here the pressure on him for controlling all aspects of his own life is reduced and he can deal with one problem such as employment, at a time.

In the latter instance, the release privilege is rescinded (probation/parole is revoked) and the community convict becomes an institutional convict. In most instances, the decision to revoke is made following a formal hearing before the appropriate authority (Court/paroling body) where both the convict and the line officer present their versions of the individual's behavior while in the community.

Within a typical work week, a line officer is usually called upon to be an investigator, a biographer, a watchdog, counselor, friend, confidant, reporter, expert witness and broker of outside services. His is an exciting challenge, demanding responsibility and creative opportunity.

The Line's Vision

Ask any line officer what the main purpose of probation and parole is and almost without exception the response will be: protection of the community. Since most convicts are of the community variety, probation and parole services are the community's first line of defense against further violations, transgressions and victimizations.

The prohibition against further violation of law is usually the first condition of any community conditional release. On the simplest of levels, it is hoped that a community convict's negative tendencies to continue antisocial behavior will be inhibited due to the line officer's knowledge of him, his situation and his activities; i.e., the "looking over my shoulder" effect.

Next, the line officer understands that the person under supervision is serving a sentence: i.e., a punishment. The basic desire here is that the probationer or parolee will make the causal connection between negative behavior and receiving a punishment and as a result of this understanding, then be motivated to positively alter behavior so as to avoid such punishment in the future.

It is at this point that the third and much more complex goal comes into play. What is it that can be provided through the intervention of the line officer in the community convict's life so as to assist that individual in making the transition from self-created unhappiness to self-fulfillment? Whereas in the two goals cited above, society's needs are first, here the needs, wants and desires of the person under supervision become paramount; and, it is here that the major dichotomy in the practice of this profession exists. The line officer must be able to "work both sides of the fence," while at the same time being responsible to a third dimension: an impartial authority set by law above the fray.

The question of how much knowledge or information should the non-convict community members who come in contact with a community convict through residential, employment and/or leisure activities be given about the offender is the most obvious everyday conflict. What knowledge is needed by the community so as to be protected from the offender has to be balanced against what effect disclosure of information about the offender has on his efforts to establish a law-abiding, self-supporting, positive attitude producing lifestyle. Examples of this particular conflict are legion and no single rule can be applicable to all cases. The solution in each case has to be tailor-made with the adeptness of a fine watchmaker and the wisdom of a Solomon.

The line officer "may find it necessary to request a special condition of probation or parole restricting an offender's employment, conduct, social, or business contacts in the interest of protecting the public..."[15] On the other hand, the line officer's obligation to assist in the rehabilitation of the community convict demands that the situation be assessed thoroughly and that an option of action most compatible with the interests of both sides be employed.

By performing their profession, line officers feel they are truly protecting their fellow law-abiding citizens, verifying the fulfillment of the punishments dispensed, assisting in the prevention of new crime and providing the climate and support to allow individuals to change (habilitate themselves).

Community convicts do not always perceive the process in the same fashion. Most likely their first observation is that their liberty is being restricted and that their "fate" is being placed in the hands of another. If they are able to work through this initial impression, they then come to realize they now have a new "significant other" in their lives and they must develop a strategy to deal with him. The responses to this are as individual and unique as are fingerprints. At one end of the spectrum is complete avoidance: the rabbit approach—absconding. While at the other end is delegation of total personal responsibility: "I'm not responsible, you tell me what to do."

In between comes all possible combinations of hostility, acceptance, cooperation and gratitude. The average individual under supervision goes through an initial phase of resistance and/or at least distance. As the relationship between he and "his PO" develops, there comes acceptance and then an understanding of agreed upon expectations. This is followed by a period of mutual checking to see if the other performs as expected. There are some short periods of reassessment with the end result being a firmed up understanding. The possibilities are: both parties negatively view one another; one party has a negative view while the other has a positive view (actually two options); and, both parties hold positive perceptions. This last, of course, is the most desired option as it holds the best promise for satisfying the system's needs and goals. Which possibility the relationship will develop into depends upon the personality of both the probation officer and the offender. However, the relationship can be characterized by any of the options-and still be successful while maybe not as psychologically rewarding to one or both of the participants.

Given the fact that research indicates somewhere between 70 and 80 percent of all people under community supervision complete that supervision in the community without being classified as failures, the majority of both officers and clients view the community supervision process as successful. All goals are not always met; nor are all needs always met. Considering the alternative of locking up all convicts in an ever increasing number of costly structures, community corrections is a very attractive alternative.

Bumps, Jogs and Prizes for the Line

Many of the sources of strain and frustration in the work of a community line officer have already been alluded to above. The most obvious are increasing workloads, diminishing resources, increasing responsibilities, static compensation, lack of public awareness and acceptance, sometimes hostile clientele and somewhat indifferent administration. A larger caseload means more unique individuals the officer has to relate to. Human nature being what it is, an officer's personality will work well with most, but on other occasions, can be quite counterproductive. Frustration can arise; and, professional judgment, knowledge and adaptability must prevail.

As the body of knowledge in the field continues to grow and the line officer becomes better informed and aware of solutions to problems presented to him, the reality of diminishing resources floods in. Knowing what's available versus what "should be" available can produce strain. To deal with this, the major ally must be the community. The line officer must be well armed with knowledge of what services the community can provide to supplement his individual efforts. While at the same time, he must work with the community to develop an awareness of what is needed, organize the effort to secure it and support the organizations which attempt to provide it. Like everyone else, the line officer must learn "to do more with less."

Doing more with less is also being required in the line officer's personal life as his family needs grow, inflation grows and due to the public outcry to hold the line on public expenditures, the income does not grow. No matter how sympathetic one may be as a taxpayer, as a wage earner feeling uncompensated for increased expertise and performance, tension over compensation is bound to arise.

Even though one cannot take recognition and praise to the bank, it is a necessary element of what fuels the engines that drive us all. Being involved in public safety, reduction in crime and rehabilitation of offenders is dealing at the forefront of one of society's major concerns. Yet while being numbered among those individuals who are the pointpersons in this effort, line officers do not see much public acceptance or recognition of their exertions.

The very nature of the process of dealing with involuntary clients who in many cases would rather be almost anywhere else, even Philadelphia, has its own set of unique pitfalls. The helping professions of which community corrections is a substantial part, are extremely susceptible to the phenomenon known as "burnout." Trying to be all things to all people takes its toll and attempting that trick with individuals who don't want to be involved makes the process even more of a Gordian knot.

Finally, as related above, even with these and other sources of strain and frustration, the practice of the profession can be very rewarding. When the line officer feels secure in his own system, has a sense that his best interests are being looked out for by those above him, that his efforts and position in these various conflicts are well understood and appreciated, these potholes along the way appear very minor. However, what is just outlined above is the ideal and throughout the field in general, this is most likely not the case. The reality is that line officers operate in public organizations subject to political pressures and shifts of societal mood. The support to back up the officer and provide him a secure, firm and supportive place from which to operate is not always forthcoming.

Even given this somewhat gloomy assessment, people attracted to this profession for the most part stick with it. In certain instances, under certain circumstances, the monetary rewards are very good. However, this is not the most important reward which binds these practitioners to their profession. The incalculable rewards received from knowing that you are instrumental in achieving a safer community and in observing an individual shy away from self-destructive tendencies, gradually question alternatives and eventually turn to productive behavior more than makes up for the bumps and jogs encountered while traveling down the line to that achievement.

Line on the Future

As with rock and roll, community corrections is here to stay. What form it may evolve into and what system may be its prime conveyance is currently under constant debate and review. No profession operates in a vacuum alone unto itself impervious to outside influences; least of all community corrections. Since it is a public function and a publicly provided service, what happens with the profession depends on many factors.

The primary responsibility for its existence, its mission and its support lies with the community at large. Authority is delegated to the community's elected officials upon whose shoulders rests the burden of educating the community to its benefits and rallying the community to provide the support and consensus so as to be able to acquire adequate resources. Next down the line come the administrators and supervisors who must take these resources and establish functioning systems which deliver the services the community wants. How valuable these services actually are is determined by the line staff's efforts with the Court, the paroling authorities, the community, the probationer and the parolee. How each line officer views the task and then translates it into actions aimed at performing the tasks can and does have a very profound effect on how the community, the elected officials and the administrators respond to the system's needs.

Unfortunately, while the majority of community convicts who enter the system adapt to the program, achieve its goals and are released back into the non-convict class; they get no headlines or major publicity. On the other hand, it is the approximately one-fifth of the convict class that fails to adjust successfully whose negative activities are rapidly brought to the public's attention. It is on these human failures that the probation and parole system is judged. The remaining four-fifths are to one degree or another very fulfilling human success stories. They go unreported, unnoticed and unappreciated.

In the future for line officers to receive the support and recognition they perceive the system needs and to have the greatest effect possible on public policy, they must become more actively involved in communicating to the public the goals, functions and achievements of their profession. The line must become more actively involved with appearances at community organizations, providing interviews to print and electronic media and publish at an increased rate the facts as to what is going on in community corrections. The public must be informed about what studies, innovative ideas and pilot projects are being conducted to better satisfy both the community's goals and at the same time provide a more desirable, productive atmosphere for the client. Educating the public is the foundation upon which a successful growing community corrections profession must be based.

Once this foundation is properly laid, the necessary building blocks will be forthcoming. Appropriate staffing will allow time for greater line training and advanced education. More individuals involved in those activities will promote an expanding body of technical knowledge and approaches. This will encourage greater specialization among institutions of higher learning who will seek out individuals with proven and widely accepted expertise. These individuals will no doubt seek out, contribute to and help expand the reputation and acceptability of one or more nationally recognized community corrections associations.

If community convicts receive more "professional treatment," more of them will grow out of that stigma class; there will be less of them continuing to victimize themselves and the community around them.

Incidences of brother wronging brother and neighbor wronging neighbor are as old as human kind. Such events have been listed since the dawn of recorded history. Human nature, being what it has been, is and will be, will always produce "community convicts." Can community services improve its response to community convicts and keep their negative effects to a minimum? The answer lies in history. The organized effort began in Massachusetts just slightly over 100 years ago has developed into today's vast system. Today the extent of the problems and the magnitude of the effort applied has never been greater.

We can, we are and we will meet these challenges — the solution is on the line.

Endnotes

[1]"Probation and Parole 1982"; *Bureau of Justice Statistics Bulletin,* U.S. Department of Justice, September, 1983. Page 2.

[2]*Ibid.*

[3]*Ibid.*

[4]"The Supervision Process, Publication 106"; Probation Division of the Administrative Office of the United States Courts, Washington, D.C., 1983. Pages 1-2. (Taken from the introduction to "Standards Relating to Probation" published by the American Bar Association.)

[5]"Probation and Parole 1982", Page 1.

[6]"Setting Prison Terms," *Bureau of Justice Statistics Bulletin,* U.S. Department of Justice, August, 1983. Page 1.

[7]Fogel, David. "Probation in Search of an Advocate," a paper presented at the 13th Annual John Jay Criminal Justice Institute, New York, May 15, 1981. Pages 2-6.

[8]Gartner, Allen. *The Preparation of Human Service Professionals.* Human Service Press, New York, New York (1976). Page 27.

[9]Thomas, R.L. "Professionalism in Federal Probation, Illusion or Reality? The Role of Continuing Education." *Federal Probation,* March, 1983. Page 3.

[10]"Probation and Parole 1982." Page 3.

[11]Trester, Harold B. *Supervision of the Offender,* Prentice/Hall, Inc. Englewood Cliffs, New Jersey. (1981) Page 58.

[12]"A Guide to Judiciary Policies and Procedures, Probation Manual," Administrative Office of the United States Courts, Washington, D.C., Vol. X/A. Pages 1-3 and 1-4.

[13]"The Presentence Investigation, Publication 105," Division of Probation, Administrative Office of the United States Courts, Washington, D.C. (1978). Page 16.

[14]"The Supervision Process, Publication 106," Page 15.

[15]*Ibid.,* Page 17.

VI
Treatment Programs

Treatment Innovations in Probation and Parole

Robert G. Culbertson
Thomas Ellsworth
Illinois State University

Introduction

Probation and parole systems are part of the broader area of community-based corrections. Courts place offenders on probation, and parole-granting authorities place incarcerated offenders on parole. Probation is often granted as part of a court-ordered, supervised release which does *not* include incarceration in prison. Parole is granted *after* a person has served part of his or her sentence in a penal institution. The two forms of supervision, while having many similarities, also have some significant differences. Each has a distinct historical development. The bureaucratic organizational structures for each are also quite different, and the client systems (i.e., persons supervised) generally have quite different life experiences. Procedures regulating supervision and methods of supervision are also somewhat different.

Probation Supervision

The social setting in which probation developed in the United States contributed substantially to its history. John Augustus, a Boston shoemaker, is considered by most to have begun the first systematic use of probation (Abadinsky, 1982). Augustus bailed offenders after conviction, and, in addition to providing them with friendship and emotional support, he made efforts to find his probationers jobs. He would report his progress to the judge, who would order a small fine and court costs rather than incarceration. Between 1841 and 1858, Augustus bailed almost 2,000 defendants

(United Nations, 1951). In 1878 the state of Massachusetts recognized the success of the practice and enacted the first probation statute in the United States. Probation emerged because reform-minded persons were aware of the brutal effects of incarceration and the necessity of developing alternatives to institutions which would meet the needs of individual offenders.

Minnesota is credited with enacting the first state law, passed in 1889, authorizing the hiring of county probation officers; however, the granting of probation was limited to those under 18. The early development of probation was directly related to the establishment of the first Juvenile Court in Cook County, Illinois in 1899 (Abadinsky, 1982). As a formal system to investigate, supervise and treat offenders, juvenile probation advanced more rapidly than did adult probation. Juvenile probation was available in forty states by 1910, providing non-punitive, treatment oriented programming for children (President's Commission on Law Enforcement and the Administration of Justice, 1967). By 1925, probation was available to juveniles in every state; however, not all states provided probation for adults until 1956 (President's Commission on Law Enforcement and the Administration of Justice, 1967).

Over the years, probation developed as a program which focused on the rehabilitation and reintegration of the offender. Traditional casework approaches emphasized both individual and family counseling, job assistance, and psychological and psychiatric counseling when appropriate. In some respects, probation, through the 1960s, reflected early historical foundations. However, during the late 1970s and the early 1980s, both probation and parole were affected by political and philosophical movements in criminal justice which placed a greater emphasis on punishment. Examples of policies reflecting these movements include mandatory incarceration with longer prison sentences, selective incarceration, determinant sentencing, and intensive supervision of offenders with an emphasis on surveillance. Some authorities are calling for an even greater emphasis on punishment, with less of an emphasis on rehabilitation and related activities. The controversy is intense, with deep philosophical differences reflected in the goal statements for probation.

A major problem in the field of criminal justice, and especially corrections, is the lack of an articulated goal structure (Marshall and Vito, 1982; Culbertson, 1977). As a result, goal statements are sometimes contradictory, depending on the perspectives of those who develop the statements. The following statements provide some insight into these controversies and conflicts as we examine the conflicting perspectives of the "traditionalists," who are strong supporters of rehabilitation, and their "critics," who support crime control and surveillance.

The first goal of probation is community protection. Traditionalists believe this goal can best be accomplished by rehabilitation of the offender.

The offense, for the traditionalist, is important to the extent that it is symptomatic of problems in the offender's life which ultimately must be resolved. Recommendations, reflecting the needs of the offender, are made to the court. Implementation of the treatment plan includes a heavy emphasis on individual counseling. The traditionalist denies that this approach ignores the offense and, concurrently, protection of the community. Rather, the traditionalist argues the only way to successfully protect the community is through the successful rehabilitation of the offender.

Critics of traditional methods of supervision, with an emphasis on the individual offender, have called for new goals and classification methods which place an emphasis on the offense committed, the prior record of the offender, and the prognosis for non-criminal behavior in the future. Critics argue the traditionalists have emphasized the needs of the offender to the exclusion of protection of the community. Screening, prediction and classification are central to the critics' beliefs that the public's interests are paramount to those of the offender. The supervision of the offender has an underlying philosophy, the goal of which is to achieve a secure community (Allen, Carlson, and Parks, 1979). Classification schemes espoused by the critics place less emphasis on the needs of the offender and more emphasis on the protection of the community. In this controversy, one begins to understand the philosophical conflicts in criminal justice which pervade the policies and procedures utilized in community supervision of offenders.

While traditionalists argue the best way to protect the community is through the rehabilitation of the offender, critics contend that rehabilitation programming has failed. The community is then best protected by programs emphasizing supervision and surveillance, depending on the offense background of the individual offender. The debate over "what works" is extensive (Martinson, 1974; Palmer, 1975, 1978).

A second and closely related goal of probation is reintegration of the offender. Reintegration, according to the traditionalists, is accomplished by carefully assessing the needs of the offender in order to enhance the delivery of appropriate treatment and rehabilitation programming. The goal is a successfully adjusted offender who is a full participant in his or her community.

Critics of the traditional approach generally agree with the goal of reintegration; however, there is less concern for the offender's behavior and the extent to which the offender does not violate the law. Critics contend the rehabilitation and reintegration goals of the traditionalists are extremely elusive, whereas the goal of no further criminal behavior can be easily documented. That is, critics contend probation should be evaluated on the basis of a criterion emphasizing offense records rather than whether an individual has improved in his or her "life situation." These controversies are reflected in a variety of court documents, including probation contracts which call for behavioral change, community service, and restitution and related programs which place a high degree of accountability on the individual offender.

Parole Supervision

Parole, as indicated earlier, has a different origin than does probation. Captain Alexander Maconochie, who was in charge of an English penal colony, Norfolk Island, is considered to be the "father of parole" (Dressler, 1969). Maconochie developed a Ticket of Leave system which resulted in prisoners having an opportunity to leave the island before completing their sentences. The holder of a Ticket of Leave could have his freedom revoked if he associated with "notoriously bad characters" or led an idle or "dissolute life," or had no visible means of obtaining an honest livelihood (p. 86).

Parole was first introduced in the United States by Boston penal reformer, Samuel G. Howe, in 1847 (Dressler, 1969). Parole is the status one holds once released from a prison or reformatory after having served part of a sentence. The release is on condition that the person on parole maintain "good behavior." During the parole period, the individual is under the supervision of an agency of the state until a final discharge is granted. The goals for parole reflect the status of the offender considered for parole.

The first goal of parole, according to the traditionalists, is to provide a timely release from prison, enhancing the potential that the sentence served will meet the needs of the inmate and adequately protect society. Individuals who are incarcerated in prison change, but the rate of change is different for each offender. Traditionalists argue it is important that this be recognized because the timing of release is important in the reintegration process. If an offender is released too early, potentials for further criminality may be increased. On the other hand, if the offender is held an "unreasonable" period of time, there is the potential for bitterness which can function to enhance criminality.

Critics contend that the methods used to determine when an offender should be released are unscientific and subjective, and the result has been too many early releases for too many offenders (Martinson, 1974, Martinson and Wilks, 1977). The critics call for longer prison terms before parole can be considered, raising two issues in support of their position. First, is the notion of "just deserts" (von Hirsch, 1976). Under this concept, if one commits a crime, one should be incarcerated for a reasonable amount of time which is *proportionate to the crime,* regardless of adjustment progress. The second issue is that of community protection and the perceived need for firm control of the parolee, with an emphasis on surveillance. Calling for stronger controls, critics point to the failure of a number of traditional parole-related programs.

The critics' philosophical perspectives have important policy implications. The traditional notion of the halfway house, where one resided in order to facilitate adjustment prior to returning to the community, has changed. As punitive philosophies gain support, the concern with adjustment has been increasingly replaced with a concern for control. Thus, the halfway house becomes one of several mechanisms for attaining greater control over the offender, as opposed to a means of obtaining the traditional goals of rehabilitation and reintegration.

A second goal of parole is to lessen the harshness of some long prison sentences. Traditionalists argue there is substantial "sentencing disparity" throughout the United States, and there are a large number of individuals who have committed the same or similar offenses who have very different sentences. That is, some offenders receive very long sentences which are reflective of the punitive philosophy of the sentencing judge, while others may receive moderate or light sentences which reflect a different philosophy. Traditionalists argue it is important that we have a mechanism to insure that sentences are just and fair and that these disparities are reduced. Parole has served this function.

Critics acknowledge the importance of reducing sentencing disparity but contend it should be accomplished legislatively, not administratively. That is, sentencing disparities could be reduced by increasing the number of fixed or determinant sentences. Also, critics contend that, while some individuals may receive sentences which appear to be harsh, the appearance of harshness is an illusion created by comparing longer sentences to shorter sentences, which were inappropriate for similar offenses. According to the critics, the resolution is to remove sentencing disparity by eliminating the short term sentences by adopting longer determinant sentences for a number of offenses.

A third goal of parole is to provide a "safety-valve" for overpopulated prisons. This is a controversial practice; however, traditionalists note that prison populations outstrip prison capacities in most states. Traditionalists contend it is imperative we have a procedure to reduce the levels of violence and dangerousness caused by overpopulation. Few parole systems openly recognize this as a goal; however, one cannot ignore the increased granting of paroles and the greater number of reduced sentences as prison populations increase.

Critics contend these informal safety-valve policies produce an increased possibility that offenders may be released both too soon and without adequate parole planning. Critics also argue this practice increases the level of uncertainty in the sentencing process, and punishment loses its potential as a general deterrent. That is, when individuals are aware their sentences may be determined by prison population problems rather than by the crime they committed, the deterrent effect of punishment is lost. Critics claim the resolution should come through determinant sentences applicable to all offenders, not through early release. They also believe more prisons should be built if population increases mandate construction. Traditionalists counter, arguing the taxpayers will never pay for prison construction necessary to keep up with present incarceration rates, and, as a result, the safety-valve function is critical if we are to avoid large-scale disturbances and riots.

Problems emerge when a parolee commits another crime because of early release and inadequate supervision. The parole process is immediately blamed, ignoring the possibility the supervising parole office might be understaffed and overwhelmed with supervision responsibilities. This is an example of "structured failure." That is, parole is guaranteed to fail because demands on the agencies and personnel exceed resources available to meet those demands adequately. This is a common problem in the field of corrections, reflecting the absence of philosophical and political agreement on goals we should pursue.

A fourth goal of parole is to provide prison authorities with a tool which can be used to maintain social control over prison populations. The importance of parole as a control mechanism has been reduced by recent trends which have established mandatory sentences for some crimes. In some states, which have abolished parole, the threat of denial of release is no longer an effective control mechanism for those inmates who are inclined to be disruptive. That is, fixed sentencing statutes have tended to eliminate official discretion regarding early release.

Rules, Roles and Relationships

Practitioners entering the fields of probation and parole often begin their professional careers with idealistic visions of the "rehabilitation process." Probation and parole officers work in administrative bureaucracies which impose constraints on what they do, how they do it, and how effectively they can work with the persons they supervise.

Probation systems vary substantially across the United States. In most states, probation is administered by a state executive agency. In twelve states, probation is a county function (Johnson and Smith, 1980). In states in which probation is a county function, individual probation officers are generally appointed by a judge. Some county probation systems are intensely political, and probation officers are selected because of their involvement in local politics. Also, in county systems, supervision strategies may be determined by the political philosophy of the judge, rather than by the professional standards accepted in the field. However, county probation departments in some states *are* highly professionalized. Differences in professionalism and effectiveness of county probation departments can be substantial, depending on the financial support provided by the county governing bodies with taxing powers.

Comparing an under-funded probation department with an adequately-funded department will reveal significant variations. For example, salaries between the two departments are likely to be quite different, with probation officers paid as little as $8,000 per year in some departments and as much as $20,000 per year in other departments, with variation from state to state. Differences also affect the service area. Adequately-funded probation departments are likely to have well-credentialed probation officers, psychological and psychiatric services, a foster home placement program, and related types of programming which increase the ability to meet the probationer's individual needs as well as protecting the community. Under-funded probation departments are likely to have untrained officers, minimal resources, and low commitment to programming.

In states in which probation is a state function, there tends to be a high degree of uniformity in the development of procedures and policies for the entire state. Regardless of the county of residence, probationers are likely to receive similar treatment in the probation process under a state-administered system. State control of the probation process reduces the potential for disparity in the decision-making process. A professional executive trained in various aspects of field supervision is likely to head a state executive agency responsible for probation supervision.

Parole is a function of the state. Although the parole-granting authority is uniformly autonomous from the state's Department of Corrections, the parole supervision bureaucracy is often part of the state's correctional system. In a few states, the parole function is directly subordinate to the governor. The preferred organizational structure places parole supervision in the Department of Corrections in order to enhance potentials for developing pre-release planning for the inmate and to increase the quality and quantity of information from institutional counselors which is available to parole officers (National Advisory Commission on Criminal Justice Standards and Goals, 1973).

In a well-managed parole system, there are pre-release counselors in the correctional institutions. The parole process may include two distinct units. The parole board may be a highly autonomous body, while the supervisory aspect of the parole process may be managed by a separate unit answerable to the state's Department of Corrections. This separation is recommended for a number of reasons, including lessening administrative responsibilities for the parole board and making supervision more effective through independence.

The roles adopted by probation and parole officers as they carry out their responsibilities are determined by a variety of issues, ranging from the personality of the officer to the political-social-legal philosophy of the agency administering the supervision. It is important to examine the potential roles probation or parole officers might assume. Several studies have focused on role types in the supervision process, and a number of typologies have been developed.

A typology is an attempt to categorize different styles of probation or parole supervision. A typology provides a framework from which to evaluate different supervision styles and to reach tentative conclusions about how probation and parole officers should meet their responsibilities to the offenders they supervise and the communities they protect. There are very few officers who exclusively "fit" into one "type." Most officers perform tasks reflecting each of the types of roles. Also, typologies of roles are seldom "value-free." That is, a particular typology is likely to reflect the biases of the person who developed the typology. The typology discussed below includes three types of officers: the punitive officer, the welfare officer and the protective officer (Carlson and Parks, 1979).

The *punitive officer* tends to view supervision as a law enforcement function. The punitive officer is likely to emphasize control and surveillance in the supervision process and may attempt to coerce the offender into conforming by threats of punishment. Supervision by punitive officers tends to be highly routinized, with contracts setting strict limits on the probationer's or parolee's associates, hours, travel, employment and other aspects of life. Some probationers and parolees undoubtedly benefit from this type of supervision.

However, the punitive officer may have a tendency to use a punitive style with an entire caseload. As a result, the distinct needs of probationers and parolees may not be served. For example, a youth on probation may also be a school truant because of serious learning disabilities. The truancy could be a contributing factor to more serious legal problems. A punitive probation or parole officer who is concerned with conformity and who has little interest in the individual needs and problems of the offender, will likely miss the unique problems of this probationer. Outward conformity does not resolve the important issues of social development and the problems which contributed to the individual's delinquency or criminality. Compliance is not a measure of change (Street, Vinter and Perrow, 1966).

The major problem with punitive supervision is that it tends to address symptoms rather than problems. At the same time, the task of the probation and parole officer is one of insuring compliance with the conditions of probation or parole. The notion of officer as counselor has tended to confuse the issue because the protection of society has always been paramount, and the counselor role has always been secondary (Marshall and Vito, 1982).

The *welfare officer* can be contrasted to the punitive officer in that the two types are near opposites. Unlike the punitive officer, the welfare officer has as the ultimate goal the improved welfare of the probationer or parolee. This type of officer is committed to the philosophy that the only guarantee of community protection lies in the successful personal adjustment of the client. Ideally, this type of officer is emotionally neutral and works from diagnostic categories and treatment skills which are objective and theoretically based on an assessment of the client's needs and potentials.

Various writers have used positive labels to describe the welfare officer and negative labels to describe the punitive officer, reflecting the biases of the author of the typology. However, the welfare officer may place an emphasis on the rehabilitation of the offender, ignoring the importance of protecting the community. Some welfare officers see repeated acts of delinquency or criminality as indicative of problems the probationer or parolee has not resolved. However, the probationer or parolee may have strong commitments to delinquency or, in the case of an adult, to criminality and may be manipulating the officer in order to remain free from any control.

The *protective officer* tends to alternate between protecting the offender and protecting the community. In some instances, the officer may provide direct assistance, and in other instances he may be somewhat punitive. This officer type is sometimes portrayed as vascillating, providing inconsistent supervision for the offender. However, probation and parole include responsibilities to provide programs and supervision of offenders within a legal framework. This issue cannot be ignored, regardless of the needs of the offender.

While the protective role may seem confusing, with the officer appearing to help at times and to punish at others, this is probably an accurate portrayal of the role, because the role of probation or parole officer involves substantial role conflict (Marshall and Vito, 1982). That is, a wide array of expectations of the officer exists, some of which may appear contradictory. For example, at one extreme, the officer may be expected to provide crisis counseling during moments of acute trauma in the probationer's or the parolee's life. The counseling in this setting may require unlimited patience, empathy skills and considerable professional expertise. At the other extreme, the officer may be expected to deliver an arrest warrant which will result in incarceration or reincarceration of the probationer or parolee. This type of conflict is an inherent part of the role and can create confusion for the probationer and parolee. The officer must have the capacity for performing at both ends of the treatment/punishment continuum, depending on the behavior of the client and the situational context in which the behavior occurs.

The protective role recognizes the possibility that probation and parole officer roles cannot simply be typed as surveillance or treatment. Rather, the roles include elements of both surveillance and counseling. The role utilized in a specific situation will be dependent on a number of factors, not the least of which will be the offense and behavior of the offender. For example, if the offender is an active member of a crime syndicate, it is highly improbable that he will be interested in "counseling services" offered by a probation or parole officer.

A major issue relating to supervision style, outlined by Marshall and Vito (1982) and others, is that the client is not seeking help. Rather, the officer and the client interact as a result of involvement in the adversary justice system in which the offender was a defendant before he/she was given the status of "client." The label "probationer" or "parolee" is a label *imposed* by the criminal justice system. While professional jargon refers to probationers and parolees as "clients," they are actually "involuntary clients," a notion which is inherently contradictory. McCleary (1978) has simplified the issue, noting that the goals of the process include rehabilitating those clients who are amenable to rehabilitation. At the same time, it is equally important to protect society from those persons who are not amenable to rehabilitation and who require surveillance.

A Time for Reassessment

Probation and parole have come under severe criticism in recent years. The result is a reassessment of the goals, roles, and responsibilities for probation and parole personnel. Past practices tended to reflect commitments to the "medical model," a major problem that has pervaded the field of corrections since the 1950s. Utilization of the medical model in the field of corrections resulted from excessive power held by psychiatrists and intensive lobbying by professional social work organizations. The general theme of the medical model, was that the offender was *sick* and, therefore, needed treatment for an *illness*. A number of authorities have criticized the medical model, noting that, contrary to the contentions of psychiatrists and social workers, most offenders are not *sick*. [1]

The medical model tended to grossly oversimplify the problems of the probationer and the parolee. Treatment included an attempt to locate some form of pathology which could be identified as the "cause" of the delinquent or criminal behavior. The context in which the offense occurred and an array of family, work, social and community experiences which may have contributed to the offender's behavior were often ignored. Critics, following the general theme developed by van den Haag (1975) and others (Wilson, 1975; Lerman, 1975), contend that the notion criminals are sick only functions to shift responsibility for criminal behavior to some unknown cause, thereby insulating the criminal from accountability for criminal behavior. "Since they are not responsible, we would not have to worry about guilt, punishment, and justice, only about treatment or incapacitation. Moral choices would be needed no more" (van den Haag, 1975:118).

Resource Brokerage

The reassessment of roles in probation and parole has taken different directions; however, the general theme is that there should be a break with traditional approaches—whatever they are. In this process, a new concept has emerged—*resource brokerage*. Resource brokers are less concerned about understanding and changing behavior and more concerned with assessing the concrete needs of the individual offender, making certain the individual receives services from a variety of sources which will directly address those needs. The basic principles of resource brokerage are rather simple.

1. When probationers and parolees are released from supervision it will be expected that they have been prepared to meet community responsibilities.
2. Each individual is accountable for his or her behavior, and responsible behavior is required for freedom.
3. Probationers and parolees generally need the opportunity to learn new workable strategies for handling their life roles while receiving supervision (U.S. Department of Justice, Improved Probation Strategies 1979).

Under the concept of resource brokerage, the goals of probation and parole can be accomplished through a highly-structured community resource program which provides selective services appropriate to the needs of the offenders. The resource program must include opportunities for offenders to change themselves *and* those conditions which brought them into the juvenile justice or criminal justice system.

The key to the program is the assumption that most offenders are *not* pathologically ill, and for this reason, the role of the counselor/therapist is usually inappropriate (Dell'Apa, 1976). A new role emerges for probation and parole officers—that of "advocate-broker." Community resources are seldom organized in the highly-structured system envisioned by the authors of resource brokerage. To the contrary, service agencies have their own histories, traditions, biases and myths which may actually impede the delivery of services, especially to persons who have violated the law.

As we attempt to move away from traditional supervision methods in probation and parole to approaches which require different types of assessment methods, we find that those methods have yet to be developed. A major problem limiting the development of new assessment methods and supervision strategies is the absence of scientifically validated procedures which can be used to assess offenders. The validation problem has a number of sources, including lack of agreement on techniques which are appropriate for the assessment and treatment of offender behavior. Before appropriate treatment can be provided through a probation or parole reintegration program, it is imperative that causal factors be accurately defined and classified.

Classification

The development of offender classification techniques is a complex process. The problems involved in classifying varieties of human behavior have plagued the professions of psychiatry and psychology for years (Glaser, 1983). Problems of classification are even more complicated in the field of corrections. In addition to attempts to develop classification systems to deal with a large variety of human emotions and behaviors, corrections must also consider and assess the individual's criminal behavior. Classification is an attempt to place individuals in various categories, according to criteria based on assumptions and, hopefully, data concerning the offender and his or her behavior. The category in which one is placed requires a supervision plan reflecting the rationale for category placement. The problem is that there is little agreement on the criteria which should be used, and there is even less agreement as to what should be accomplished with individuals once they are classified.

Typologies, as indicated earlier, are artificial creations of professionals which reflect personal and research biases. There is considerable debate surrounding classification, and the debate becomes even more intense in the arguments regarding typologies. The political, social and professional biases of individuals developing classification schemes and typologies must be considered. It is difficult to determine the goals of a classification system unless one is aware of the reason for the development of the system. For example, in some agencies, the classification system may emerge from scientific research, and the typologies may reflect the results of empirical data. In other agencies, the classification system may emerge as a response to budget reductions. The goals of the classification system then reflect the political-budgetary problems of the agency. Obviously, the classification systems developed from these types of agency situations will vary considerably. It is important to understand the goals of the classification system. Is the goal to improve individualized treatment programming, or is the goal to increase agency cost-effectiveness? While these goals are not incompatible, there are strong potentials for conflict which could be reflected in the classification systems.

There are serious limitations on the development of typologies and classification schemes, and the work in this area has been marked with a number of failures. The reasons for some of these failures have been discussed by Solomon and Baird (1981), who note four general factors which have contributed to the failure of classification systems.

First, there is a general misunderstanding of the intent and, more importantly, the capabilities of classification systems. Practitioners have expected too much because they failed to realize that classification was plagued with the same problems as other areas of prediction. There is a great deal about human behavior we do not understand and, therefore, cannot quantify. Our failure to acknowledge the extent to which we *do not understand* often limits the potential to which we *can* understand.

Second, the emphasis on research and development of classification systems has sometimes occurred in a vacuum. As a result, adequate attention has not been given to implementation of the classification system. Very important in the implementation process are the training needs of personnel responsible for the successful application of the system on a day-to-day basis. Often, these training needs have been ignored.

Third, classification is often not utilized as an integral component of overall operations in the probation or parole agency. Classification systems have the potential for generating substantial amounts of helpful data in the policy- and decision-making processes. However, agency administrators may ignore the data for a variety of personal and, perhaps, political reasons. For example, data generated by the classification system may call for new staff or for specialized staff. A request for funding these additional positions might be politically unpopular. As a result, the agency continues to function with an inadequate number of staff positions, providing inadequate supervision of probationers or parolees. Recidivism rates may increase. Even though data produced by the classification system was ignored, the classification system itself might possibly be blamed for agency ineffectiveness. This problem demonstrates the difficulty in initiating change in the criminal justice system.

Fourth, and perhaps most importantly, there has been a general failure to recognize and address the constraints imposed by agency policy and politics when there is an effort to implement new strategies. Most corrections policies emerge from politicians and political processes, not from research and scientific application of knowledge. As long as corrections policies are determined through political processes, rather than through administrative processes, it is likely there will be little change in the outcomes.

Ellsworth and Culbertson (1982) found indications of distrust resulting from agency utilization of a classification system in Illinois. Survey results indicated some probation and parole officers believed the classification system provided an excellent management tool, but they contended that some agency administrators manipulated the scoring systems in order to artificially reduce supervision levels, thereby justifying increased caseloads. These concerns were compounded by perceptions that criminal justice officials, including judges and prosecutors, did not understand the classification system. As a result, decision-makers in the system were seen as disregarding the classification system. Some officers became cynical, questioning the value of classification when, from their perspective, the only outcome seemed to be increased paperwork.

A number of classification systems have the potential for enhancing decision-making in probation and parole agencies and lowering the levels of subjectivity in the decision-making process (Clear and O'Leary, 1983). Historically, classification has served to optimize the allocation of resources through the deployment of staff to meet agency and client needs. In addition, classification serves the purpose of providing a structured, uniform, screening process which permits more accurate, consistent and equitable decision-making. Although virtually all classification systems grew out of some agency need, the method of data collection differs in many jurisdictions. In a national survey, almost half the probation and parole agencies now using some type of classification scheme acknowledged that the system was "borrowed" from another jurisdiction (U.S. Department of Justice, Probation and Parole Supervision, 1979). Only 26% of the agency classification systems were developed from local research efforts (U.S. Department of Justice, Probation and Parole Supervision 1979).

Many classification systems collect virtually the same client information on which to make the classification decision. Examining present and past criminal behavior patterns, data collection instruments also focus on the areas of assaultive behavior, employment, alcohol and drug use, and attitude. Additional data may be collected concerning academic/vocational skills, finances, family relationships, education, emotional stability, physical health, and sexual functioning. While classification systems tend to be similar, there are also significant differences, which reflect the political and philosophical variations between jurisdictions as well as differences in research methodologies. In this chapter, we will discuss one type of classification system because it has been adopted in a number of jurisdictions.

The Wisconsin Case Classification System

In examining a classification system, it is important to understand the objectives of the system. The system presented here was initially developed in 1973 in Wisconsin, as a result of a legislative mandate to justify requests for additional staff positions and funding for new programs. It is referred to as the Wisconsin Case Classification System. In evaluating the classification system, Wisconsin authorities made two assumptions about probation and parole supervision: 1) Available data did not suggest that a reduction in caseload size would result in a reduction in criminal behavior, or improve the effectiveness of probation and parole supervision. 2) The first six to twelve months of supervision are critical to the successful completion of the probation or parole term. Violation rates tend to decline as time on supervision increases (Wisconsin Department of Health and Social Services, Project Report #14, 1979).

The first objective of the Wisconsin Case Classification System, risk assessment, is accomplished through the administration of an "Assessment of Risk" instrument. An instrument was needed to assess the client's propensity for violating probation and parole rules and criminal statutes. The result was the development of a ten-item scale which addressed the following areas: address change, employment, alcohol and drug use, attitude, and present and past criminal behavior. An eleventh item, which identified the client's aggressive/assaultive behavior during the five-year period prior to placement under probation or parole supervision, was incorporated for the purpose of community protection. Completion of the "Assessment of Risk" instrument produces a Risk score, which assists the officer in determining the client's supervision level.

A second objective of the System, needs assessment, is accomplished using an eleven-item "Assessment of Needs" instrument. These data generate a Need score, which describes the client's "need" for supervision. The items reflect problem areas common to probationers and parolees. The weighting of these items corresponds to the amount of time probation and parole officers spend in addressing the particular problem areas. For example, the highest weighted item on the "Need" scale, "Emotional Stability," reflects the amount of time officers spend supervising clients with emotional problems. Areas assessed on the "Needs" scale include academic/vocational skills, employment, financial management, marital/family relationships, companions, emotional stability, alcohol/drug use, mental ability, health, sexual behavior and probation/parole officer perceptions of client needs. (Wisconsin Department of Health and Social Services, 1978). Some items found to be predictive of potential "risks" are also related to assessing the "needs" of the offender. These items are alcohol/drug use and employment.

Assume we are assessing an offender, John Smith, who has been placed on probation for aggravated assault. First, we complete the Risk instrument (see Table 1, p. 148). Mr. Smith has moved once in the last twelve months (+ 2), has been employed 40-59% of the time (+ 1), has occasionally abused alcohol (+ 2), has occasionally abused drugs (+ 1), has refused to accept responsibility (+ 3), was twenty-two when first convicted (+ 2), has three prior periods of supervision on probation (+ 4), has never had probation revoked (0), has one prior felony conviction (+ 2), has a pior juvenile conviction for auto theft (+ 2), and has been convicted for an assaultive offense (+ 15). The offender has a Risk Score of 34. The Risk Score is posted on the Scoring Guide.

The next step is to complete the Needs instrument (see Table 2, p. 149). Mr. Smith has adequate skills (0), an unsatisfactory employment record (+ 3), minor financial problems (+ 3), a relatively stable marital relationship (0), no adverse companions (0), symptoms of emotional instability (+ 4), occasional abuse of alcohol (+ 3), occasional drug abuse (+ 3), needs mental health assistance (+ 3), has a minor health handicap (+ 1), has situational sexual problems (+ 3), and is perceived as being in the "Medium" need category by the probation officer (+ 3). Mr. Smith has a Needs score of 26. That score is also posted on the Scoring Guide.

The client's supervision level is determined by the highest score on either scale (see Table 3, p. 149). For example, our client, who has a Risk Score of

34 and a Need Score of 26, would be placed in the Maximum supervision category. A high score on the Risk instrument is more likely to place the client in the Maximum Supervision category than if he has a similarly high Needs Score. The supervision level (maximum, medium, minimum) specifies the number of client contacts the officer must have with the client during a reporting period (usually from three to six months). Typically, probation and parole agencies have adopted specific "Contact Standards" relating to each supervision level. These standards also dictate the context in which the contact should occur (i.e., agency office, client's home, client's workplace, etc.)

The generally accepted contact standards in probation and parole agencies are as follows:

> *Maximum Supervision:* At least one face-to-face contact every fourteen days, as appropriate; monthly verification of employment and residence; collateral contacts (police, family, agencies), as appropriate.
>
> *Medium Supervision:* At least one face-to-face contact every thirty days; monthly verification of employment and residence; home visits and collateral contacts, as appropriate.
>
> *Minimum Supervision:* Client shall be seen at least once every ninety days in personal, face-to-face contact; verification of residence and employment every ninety days. **Or**—receipt of a mailed report every 30 days; home visits, as appropriate; verification of residence and employment at least prior to discharge (Wisconsin Department of Health and Social Services, Project Report #14, 1979).

Each probation and parole case is periodically "Reassessed," using the Risk and Needs Assessment Instruments. This is usually done between three and six months after the initial placement on supervision, depending on agency policy. The reassessment instrument includes items which reflect the probationer's or parolee's performance during the initial period of supervision. The reassessment process allows the client to "move" through the system, perhaps from maximum to medium supervision or from medium to minimum supervision. The decreased time spent with clients who "move" through the system to lower supervision levels allows officers to focus their attention on more problematic and complex cases.

Risk and needs assessment specify the quantity of client-officer contacts; however, the instruments are of little help in determining treatment strategies or anticipating problems in the relationship between the client and the officer. Often, failure in the probation and parole supervision process can be attributed to an inability to treat or rehabilitate the offender because basic client needs are not addressed. Typically, the rehabilitation process is a "reaction to crises," with little planning or anticipating of client problems or treatment needs. When caseload sizes in many jurisdictions are considered, it is clear how an officer could fail to identify the treatment needs of the client.

The third objective of the classification system is the determination of an appropriate supervision strategy for the probationer or parolee. To do so, the Wisconsin staff developed the Client Management Classification System (Wisconsin Department of Health and Social Services, 1977). This pragmatic treatment approach outlines four different case-management treatment strategies to assist the probation and parole officer in the development of a case plan. Clients are assigned to the appropriate casework group on the basis of their responses to an objectively scored, 45-item, semi-structured interview. The Client Management Classification interview (C.M.C.) was developed with the knowledge that burglars, check writers, robbers, rapists, drug pushers, prostitutes, white-collar offenders, and those who fail to pay child support are all labeled criminals, although they differ considerably in offense patterns, living stability, commitment to criminal values, family background, finances, emotional needs, educational level, work record, and other factors (Wisconsin Department of Health and Social Services, 1977).

Providing effective treatment to persons on probation and parole supervision requires both a knowledge of the individual and an ability to develop various rehabilitative techniques appropriate to a client's individual situation and needs. The relationship between the client and the officer has considerable impact on the final outcome of the supervision process. Probation and parole officers who develop an understanding of their clients and who apply appropriate rehabilitative techniques can be more effective with a greater number of clients. Knowing what type of treatment technique to use, under what circumstances, and for how long is the key to successful rehabilitation. Officers who apply similar treatment techniques to all types of clients are found to be effective with only a select group of offenders who respond to the officer's particular style and approach. Through the use of the Client Management Classification interview, the officer is able to assess client problem areas and gain a proactive stance in the supervision process.

Following the Client Management Classification interview is the placement of the client in one of four Supervision Groups: Selective Intervention, Casework Control, Limit Setting, or Environmental Structure (Wisconsin Department of Health and Social Services, 1977). Each title is indicative of the supervision strategy which the officer would use in working with clients in that group. A treatment guide, which identifies issues in the supervision process, accompanies the Client Management Classification interview. The guide helps the officer to anticipate problems in the relationship and to utilize appropriate treatment, supervision and authority. Research on the C.M.C. has shown it to be effective in predicting success/failure while under supervision. It has also been shown to enhance the quality of officer/client relationships.

Researchers have attempted to establish an ideal or maximum caseload the probation and parole officer should supervise. Professionals generally agree that officer/client ratios are inadequate because these ratios assume that caseloads of equal size require the same supervision plan on the part of the probation and parole officer. Obviously, not all clients are the same. Some require virtually no supervision, while others require almost constant supervision. In most traditional probation and parole systems, cases requiring minimum and maximum supervision are considered equivalent for statistical purposes.

Wisconsin staff initiated a system which replaced the traditional caseload concept with the concept of "workload." Initial time studies, which the workload concept was based on, indicated that approximately three hours was needed each month by the officer to supervise a client classified as needing maximum supervision; one and one-half hours was needed each month for a client classified as needing medium supervision; one-half hour each month was needed for a client classified as needing minimum supervision (Wisconsin Department of Health and Social Services, Project Report #9, 1979). For the purpose of comparison, time spent per month supervising one case classified as "maximum supervision" would be the same as that needed to supervise two cases classified as a "medium supervision" or six cases classified as "minimum supervision." The workload concept allows assignment of cases based on the time needed to supervise each case.

The final component of the Wisconsin Classification System is the Management Information System. Used primarily to monitor policies and procedures in the jurisdiction, the Information System also compiles information about clients receiving probation and parole supervision. When supervision begins, an initial profile containing demographic data, offense history, sentence information, risk and needs data, and referral information is compiled. Similar data, obtained at termination, is merged with intake data to provide a before/after picture of the client while under supervision. These data provide additional measures of agency effectiveness by showing changes in classification, education, alcohol/drug use, employment training and related measures of adjustment (Wisconsin Department of Health and Social Services, Project Report #14, 1979). Unlike approaches which evaluate system effectiveness on the basis of legal factors (arrests, convictions, violations), the Wisconsin System is able to evaluate the various treatment efforts.

Summary

While both probation and parole have roots in treatment and concern for the offender, many political, philosophical, and social changes have served to confuse the role of probation and parole systems in the 1980s. Various studies have shown the need to provide greater support for probation and parole officers through the reduction of caseloads, employment of increased staff, and the development of innovative programs.

The history of treatment programs in probation and parole reflects a rocky road, with little evidence that many of these programs are effective. The reality of most probation and parole systems is that little is known about the effectiveness of supervision techniques or treatment methods. What is now in use is assumed to work. Historically, this has proved to be a dangerous assumption. New directions in community-based corrections, especially in probation and parole systems, are indicative of the need to empirically evaluate our efforts. The Wisconsin Classification System is only one of several innovative, treatment-oriented approaches for addressing client treatment needs and safeguarding the public. The continued use of classification systems will enhance the effectiveness of both probation and parole officers as well as agency operations.

Endnotes

[1]For a detailed critique of efforts to utilize the medical model in corrections see H. H. Allen and N. Gatz (1974) "Abandoning the Medical Model in Corrections: Some Implications and Alternatives," *The Prison Journal 54* (Autumn) 4-14; L. Coleman (1974) "Prisons: The Crime of Treatment." Psychiatric Opinion *11* (June) 5-16; R. Culbertson (1977) "Corrections: The State of the Art," *Journal of Criminal Justice, 5,* 1, 39-47; R. Culbertson (1981) "Achieving Correctional Reform," in *Critical Issues in Corrections,* edited by V. Webb and R. Robert. St. Paul: West Publishing Company; A. Dershowitz (1976) Fair and Certain Punishment, New York: McGraw-Hill Book Company; D. Fogel (1975) "...We are the Living Proof..." The Justice Model for Corrections. Cincinnati: Anderson Publishing Company.

References

Abadinsky, H. (1982). *Probation and Parole: Theory and Practice.* Englewood Cliffs, NJ: Prentice-Hall.

Albanese, J., Fiore, T., Powell, and Stori, J. (1981) *Is Probation Working: A Guide for Managers and Methodologists.* Washington, D.C.: University Press of America.

Allen, L. and Carlson, E. (1984). "The Development of Probation." In R. Carter, D. Glaser and L. Wilkins (Eds.), *Probation, Parole and Community Corrections* (pp. 3-11). New York: John Wiley and Sons.

Carlson, E., and Parks, E. (1979). *Critical Issues in Adult Probation.* Washington, D.C.: U.S. Department of Justice, Law Enforcement Assistance Administration.

Clear, T. and O'Leary, V. (1983) *The Supervision of the Offender in the Community.* Lexington, MA: Lexington Press.

Coleman, L. (1974). "Prisons: The Crime of Treatment." *Psychiatric Opinion, 11,* 5-16.

Conrad, J. (1979). "Who Needs a Door Bell Pusher?" *The Prison Journal, 59,* 17-26.

Culbertson, R. (1977). "Corrections: The State of the Art." *Journal of Criminal Justice, 5,* (1), 39-47.

Culbertson, R. (1981). "Achieving Correctional Reform." In V. Webb and R. Robert (Eds.), *Critical Issues in Corrections,* 308-345. St. Paul: West.

Dell'Apa, F., Adams, W., Jorgensen, J., and Sigurdson, H. (1976). "Advocacy, Brokerage, Community: The ABC's of Probation and Parole." *Federal Probation, 40,* 37-44.

Dershowitz, A. (1976). *Fair and Certain Punishment.* New York: McGraw-Hill.

Dressler, D. (1969). *Practice and Theory of Probation and Parole.* New York: Columbia University Press.

Ellsworth, T., and Culbertson, R. (1982). *Probation and Parole Attitudes Toward Classification.* Paper presented at the meeting of the American Society of Criminology, Toronto, Ontario, Canada.

Fogel, D. (1975). "...We Are The Living Proof..." *The Justice Model for Corrections.* Cincinnati: Anderson Publishing Company.

Glaser, D. (1983). "Supervising Offenders Outside of Prison." In J. Wilson (Ed.), *Crime and Public Policy.* San Francisco: Institute for Contemporary Studies.

Johnson, C., and Smith, B. (1980). "Patterns of Probation and Parole Organizations." *Federal Probation, 44* (4), 43-51.

Killinger, G., Kerper, H., and Cromwell, P. (1976). *Probation and Parole in the Criminal Justice System.* St. Paul: West Publishing Company.

Klockars, C. (1972). "A Theory of Probation Supervision." *Journal of Criminal Law, Criminology and Police Science, 63,* 550-557.

Lerman, P. (1975). *Community Treatment and Social Control.* Chicago: University of Chicago Press.

Marshall, F. and Vito, G. (1982). "Not Without Tools: The Task of Probation in the Eighties." *Federal Probation, 34* (4), 37-40.

McCleary, R. (1978). *Dangerous Men: The Sociology of Parole.* Beverly Hills: Sage.

Martinson, R. (1974). "What Works? Questions and Answers About Prison Reform." *The Public Interest, 35* (2), 22-54.

Martinson, R., Palmer, T., and Adams, S. (1976). *Rehabilitation, Recidivism and Research.* Hackensack, NJ: National Council on Crime and Delinquency.

Martinson, R. and Wilks, J. (1977). "Save Parole Supervision." *Federal Probation, 41* (3), 23-27.

Miles, A. (1965). "The Reality of the Probation Officer's Dilemma." *Federal Probation, 29,* 18-22.

National Advisory Commission on Criminal Justice Standards and Goals. (1973). *Corrections.* Washington, D.C.: U.S. Government Printing Office.

Ohlin, L., Piven, H., and Pappenfort, D. (1956). "Major Dilemmas of the Social Worker in Probation and Parole." *National Probation and Parole Association Journal, 2,* 211-225.

Palmer, T., (1975). "Martinson Revisited." *Crime and Delinquency, 21* (3), 133-152.

Palmer, T. (1978). *Correctional Intervention and Research.* Lexington, MA: D.C. Heath.

President's Commission on Law Enforcement and the Administration of Justice.

Treatment Innovations in Probation and Parole 147

(1967). *Task Force Report: Corrections.* Washington, D.C.: U.S. Government Printing Office.

Sigler, J., and Bensaason, T. (1970). "Role Perceptions among New Jersey Probation Officers." *Rutgers Camden Law Journal, 2,* 256-260.

Solomon, L. and Baird, S. (1982). "Classification: Past Failures, Future Potentials." *Corrections Today, 43,* 4.

Street, D., Vinter, R., and Perrow, C. (1966). *Organization for Treatment.* New York: Free Press.

Studt, E. (1978). *Surveillance and Service in Parole.* Washington, D.C.: U.S. Department of Justice, National Institute of Corrections.

Tomaino, L. (1975). "The Five Faces of Probation." *Federal Probation, 39* (4), 41-46.

United Nations, Department of Social Affairs. (1951). *Probation and Related Measures.* New York: United Nations.

U.S. Department of Justice, Law Enforcement Assistance Administration. (1979). *Critical Issues in Adult Probation.* Washington, D.C.: U.S. Government Printing Office.

U.S. Department of Justice, National Institute of Corrections. (1979). *Classification Instruments for Criminal Justice Decisions: Vol. 2. Probation/Parole Supervision.* Washington, D.C.: U.S. Government Printing Office.

U.S. Department of Justice, National Institute of Justice. (1979). *Improving Probation Strategies.* Washington, D.C.: U.S. Government Printing Office.

van den Haag, E. (1975). *Punishing Criminals, Concerning a Very Old and Painful Question.* New York: Basic books.

von Hirsch, A. (1976). *Doing Justice: The Choice of Punishments.* New York: Hill and Wang.

von Laningham, D., Tauber, M., and Dimants, R. (1966). "How Probation Officers View Their Responsibility." *Crime and Delinquency, 12* (2), 97-104.

Wilks, J. and Martinson, R. (1976). "Is the Treatment of Criminal Offenders Really Necessary?" *Federal Probation, 40* (1), 3-8.

Wilson, J. (1975). *Thinking About Crime.* New York: Basic Books.

Wisconsin Department of Health and Social Services, Division of Corrections. (1976). *Project Report #2: Development of the Wisconsin Risk Assessment Scale.*

Wisconsin Department of Health and Social Services, Division of Corrections. (1977). *Project Report #7: Client-Management Classification Progress Report.*

Wisconsin Department of Health and Social Services, Division of Corrections. (1979). *Project Report #9: Staffing by Workload.*

Wisconsin Department of Health and Social Services, Division of Corrections. (1978). *Project Report #12: Analysis of the Client Needs Assessment Scale.*

Wisconsin Department of Health and Social Services, Division of Corrections. (1979). *Project Report #14: A Two-Year Follow-up Report.*

Table 1

ILLINOIS ADULT PROBATION CLASSIFICATION SYSTEM

_____ County _____ Judicial Circuit

ASSESSMENT OF ADULT PROBATIONER RISK

Probationer's Name _____   Dept. ID # _____

       Last   First   Middle

Assessment Date _____   Officer's Name _____

       Mo.   Day   Year

Sentencing Date _____   Expiration Date _____

       Mo.   Day   Year   Mo.   Day   Year

				SCORE
Number of Address Changes in Last 12 Months: ……	0	None		
	2	One		
	3	Two or more		2
Percentage of Time Employed in Last 12 Months: ……	0	60% or more		
	1	40% - 59%		
	2	Under 40%		
	0	Not applicable		1
Alcohol Usage Problems: : ……………………	0	No interference with functioning		
	2	Occasional abuse; some disruption of functioning		
	4	Frequent abuse, serious disruption; needs treatment		2
Other Drug Usage Problems: ………………………	0	No interference with functioning		
	1	Occasional abuse; some disruption of functioning		
	2	Frequent abuse; serious disruption; needs treatment		1
Attitude: ………………………………………	0	Motivated to change; receptive to assistance		
	3	Dependent or unwilling to accept responsibility		
	5	Rationalizes behavior; negative; not motivated to change		3
Age at First Conviction: ……………………… (or Juvenile Adjudiction)	0	24 or older		
	2	20 - 23		
	4	19 or younger		2
Number of Prior Periods of Probation/Parole Supervision: …………………… (Adult or Juvenile)	0	None		
	4	One or more		4
Number of Prior Probation/Parole Revocations: ……… (Adult or Juvenile)	0	None		
	4	One or more		0
Number of Prior Felony Convictions: ……………… (or Juvenile Adjudications)	0	None		
	2	One		
	4	Two or more		2
	0	None		
Convictions or Juvenile Adjudications for: …………… (Select applicable and add for score. (Include current offense.)	2	Burglary, theft, auto theft, or robbery		
	3	Worthless checks or forgery		2
Conviction or Juvenile Adjudication for Assaultive Offense within Last Five Years: ………… (An offense which involves the use of a weapon, physical force or the threat of force)	15	Yes		
	0	No		15
			TOTAL	34

Table 2

STATE OF ILLINOIS

ILLINOIS ADULT PROBATION CLASSIFICATION SYSTEM

_____ County _____ Judicial Circuit

ASSESSMENT OF ADULT PROBATIONER NEEDS

Probationer's Name _____   Dept ID # _____
                    Last   First   Middle

Assessment Date _____   Officer's Name _____
                Mo. Day Year
Sentencing Date _____   Expiration Date _____
                Mo. Day Year   Mo. Day Year

Category	0	+/-	higher			SCORE
ACADEMIC/VOCATIONAL SKILLS -1 High school or above skill level	0 Adequate skills; able to handle everyday requirements	+2 Low skill level causing minor adjustment problems	+4 Minimal skill level causing serious adjustment problems			0
EMPLOYMENT -1 Satisfactory employment for one year or longer	0 Secure employment; no difficulties reported; or homemaker, student or retired	+3 Unsatisfactory employment; or unemployed but has adequate job skills	+6 Unemployed and virtually unemployable; needs training			3
FINANCIAL MANAGEMENT -1 Long-standing pattern of self-sufficiency; e.g., good credit	0 No current difficulties	+3 Situational or minor difficulties	+5 Severe difficulties; may include overdrafts, bad checks or bankruptcy			3
MARITAL/FAMILY RELATIONSHIPS -1 Relationships and support exceptionally strong	0 Relatively stable relationships	+3 Some disorganization or stress but potential for improvement	+5 Major disorganization or stress			0
COMPANIONS -1 Good support and influence	0 No adverse relationships	+2 Associations with occasional negative results	+4 Associations almost completely negative			0
EMOTIONAL STABILITY -2 Exceptionally well adjusted; accepts responsibility for actions	0 No symptoms of emotional instability; appropriate emotional responses	+4 Symptoms limit but do not prohibit adequate functioning; e.g., excessive anxiety	+7 Symptoms prohibit adequate functioning; e.g., lashes out or retreats into self			4
ALCOHOL USAGE	0 No interference with functioning	+3 Occasional abuse; some disruption of functioning	+6 Frequent abuse; serious disruption; needs treatment			3
OTHER DRUG USAGE	0 No interference with functioning	+3 Occasional abuse; some disruption of functioning	+5 Frequent abuse; serious disruption; needs treatment			3
MENTAL ABILITY	0 Able to function independently	+3 Some need for assistance; potential for adequate adjustment; possible retardation	+6 Deficiencies severely limit independent functioning; possible retardation			3
HEALTH	0 Sound physical health; seldom ill	+1 Handicap or illness interferes with functioning on a recurring basis	+2 Serious handicap or chronic illness; needs frequent medical care			1
SEXUAL BEHAVIOR	0 No apparent dysfunction	+3 Real or perceived situational or minor problems	+5 Real or perceived chronic or severe problems			3
P.O.'S IMPRESSION OF PROBATIONER'S NEEDS -1 Indirect; Unsupervised	0 Minimum	+3 Medium	+5 Maximum			3
					TOTAL	26

Table 3

SCORING GUIDE
SUPERVISION LEVEL CUT-OFF SCORES

Risk		Needs	
15 and above	— Maximum	30 and above	— Maximum
8 - 14	— Medium	15 - 29	— Medium
7 and below	— Minimum	14 and below	— Minimum

The probationer is to be assigned to the highest level of supervision indicated by either scale.

Halfway House Programs
for Offenders

George P. Wilson
North Carolina Central University

The continued growth of the Community-Based-Corrections ideal and the utilization of halfway houses for criminal offenders is a rather recent phenomenon. However, criminal justice and correctional administrators have erroneously assumed that the development of halfway houses for criminal offenders was a by-product of rehabilitation oriented, rather than the punishment and deterrence philosophy associated with earlier years of the United States prison system. A close examination of the historical development of the United States halfway house will suggest the inaccuracy of this assumption (Carlson, Seiter, 1977).

Confusion also exists in defining the concept of community-based corrections and the adoption of the halfway house idea as its primary model for reintegration. The major assumption and misconceptions about the community based concept are:

1. It is community-based because it is so labeled.
2. It is community-based because others are not.
3. If it is located in a community, then it is community-based.
4. Programs with minimal control or supervision are community-based.
5. Programs operated by private agencies rather than by the state are community based (Coates, 1976).

R.J. Coates has vehemently criticized each of the aforementioned methods of defining the community-based idea. He defined community-based corrections as "any correctional-related activity purposively aimed at directly assisting and supporting the efforts of offenders to establish meaningful ties and function in legitimate roles in the community.'' Clearly and unmistakably, then the goal of community-based corrections is the successful reintegration of the offender into the community (Doeren and Hageman, 1982). The vehicles best suited to accomplish this goal are community-based halfway houses. Therefore it is important that the halfway house model (community, residential approach) with its strengths and weaknesses be properly understood.

The following pages will attempt to place halfway houses in the larger context of community-based corrections. The article will trace the historical development of the halfway house movement, treatment models, present and potential use of the halfway house model, cost of operations, effectiveness of the programs, and finally, future trends and the resurgence of the halfway house model.

Historical Development of the American Halfway House

The halfway house concept, defined as a transitional residence for criminal offenders, originated in England and Ireland during the early 1800's. The concept was shortly thereafter adopted in the United States when the Massachusetts Prison Commission in 1917 recommended the creation of a temporary refuge to house destitute released offenders. In making this recommendation to the Massachusetts Legislature, they recognized that:

> The convicts who are discharged are often entirely destitute. The natural prejudice against them is so strong, that they find great difficulty in obtaining employment. They are forced to seek shelter in the lowest receptacles; and if they wish to lead a new course of life, are easily persuaded out of it; and perhaps driven by necessity to the commission of fresh crimes. It is intended to afford a temporary shelter in this building, if they choose to accept it, to such discharged convicts as may have conducted themselves well in prison, subject to such regulations as the directors may see fit to provide. They will here have a lodging, rations from the prison at a cheap rate, and have a chance to occupy themselves in their trade, until some opportunity offers of placing themselves there they can gain an honest livelihood in society. A refuge of this kind, to this destitute class, would be found, perhaps, humane and political. (Cohen, 1973)

The commission believed the establishment of these facilities might reduce the high recidivism rates of released offenders. They were also motivated by the search for a mechanism by which the offender could be offered an accepting transitional environment immediately following release and before the resumption of the normal independent existence (Carlson and Seiter, 1977).

The Massachusetts Legislature did not act on the Commission's recommendations. The reason given for this negative reaction was that the prisoners might "contaminate" one another. They were afraid that ex-prisoners in contact with each other would tend to unlearn all the formidable behavior that had been instilled by the silent and separate Pennsylvania system of prison life then in use (Powers, 1959).

Although the official criminal justice system was not very responsive to the need for transitional steps between custody and freedom, the halfway house concept continued to spread and several halfway houses opened under private auspices. The Isaac T. Hooper Home in New York was established by a group of Quakers in 1845 and is still in operation today. In 1864 a group of Bostonians opened the "Temporary Asylum for Disadvantaged Female Prisoners" for women discharged from jails and prisons in Boston and operated for twenty years. The halfway house movement spread to Pennsylvania with the establishment of the "House of Industry in Philadelphia." This halfway house began in 1889 and has continued to receive parolees from the Pennsylvania prison system today.

Despite the unpopularity of halfway house programs among correctional officials, Maud and Ballington Boothe opened what was eventually called Hope House in 1896 in New York City. The program received financial and moral support from the Volunteers of America, a missionary religious society, and not an institution. The success of this program enabled the Boothes to open other Hope Halls in Chicago, San Francisco and New Orleans. However, the introduction of parole during the 1900's, a mechanism for controlling released offenders, and the continued belief that ex-offenders should not associate with ex-inmates, strengthened the position of those opposed to halfway houses and began their demise. The onset of the Depression finished off the majority of already inadequately financed programs. Consequently, little if any activity related to halfway house development occurred between the 1930's and 1950's.

The revival of the halfway house movement during the 1950's seems to be a classic example of "independent multiple (re)discovery" (Beha, 1975). In 1954, Merfyn Turner opened Normal House in London, shortly followed by the estabishment of Beverly Lodge in Toronto, Crenshaw House in Los Angeles, St. Leonard's House in Chicago, 308 West Residence in Delaware and the infamous Dismas House in St. Louis by Father Charles Dismas Clark (the "Hoodlum Priest"). This revival of the halfway house movement is generally attributed to a growing concern and dissatisfaction with the ineffectiveness of institutional corrections. The increasingly high recidivism rates indicated that prisons were ineffective as an instrument of rehabilitation. These findings coupled with a new appreciation of the problems confronting the offender released from prison provided ample evidence essential that supportive services were needed to assist the offenders' transition from institutional to community living (Doeren and Hageman, 1982). It is also worth noting the pivotal role of private and religious groups in the historical development and revivial of the halfway house movement.

During the 1960's halfway house programs began using the individualized team treatment model that had already been adopted in correctional institutions. In addition, parole officials began to see that halfway houses could work with the correctional system by providing community ties and assistance in job placement that was otherwise unavailable to inmates. However, the impetus to legitimize halfway houses came in 1961 when Attorney General Robert F. Kennedy recommended funds be appropriated for the establishment of the first publicly operated halfway house under federal auspices (Goldfarb and Singer, 1973).

The first "pre-release" halfway houses were limited to juvenile and youthful offenders. However, by 1964 Kennedy was satisfied that the programs were successful and the following year asked Congress to authorize expansion of the program to include adult offenders. Under the Prisoner Rehabilitation Act of 1965, the Bureau of Prisons was authorized to establish community-based residences for adult and youthful pre-release offenders, and to transfer federal prisoners to approved halfway houses that were operated by non-federal agencies. In addition, the establishment of the Law Enforcement Assistance Administration (LEAA) in 1968 served as a principal means for providing substantial funding for halfway house programs which continued through the 1970's.

Another key event in the remarkable growth of halfway houses in the 1960's was the formation and development of the International Halfway House Association (IHHA). This group was prompted by the fact that few states or countries followed the lead of the federal government in establishing halfway houses. Most of the programs for released offenders and halfway houses for adults remained privately operated. In 1964 a group of concerned operators of halfway houses met in Chicago, Illinois and established a professional organization related to the goals and objectives of community-based treatment programs (Doeren and Hageman, 1982). This was the beginning of the International Halfway House Association. The newly formed association developed a directory of halfway houses operated in the United States and Canada with only 40 names listed in 1966. In 1968 IHHA was accepted as an affiliate of the American Correctional Association and by 1982 the IHHA directory listed more than 1800 programs. Today only a few cities and counties administer their own halfway house programs, and most states operating halfway houses contract with private non-profit agencies to perform this service.

There is no single definition that would encompass or describe the wide range of places and facilities that call themselves halfway houses. The halfway house also serves a wide variety of offenders that generally fall into two distinct categories: the "halfway in," and the "halfway out." The halfway-in house is relatively new and is primarily a diversion program for younger, first-time offenders with special problems that would be better served in the community (drugs, alcohol, etc.). This group is composed of probationers, or those who fail probation, but who the court considers worthy of another opportunity to remain in the community (Keller and Alper, 1970).

The halfway-out house is the traditional and better known halfway house facility. It is designed to provide specific and substantial support and assistance to the offender during this critical period of readjustment to the outside community. The house provides a clean and reasonably comfortable environment that is shared by other offenders in the same situation. The offender quickly learns that he/she is not totally unique and that other offenders share his/her fears, frustrations and difficulties. The stafff also provides many essential supportive services including: counseling, job placement, educational opportunities and financial support, to name a few. It is hoped that the combination of the staff, residents and the offenders' own initiative will enable him/her to emerge from this "decompression chamber" with the requisite tools and confidence to make a successful post-release adjustment (Miller, Montello, 1977).

Although halfway houses serve a wide variety of offenders, and programs vary from just being a place to live to specific treatment centers, they are all based on the same theoretical assumptions. Seiter, in his review of the historical development of halfway houses, found that all halfways were based on three major theoretical premises: (a) the treatment of offenders in the community is more humane than are traditional methods; (b) gradual reintegration in the realistic setting of the community is more effective in reducing recidivism than in the prison/rehabilitation ideology; and (c) offender reintegration in the community can be accomplished at a cost less than that of incarceration (Carlson, Seiter, 1977).

If we believe the period of transition from institutional to community living is a crucial and extremely stressful period for offenders, that a gradual re-entry from institutions to halfway houses to community has a positive effect on the ex-offender's adjustment, and that the community must be involved in the reintegrative process; then the halfway house is an attractive solution for easing the transition from incarceration to the community.

Programs and Treatment

The list of halfway programs and modes of treatment for halfways would be a monumental task to accomplish. However, we do find some common ground when discussing programs and treatment. For the most part, halfway house programs depend on whether the offenders are "halfway-in or halfway-out." The halfway-in programs are designed for probationers and deliberately create an uncomfortable climate for the offender. It hopes that this discomfort and uncertainty will foster self-examination which will ultimately induce a personality change (Keller, Alper, 1970).

Unlike the previously mentioned programs, halfway-out programs are designed for offenders released on parole. These programs provide the offender with the security of a place to live, a supportive environment, job placement, opportunities for education, and counseling to aid in family and personal readjustment problems. In other words, this program would be a homelike environment for offenders.

On the other hand, treatment, whether formal or informal, is a part of all halfway house programs. Usually counseling falls into two general types — individual and group treatment. One-to-one, or individual counseling, is made available to all offenders and is specifically directed to assist the offender in coping with readjustment problems. The group treatment approach often varies from program to program but can be distinguished as group counseling, group psychotherapy and guided group interaction. Group counseling is the least demanding with regard to frequency of meeting and depth of training required. The other two group treatment approaches tend to be more therapeutic and require frequent meetings and in-depth training (Keller, Apler, 1970).

Many halfway houses, however, have been established to serve a particular type of offender and are designed around a specific treatment model. For example, programs for drug addiction would gear their treatment toward the specific and unique needs of residents. The supervision and structure of the program would be very structured with mandatory daily meetings and personal responsibilities would be stressed. The periodic taking and analysis of urine samples would be mandatory to ensure the offender is remaining drug free or stabilized on alternative maintenance such as methadone. These programs attempt to change the drug addicted offender's entire lifestyle and stresses a therapeutic community orientation within the community. The programs are long term, 12 to 18 months, compared to the normal 1 to 3 month requirement for the halfway house programs.

Other halfway house programs would include group foster homes for delinquent children. The optimism capacity of these programs range from five to eight with a strong family environment, including male and female house parents. Prerelease halfway programs are utilized for both state and federal offenders. The federal prereleased offender is provided an opportunity to complete his/her remaining institutional time under conditions of minimum security while still legally and administratively in the custody of the Bureau of Prisons. State prerelease offenders would include those on parole and those on furlough. The furlough programs are normally operated by the State Department of Corrections and maintain more control of the offender than the above mentioned programs. Still, another variation is the halfway houses for probationers or in lieu of imprisonment. These programs are primarily for young, first-time offenders and serve as a valuable alternative to incarceration of minor but serious offenders.

Generally all halfway houses use the same basic programmatic elements of operation irregardless of the type of offender population. During the orientation phase, the first one or two weeks, the offender becomes acquainted with the rules and procedures of the house and becomes oriented to the community. This period also provides an opportunity for staff evaluation and individual program plans for reintegration of the offender. These plans must be realistic and mutually agreed on by the staff and the offender. Since the goal of any halfway house is to prepare the offender to function independently in the community, emphasis is placed on employment training and/or educational placement. After the completion of the orientation period, the offender joins the routine of the other offenders. This routine includes weekly mandatory group meetings. The purpose of the meetings is two-fold: (1) to discuss the operation of the house and resolve any problems which may be developing before they assume crises proportions; (2) to provide group counseling in which offenders are given a role in assisting each other in their reintegration efforts (Miller and Montilla, 1977). These meetings provide a means to share common experiences and problems in an open and supportive environment. It allows other offenders to discuss and prepare successfully for coping with particular problems and allows the staff a means of evaluating progress and potential problems.

Administration and Staffing

From their inception, halfway houses developed through the efforts of private organizations and persons who have dedicated themselves to the successful operation of facilities which care for released offenders. Although correctional agencies today operate a variety of halfway house programs, the majority are still run by private organizations which include correctional agencies contracting with private groups to open and operate halfway houses. The major advantage in this contractual arrangement is that private organizations can provide the service at less cost. This can be accomplished because of the private organization's flexibility in staffing, securing of necessary goods and services, and their greater access to sources of contribution from the public sector. Other advantages include the fact that private organizations are already established, known and accepted in the community and know the available resources. The contracts specify the exact services to be provided for which the correctional agency (state or federal) may reimburse the private organization for all expenses connected with the operation of the halfway house (Miller, 1977). Many halfway houses also require purchase of a guaranteed minimum number of spaces on a per annum basis.

The staffing of halfway houses varies with the size and specific needs of the offenders in the program (i.e. drugs and alcohol problems). Generally, a program with 11 or more offenders would be composed of an administrative and counseling staff members. The program Director would provide the overall leadership and direction of the facility's operation. These duties would include responsibility for all budgetary and fund-raising matters, formal relationships with community, governmental and funding agencies. The assistant director is the primary back-up to the director and frequently handles day-to-day operations of the house. His/her duties would also include program responsibilities and counseling with residents and staff. A secretary would provide clerical support and many times basic bookkeeping functions.

The counseling staff consists of both full-time and part-time counselors. The full-time counselor normally has a college degree and/or some professional training, and primarily works during the day. He or she provides individual and group counseling in addition to assisting residents in finding jobs, training, educational and other available community services. The part-time counselor is normally considered a paraprofessional and often lacks professional training and college degrees. They provide the general supervision of the residents, insuring that they observe the rules, perform assigned tasks, and check them in and out of the halfway house. The maintenance and general housekeeping is a shared responsibility of the residents, however a cook is responsible for meal preparations. A major problem in staffing most halfway houses is finding and maintaining good halfway house personnel. With few exceptions, halfway house staff members are underpaid, especially in privately sponsored halfway houses. Although these traditionally low social status jobs are now being recognized and pay is increasing, the low salary range often discourages professionally trained persons from entering the halfway house field.

Operations Cost

The phenomenal growth of halfway houses since 1969 and the cost associated with the operations of these programs is amazingly low compared to institutional programs. A study conducted in 1975 showed the operating cost of eleven of the least expensive and eleven of the most expensive programs across the country (Thalheimer, 1975). The operating cost included personnel salaries and fringe benefits, rental of facility, food, maintenance, utilities, and other expenditures associated with the successful operations of the halfway house. The average cost to the eleven least expensive programs was $14.81 per resident per day, compared to $22.26 for the eleven most expensive programs. Some of the variables in cost can be accounted for through differences in services provided by the program, types of treatment programs, types of resources available in the community, geographic region, and location in the city.

We found that several states have taken advantage of the growing halfway house movement and the State of Ohio is an example. In 1969 Ohio allocated $40,000 to five (5) halfway house programs for treatment and care of parolees in the community. By 1976 the allocation was over 1 million dollars and Ohio halfway houses had a capacity of 538 beds (Gordon, 1977). The average institutional cost during this period was $16.33 per day compared to $10.46 for halfway house programs. In addition, offenders earned and paid taxes on $240,000 while living in halfway houses, compared to $.40 and no taxes earned by offenders confined to institutions.

Today, the State of Ohio pays a per diem rate of $28.15 and the Federal Bureau of Prisons pays $35.00 for contract services to operate halfway houses (Tilow, 1983). However, start-up costs which include purchases of the house and furniture, insurance, and renovations to the property are normally not part of the per diem rate. These are long-term, on-going expenses that compel private organizations to remain at full capacity at all times and to always seek outside funding.

Problems and Constraints

The first problem usually encountered when establishing a halfway house is the provision of adequate funding to operate the facility whether it is public or private. Public funding has the advantage of support from the public sector, which ultimately has the power to tax individuals. However, the public sector has resisted entering the halfway house arena. Instead it has preferred to use private organizations on a contractual basis. The advantage is that there is no long-term commitment of funds and these agencies are competing with each other in providing the state with a choice of services.

The constraints of this system of funding is that most states do not provide 100% funding of halfway house programs. In the majority of states, the funding is 75% state and 25% local or county. During the recent economic crisis many halfway houses closed because local governments were unable to match the state funds. This was coupled with the fact that the state reimburses the halfway house after services are rendered, causing a 30 to 90 day gap between billing and recovery of funds. Halfway houses that rely solely on state funding continue to run the risk of closing if occupancy drops below 100% and no other funding sources are available. However, the Bureau of Prisons and the Veterans Administration continue to provide 100% funding for their residents.

Another important problem is locating and firmly establishing the halfway house in a community setting. The community's attitude and reaction is extremely important; one should anticipate some hostility from the public when establishing a halfway house in their community. In the recent past, halfway houses could move into a community and become established before the community noticed them. Today, however, resistance to any residential program in a community takes the form of letters to various elected officials, sudden passage of restrictions on zoning regulations, and the filing of lawsuits.

Related to concerns regarding the location of halfway houses are the issues of anonymity of the house, type of facility, racial and economic composition and accessibility. The importance of accessibility according to McCartt and Mangogna in *Guidelines and Standards for Halfway Houses and Community Treatment Centers* states:

> The community-based treatment center should be located in an area reasonably close to public transportation, employment and vocational opportunities, medical, psychiatric, recreational and other community resources and agencies to be utilized by the center for its clients (McCartt and Mangogna, 1973).

The resident of the halfway house must be, and feel, he/she is a natural part of the community, rather than being identified and stigmatized as from the correctional center. Therefore, if the halfway house is to survive and succeed, some measure of community support is vital.

Other problems of building credibility of the program in the community is the selection of inmates who enter the program, avoiding becoming a dumping ground for the correctional institution, maintaining the quality of service to the residents, and hiring, training, and retention of the halfway house staff.

Effectiveness of Halfway House Programs

Although halfway house programs have many singular characteristics, they are established for many different reasons and different models have different expectations. These expectations are based on one or more of the following motives:

1. That humanitarian concern that incarceration has a negative impact on offenders.
2. That halfway houses are more cost effective.
3. That halfway houses reduce recidivism.

We find that most halfway houses will move back and forth across all of the previously mentioned motives in defending themselves, and in arguing for continued support of their programs and their effectiveness.

From the humanitarian perspective, the halfway house can provide an alternative to incarceration and offer a gradual reentry for released offenders. The halfway house provides basic services and relieves some of the pressure of the offender fending for him/herself immediately after release. The assumption is that the movement from strict supervision and confinement to limited supervision and confinement should be graduated, and that moving from the institution through the halfway house to the community has a more positive affect on the offenders readjustment. A review of the literature affirms this viewpoint as it states that the overall goal of halfway houses should be: "To assist in the reintegration of ex-offenders by increasing their ability to function in a socially acceptable manner and reducing their reliance on criminal behavior" (Carlson and Seiter, 1977). Several studies have attempted to measure the impact of the social environment of the halfway house, the interaction, the behavior changes, and the humane treatment of the ex-offender without success. And because of the difficulty of assessing humaneness and behavioral changes, most researchers tend to ignore these variables to pursue more quantifiable data. However, anyone who has worked in or around halfway houses has seen positive changes in the lives of many that enter these programs.

The second means of evaluating halfway house programs is based on the assumption that ex-offenders can be handled in the community at less cost than an institution (Goldfarb and Singer, 1973). It is easy to conclude that any program in the community is less costly than large institutions. However, a comprehensive cost comparison between halfway houses and correctional institutions is complex. A cost comparison assumes equal effectiveness and must take into account both the services being rendered and the cost incurred in providing these services. A review of the literature supports the assumption that halfway houses are more cost-effective than institutions based on a per diem cost and 95-90% occupancy rate. Two factors that help halfway house with their advantage are: 1) payments from residents to reduce cost (in a few cases by several thousand dollars per resident per year); and 2) the social benefits engendered by the greater opportunity for income-producing (family-supporting) employment (Beha, 1975). This edge is dependent on the economics of the county and geographic location which also accounts for the large variations in halfway house operations. However, the demand for quality treatment and the escalating cost to operating halfway houses indicate that they are rapidly approaching and could surpass the cost of institutional programs in the future.

The most commonly used measure to determine the success of criminal justice programs is the net effect it has on the crime rate. For halfway houses, this measure typically means the recidivism rate of ex-offenders. Although recidivism rates are inherent in the previously mentioned measure of effectiveness, it appears to be inconsistent with the aforementioned goal of halfway houses: "To assist in the reintegration of ex-offenders by increasing their ability to function in a socially acceptable manner and reducing their reliance on criminal behavior." It remains true, however, that effectiveness is most frequently stated in terms of subsequent criminal behavior — or lack of it (Woodring, 1969).

A review of the literature indicates that recidivism is operationally defined in diverse ways across most studies and lacks a common definition. This and other factors cloud any conclusion about the effect of recidivism on halfway houses. Several studies conclude that there is little or no significant difference between the recidivism rates of halfway houses and correction institutions. However, from the majority of the studies it appears that community residential programs are institutional alternatives, and there is fairly conclusive evidence that halfway houses are more effective than the traditional prison-parole cycle (Carlson and Seiter, 1977).

There are a variety of technical reasons why it is difficult to evaluate the effectiveness of halfway house programs. These include the diversity of research design and definition of outcome, the absence of follow-up information, following an adequate comparison group, and length of follow-up period to name a few. Even with these limitations, research findings indicate that halfway house programs can more effectively reduce cost, reintegrate ex-offenders to the community, and reduce recidivism.

The Future of Halfway House Programs

The Criminal Justice System in the United States is rapidly growing and changing to meet the present needs of our society. These changes are often a result of the public's view of crime and how the system is handling this problem. The increasing crime and recidivism rates, coupled with the public's attitude that criminals should be punished is evident.

The effect of this new "get tough" attitude can be seen in the longer sentences being given by judges and the rapid increase in the prison population. The Federal Bureau of Prisons estimates that the prison population will exceed 400,000 before the end of 1983. These figures do not include the thousands of persons sentenced to local jails or awaiting trial. The call for hard-line policies to deal with offenders by alarmed and frightened citizens has also spurred the construction of new jails and prisons. It has also caused several states to set maximum limits on prison populations. For example, the state of Michigan must release one prisoner when a new entering prisoner exceeds the maximum population. The parole board has also re-evaluated each prisoner to provide early release dates.

The average citizen is not aware that 95% of those incarcerated in prisons will eventually return to their respective communities. At the same time, correctional administrators increasingly favor the utilization of community programs as a way to reduce the overcrowding in prisons. This causes higher risk offenders and those who may not be prepared to face the challenges of a free society to be released. If there are no halfway houses to receive these ex-offenders, the possibility of their returning to prison for new crimes is drastically increased.

The future of halfway house programs appears bright. The need for pre-release programs will continue to be a constant need for correctional administrators and as an alternative to incarceration for newly corrected offenders. The correctional system will prefer the furlough programs over more open halfway houses because they provide additional spaces at the institutions without releasing control of the offender.

Halfway houses will continue to operate on a contracted, per diem rate by private agencies, and the state will have to guarantee a minimum number of ex-offenders per year at 100% funding. Halfway houses will have to double their size from the normal 17 or 18 to 34-36 ex-offenders per house, and become more cost-effective. And finally, halfway houses will have to continue good relationships with community agencies, strengthen community ties and acceptance, while insuring the safety of the community.

In conclusion, the author's review of the halfway house literature and experience working with Talbert House Inc. reinforces the conclusion of Carlson, Seiter, Allen, Latessa, Travis *et al.,* Cullen and others: halfway houses can be effective in the reintegration of ex-offenders; they are more cost-effective than institutions and they are more humane than prisons. However, until the public becomes aware that building new prisons and imposing longer sentences will not solve the crime problem and that provisions for those ex-offenders returning to society must be provided, the cycle of recidivism will not be halted. Community leaders, correctional administrators and politicians must unite to help convince the public that halfway houses and community correctional programs are here to stay; only with citizen support will they serve the dual purpose of protecting the community and reintegrating the ex-offender.

References

Beha, James. A., "Halfway Houses in Adult Corrections: The Law, Practice, and Results," *Criminal Law Bulletin,* 1975, 11(4).

Coates, Robert B., Alden D. Miller, "Neutralization of Community Resistance to Group Houses" in Y. Bakal, ed., *Closing Correctional Institutions,* Lexington Bink 1977.

Cohen, J. A Study of Community-Based Correctional Needs in Massachusetts. Massachusetts Department of Corrections, 1973.

Cullen, Francis T. and Karen E. Gilbert. *Reaffirming Rehabilitation,* Anderson Publishing Co., 1982.

Doeren, Stephen and Mary Hageman. *Community Corrections,* Anderson Publishing Co., 1983.

Goldfarb, Ronald L. and Linda S. Singer. *After Conviction,* New York: Simon and Schuster, 1973.

Gordon, Haralson, "Ohio's Halfway Houses Show Phenomenal Growth." *American Journal of Corrections,* April, 1977.

Keller, Oliver and Benedict Alper. *Halfway Houses: Community Centered Corrections and Treatment.* Lexington, Massachusetts: D.C. Heath and Co., 1970.

Latessa, Edward and Harry Allen, "Halfway Houses and Parole: A National Assessment. *Journal of Criminal Justice,* 1982, 10(2).

McCartt, John and Thomas Mangogna. "Guidelines and Standards for Halfway Houses and Community Treatment Centers." Washington, D.C.: United States Department of Justice, 1973.

McSparrow, James, "Community Corrections and Diversion: Cost and Benefit, Subsidy Modes, and Start-up Recommendations." *Crime and Delinquency,* April, 1980.

Miller, Eugene. "Furloughs as a Technique of Reintegration," in *Correction in the Community.* Resto Publishing Company Inc., 1977.

Miller, Eugene and Robert Montillo. *Corrections in the Community.* Resto Publishing Company Inc., 1977.

Powers, Edwin, "Halfway Houses: An Historical Perspective." *American Journal of Corrections,* 1959, 21(4).

Raush, Harold L. and Charlotte Roush. *The Halfway House Movement: A Search on Sanity.* New York: Appleton Century Crofts, 1968.

Seiter, Richard P. and E. Carlson, "Residential Inmate Aftercare: The State of the Art." *Offender Rehabilitation,* 1977, (4).

"Study Shows Halfway House Cost-Effective Alternative to Jail for Nonviolent," *Corrections Digest,* 1976, 7(19).

Thalheimer, Donald J. "Cost Analysis of Correctional Standards: Halfway Houses." Washington, D.C.: American Bar Association, 1975.

Tilow, N., Executive Director Talbert House, Inc. Cincinnati, Ohio. Interview, September 1983.

Travis, Lawrence F. III, Martin D. Schwartz and Todd R. Clear, *Corrections: An Issues Approach,* 2nd Edition, Anderson Publishing Co., 1983.

Woodring, E. "A dilemma: Rehabilitation and its Relationship to Recidivism." *Youth Authority Quarterly,* 1969.

VII
Effectiveness

Questioning the "Other" Parole

The Effectiveness of Community Supervision of Offenders

Timothy J. Flanagan
State University of New York at Albany

Questioning the Other Parole

As typically administered in American criminal justice systems, parole comprises two principal components: discretionary release and community supervision. Discretionary release decisionmaking by parole boards has been the center of seemingly endless controversy. Social scientists question the ability of parole boards to predict the future behavior of candidates for parole. Philosophers attack discretionary release as contrary to notions of equal treatment and just deserts. Legal analysts argue that the parole process lacks fundamental safeguards against capricious decisionmaking by government officials and that indeterminacy about release amounts to cruel and unusual punishment. Disaffection with some aspect of the discretionary release component of parole is one of those rare criminological issues that unites opponents from a wide range of political orientations.

Questions about the "other parole" (Wilson, 1977) have generated considerably less heat but perhaps no more light. One observer characterized attention focused on post-release community supervision of parolees as "the second wave of the assault on parole" (Wilson, 1977:56). Some critics favor the elimination of parole supervision on the grounds that it fails to meet accepted goals of correctional intervention (see, for example, Citizen's Inquiry on Parole and Criminal Justice, 1975). Yet recent legislative changes that have dramatically altered the standing of discretionary parole release in the criminal justice system have left the community supervision component largely intact. This is not to imply that post-release supervision has been completely ignored by legislatures. Maine and Connecticut eliminated parole supervision, and Washington will do so in 1988. However, the

167

criminal justice systems in these jurisdictions have "responded" to these changes by increased use of alternative mechanisms to insure some form of supervision in the community. (See Krajick, 1983). Moreover, the structure of parole supervision has been altered in several States (e.g., California and Illinois) in conjunction with sweeping penal law revisions. The changes in these latter jurisdictions are in the direction of providing greater determinacy of the parole term itself and limiting the "time owed" on the sentence if parole is revoked. (See Hussey and Lagoy, 1983 for a review).[1]

This paper poses a simple question: is our knowledge about the effectiveness of parole supervision sufficient to support (or even inform) public policy decisions regarding the retention or abolition of this component of parole? If not, what additional information is required, and how can it be obtained? Of course the question as stated is simplistic: the types of "knowledge" available are not always accepted as legitimate input for public policy decisions; the definition and criteria of "effectiveness" are subject to interpretation and debate; the quantity of information that would be considered "sufficient" to make the case for abolition or retention is not an absolute; and finally, consensus does not readily emerge regarding the nature of the beast called "parole supervision." Muddying the waters by recognizing these complicating factors certainly makes the question more interesting, but legislators and policymakers seeking easy answers to these complex questions are likely to be disappointed.

In the next section, a brief review of the origins and objectives of post-institutional community supervision illustrates the problems inherent in any attempt to unambiguously define "parole supervision." A review of research on the effectiveness of parole supervision is then presented, designed to highlight broad categories of research and assess the findings generally rather than to catalog and detail each report. The third section of the paper discusses methodological issues in the study of parole supervision effectiveness, illustrating the reasons why definitive answers to the question, "Does It Work?" are hard to obtain. Finally, the options available to public policymakers under present conditions of uncertainty are outlined.

Origins and Objectives of Parole Supervision

Parole developed as a managerial tool for institutional administrators. Commenting on the history of parole in California, Eliot Studt (1972) observed:

> As in most other states, the initial urgency to use parole grew out of problems of prison management; at first, parole was actually an adjunctive program to the prison, used to reduce overcrowding and to induce the incarcerated inmates to conform to the official requirements (1972:2).

'The chronological development of the many functions of contemporary parole is not helpful in deciding the contemporary retention/abolition debate. Rather, cognizance of the historical origins of parole should remind us that the "institutional behavior control function" of *early release* and the functions served by *supervision in the community* are discrete and separable dimensions of parole that can (and should) be examined independently.

Post-release supervision of the offender developed from a desire to cushion the "re-entry shock" that has been described as a key factor in the post-release experience of offenders. Providing assistance and control to ex-offenders was viewed as a means of simultaneously protecting community safety and promoting the reintegration of the offender into the community. The re-entry shock phenomenon is described in the oft-quoted passage from Studt:

> The parolee moves directly from the subservient, deprived and highly structured life of the prison into a world that bombards him with stimuli, expects behavior to which he has long been unaccustomed, and presents him with multitudinous problems about which he must make decisions. Food does not taste right, and often does not "sit well" after a meal; making change in a restaurant or on a bus proves unexpectedly troublesome; people and traffic seem to move with unsettling speed; and small events, anticipated with pleasure, result in exhaustion. Coming from a setting in which all time is structured for him, the parolee suddenly has no schedule except that which he can create for himself, often without the benefit of a timepiece to mark the hours (1972:16-17).

The dual objectives of community protection and reintegration assistance are reflected in the preamble to the California parole statute:

> The legislature finds and declares that the period immediately following incarceration is critical to the successful reintegration of the offender into society and to positive citizenship.

> It is in the interest of public safety for the State to provide for the supervision and surveillance of parolees, and to provide educational, vocational, family and personal counselling necessary to assist parolees in the transition between imprisonment and discharge.

Neither historical nor contemporary statements need be traced further to conclude that the primary obstacle preventing rigorous and unequivocal evaluation of the effectiveness of parole supervision is that parole serves many functions. Indeed, asking the question, "does parole work?" amounts to an *reductio ad absurdum*. Limiting the inquiry to community supervision alters the reduction only by degree. Carter and Wilkins observe:

> Although supervision by the probation or parole officer is the operational component of probation and parole best known, most visible and of greatest interest to the public, accurate evaluation of the effect of

ervision remains a very elusive factor in terms of analysis and review
76:389).

The Elements of Parole Supervision

Parole supervision is a general term encompassing at least four elements. First, there is a "selection effect" that must be considered in evaluating the effectiveness of parole supervision. Simply stated, inmates released from prison via parole are selected by the releasing authority as *appropriate candidates* for community supervision. Although numerous factors play a role in these selection decisions (see Flanagan, 1982a) the principal determination made by paroling authorities—whether routinized through the use of prediction tables or on the basis of clinical or intuitive judgments—is a risk assessment (Dawson, 1969). Therefore, we expect to find differences in *a priori* risk of recidivism between inmates released to parole versus those discharged without supervision. These differences will be directly proportional to the paroling authorities' ability to assess risk. That is, if parole boards achieve the goal of selecting the "best candidates" for early release, then simply comparing the post-prison success of parolees versus inmates held to full term is an inherently dangerous exercise. To assess the effectiveness of parole supervision in meaningful terms, this differential risk of failure must be adequately controlled. The importance of this element of parole in evaluating the results of studies that compare parolees and sentence expiration cases is apparent: the selection factor must be adequately controlled.

The second inherent element in parole supervision is an "early release effect." The comparison of parolees and dischargees for evaluation purposes must recognize that parolees are in fact released early, relative to inmates held to the full term. Moreover, simply controlling for the absolute length of time served does not control the "early release effect" because its magnitude is proportional to the potential amount of time that the parolee *could have served* in the absence of early release.

The evaluation of the effectiveness of parole supervision must also consider two dominant dimensions of supervision itself: assistance and control. By assistance, we refer to the bewildering range of services and supports that parole officers extend to clients. The nature and extent of "assistance" provided is particularly resistant to objective measurement. Studt notes that "[H]elping activities are even more difficult than surveillance activities for agents to specify, or for researchers to be sure they are observing. For one thing, there is a widely held assumption that something of value for the parolee occurs in any contact with his agent" (1972:93). The recent work of Duffee and Duffee (1981) illustrates that measurement of assistance efforts must be taken in the context of reliable information about the nature and extent of offender *needs*. Thus, we need to know not only the frequency and dosage of "Treatment Z" that the offender received, but also whether

"Treatment Z" was the appropriate intervention in light of the offender's needs.

The fourth element in parole supervision is the well-known surveillance component. Studt reports that the technology of surveillance consists of four main approaches: contact with the parolee, the element of surprise (e.g., an unannounced visit to the parolee's residence), covering multiple bases in developing intelligence about the client (by observing the client in as many social roles as possible), and the use of the parolee's role partners (spouse, employers, etc.) to develop intelligence. In general, the magnitude of the surveillance element increases as the parole officer increases the frequency and range of these surveillance technologies.

Numerous exogenous variables must also be considered. Carter and Wilkins summarize the chief exogenous factors:

> Although supervision has both assistance and control elements, there are numerous other variables that influence the supervision process. These include caseload size, types of probation and parole officers, offenders, treatments, and the social systems within probation and parole offices to include varying administrative styles. Also significant are the law enforcement, judicial and correctional decisionmakers and their decisions, which determine input and outgo in probation and parole, the administrative organization of caseloads, the community itself, and cost and political considerations. These many factors make supervision exceedlingly complex...(1976:390).

Thus, answers to public policy questions about the effectiveness of parole supervision are likely to be piecemeal in nature. No research, however well designed and well funded, is likely to provide definitive answers that will point policymakers in an unwavering direction. Rather, evidence must be marshalled from a number of sources, each limited in specific respects. And decisions must be reached under conditions of uncertainty, requiring probabilistic assessments rather than empirically derived imperatives.

The Evidentiary Patchwork

(A) Testing the selection effect: comparative studies of parole and maxout

Direct comparison of the post-release performance of inmates released to parole supervision versus those discharged without supervision places the researcher face-to-face with the selection effect. In the absence of conditions permitting controlled experimentation with offenders, quasi-experimental research designs have been employed in an attempt to control for the differential risk of recidivism between parolees and dischargees. The approach is straightforward: if the groups can be equated on variables that are associated with *a priori* risk of failure, then increased confidence can be placed in statements that ascribe intra-group post-release performance difto some feature of parole supervision itself. In the absence of ... timates of recidivism risk, our concerns are reduced but not elim-...

A small group of studies have evaluated the comparative effectiveness of parole versus discharge with these methods. Lerner's (1977) study of misdemeanant parole in New York State employed such a design, and defined failure under community supervision as arrest within a two-year followup period. After the application of statistical controls for risk, Lerner concluded that "parole supervision reduces criminal behavior of persons released from local correctional institutions" (1977:220). Since the parolees were subject to a "greater potential threat of arrest" because of the parole supervision, Lerner concluded that the data further strengthen the hypothesis that "parole supervision reduces criminal activity."

In a study of British offenders, Nuttal et al. (1977) examined the post-release performance of several groups of offenders. A group of 381 parolees released in 1968 was compared to a group of 431 men selected randomly from the pool of offenders who were *eligible* for parole but who were released without parole during the same period. A second group was drawn by similar procedures but released during 1969 and 1970. Failure on community supervision was defined as a conviction within a two-year follow-up period. After controlling for *a priori* risk of recidivism, the researchers concluded that parole supervision did not reduce the number reconvicted.[2]

Gottfredson's (1975) study of Federal releasees employed a similar research design. After controlling for risk, Gottfredson reported that parolees recidivated at a slightly lower rate than dischargees during the two-year followup period, based on a "new conviction" criterion.[3]

Waller (1974) examined Canadian offenders using the same basic approach as the previous studies. Using the criterion of arrest for an indictable offense and/or revocation of parole, with followups at 6, 12, and 24 months, Waller reported that slight differences favoring the performance of parolees at the sixth month disappeared at both the 12 and 24 month intervals. Thus, while parole may have a delaying effect on recidivism, Waller concluded that "[T]he effectiveness of parole in terms of reducing recidivism within twelve and twenty-four months, or in the long run generally, is an illusion" (1974:190).

Gottfredson, Mitchell-Herzfeld and Flanagan (1982) studied state felony offenders, using a five-year followup period and three different criteria of parole outcome. The multiple criteria enabled the researchers to examine the effect of differential handling of "technical violations" in the criterion. As expected, the researchers found that the manner in which technical violations of the rules of parole are treated in studies of parole supervision effectiveness substantially influences the studies' findings. In fact, the rank ordering of groups (parolees, conditional releasees and maximum expiration of sentence cases) reversed under different definitions of parole failure.

Focusing on the criterion that "was arguably biased in favor of discovery of an effect for supervision, differences in the range of 10 to 15 percent were found, depending on risk group" (1982:296). In summarizing the findings, Gottfredson *et al* concluded, "much of our data does indicate an effect for parole supervision, an effect that varies by offender attributes, and an effect that appears not to be very large" (1982:296).

In a companion study, Flanagan (1982b) examined "time to failure" as a dependent variable for the same groups of offenders, applying survival analysis techniques to the five-year followup data. Again, significant differences in the community survival time distributions of the parolee, conditional releasee and maximum expiration cases were found, but the absolute differences in time to failure were not marked.

Finally, a study by Martinson and Wilks (1977) used an unusual approach to the study of the comparative effectiveness of parole supervision and non-supervised release. These researchers compared "batches" of recidivism rates that were culled from numerous studies which assessed the recidivism experience of parolees versus dischargees. Martinson and Wilks ignored methodological features of the studies that would engender differential confidence in the findings, and assigned equal value to the findings of each study. The researchers reported that "in 74 of the 80 comparisons...the mean of the recidivism rates for parole is lower than for max out" (1977:26). They concluded that "[T]he evidence seems to indicate that the abolition of parole supervision would result in substantial increases in arrest, conviction, and return to prison" (1977:26-27).

How can we evaluate the contradictory and equivocal conclusions of such a diverse body of empirical findings? Martinson and Wilks view the evidence (as distilled by their method) unequivocally, hence their report is titled "Save Parole Supervision." Stanley (1976) examines the same evidence and reaches a diametrically opposite conclusion: "[T]here are no research findings that prove the efficacy of parole supervision" (1976:180). von Hirsch and Hanrahan (1979) agree with Stanley but raise the question of the burden of proof:

> Before one can make even a *prima facie* case for supervision, therefore, the threshold criterion of effectiveness must be satisfied: there must be empirical evidence that parole supervision is capable of reducing recidivism rates among parolees. Thus far, the effectiveness of parole supervision has not been established...
>
> This research is too scanty and its results are too equivocal to warrant the inference that supervision succeeds — at least, if the burden of proof rests on the proponents of supervision, as we think it should.
>
> Since there have been so few studies, it is possible that further inquiry might show success, or at least success among certain selected subgroups of offenders. But that is not what can be concluded today (1979: 61-62, 63).

...le-ground position was offered by Gottfredson, Mitchell-Herzfeld agan:

> ...If the research...is regarded as permitting the strongest inferences about the question of supervision versus no supervision following imprisonment, some consistency seems to emerge from the research. First, none of the studies have indicated a lasting effect of parole supervision beyond the period of supervision itself. Second, the research seems to indicate an effect of supervision, particularly in the initial period of release. Third, the effect indicated by the research does not appear to be very large (1982:280).

(B) Simultaneous control of selection effects and early release effects

The studies discussed in the previous section used statistical methods to control the selection effect of the parole board. However, the fact that inmates released from prison via parole are released *early,* relative to offenders held to the maximum expiration of the sentence, must also be considered. In an unusual study, Sacks and Logan (1979; 1980) were presented with the conditions of a "natural experiment" that allowed simultaneous control of selection effects and early release effects.

When a number of minor (Class D) felons *who otherwise would have been released to parole* were released by court order without supervision, Sacks and Logan were able to make comparisons with a group of similar class felons who had been released one year earlier, but to parole supervision. A subgroup of 167 of the 400 offenders covered by the court order were in penal institutions, and thus were released *early* and *without parole supervision.* One-year and three-year followup periods were studied and several outcome criteria (e.g., success/failure, gravity of failure, time to failure) were examined. Statistical controls for risk were employed. Sacks and Logan's findings indicated that parole appeared to have a *delaying effect* on recidivism, at least during the period of supervision itself, but that post-supervision failure levels of the groups were comparable (i.e., at the three-year followup point). The overall reduction in recidivism associated with parole supervision was modest. Sacks and Logan attributed the delaying effect on recidivism during the supervision period to the surveillance and "sentence overhang" aspects of supervision rather than to rehabilitative effects.[4]

(C) Testing "more vs. less" supervision: caseload size variation studies

A common reaction to research that finds little or no difference between parolees and offenders released from prison without supervision is the notion that fiscal restraints, burgeoning caseloads, and lack of adequate referral resources in the community reduce parole to little more than an episodic reporting requirement. This is particularly appropos in the case of offenders released to large, urban parole offices where each officer may supervise hundreds of clients. Under such conditions, it is not surprising that parole supervision may be no more "effective" than outright discharge, since the functional difference between parole supervision and no supervision may be negligible. A second line of research provides information on the question of whether "more supervision is better," although for several reasons the findings of these researches are no less equivocal than the studies discussed above.

Detailed presentation of the individual studies in this area will not be undertaken here, as extensive reviews are available (see Lipton, Martinson and Wilks, 1975; Neithercutt and Gottfredson, 1973).

In the caseload size variation (CSV) studies, caseload *size* is regarded as a proxy variable for intensity of supervision. Presumably, parole officers supervising smaller caseloads have more time to devote to the surveillance and assistance elements of parole supervision than their colleagues handling larger caseloads.[5] Thus, if supervision "works," then intensive supervision ought to work even more dramatically in reducing recidivism.

Neithercutt and Gottfredson's review of the CSV studies concluded that there was "little to indicate that varying caseload size impacts parole outcome" (1973:289). They continue:

> The results thus far indicate that sometimes caseload size reduction yields indications of improved performance, sometimes no outcome changes surface, and sometimes the smaller caseloads do significantly worse than the larger. It seems reasonable to conclude from this that much more is transpiring than is being scrutinized...the mere increased availability of an officer is not enough in itself (1973:290).

That such findings emerge should neither surprise nor disappoint us, according to Neithercutt and Gottfredson. Rather, the research in this area needs to be more sensitive to the broad range of exogenous factors that mediate the relationship between the client and the parole officer. These confounding factors are discussed in the next section.

Lipton, Martinson and Wilks' review of the CSV studies is more positive. They note that reduced caseloads appear to be effective in reducing recidivism, when recidivism is defined as "remaining arrest-free during parole or a low rate of minor arrests" (1976:568). However, they note that for adult offenders, no significant reductions occur in new felony convictions or major arrests.

A second line of research on "more vs. less" supervision focuses on early termination of parole supervision or dramatic reduction in the requirement that parolees routinely report to parole officers. Star's (1978) research on the efficacy of "summary parole" is a good example. Star compared offenders released to standard parole supervision with a group of parolees who were required to contact parole officers but twice during the first year after release. Random assignment methods were used to address selection bias. Star's results indicated no significant differences between the groups in post-release arrests, convictions, time to failure or offense severity.

(D) Confounding and contamination

As Carter and Wilkins observed, caseload size is but one of a large number of variables that influence the nature of parole supervision. Manipulating caseload size exerts a crude control for one of these variables, but the control is far from complete. The mix of assistance and control efforts is not measured with precision in any of these studies, and the comparative effectiveness of different types of assistance or different forms of surveillance provided is rarely measured. Waller's study of Canadian releasees provides limited data on the relative effectiveness of assistance types; he reported that provision of assistance in locating post-release employment appeared to influence recidivism among parolees. In terms of surveillance methods, nalline testing with drug-abuser releasees in a California experiment was evaluated, but the utility of this form of surveillance was related to the revocation policy of the administering agency (Lipton, Martinson and Wilks, 1975). Controlled experiments that manipulate variables such as the use of surprise visits and type of reporting have not been conducted routinely, therefore inferences that can be drawn regarding the effects of these measures are tenuous. In brief, there is little credible evidence on the question of whether variation in assistance and/or control elements of the parole supervision process is systematically related to reduction of recidivism among supervised releasees.

There is also a dearth of empirical evidence about the "other" variables that may influence the efficacy of parole supervision. Several researchers have demonstrated that "officer orientation" (i.e., commitment to a control or assistance ideology or work style) can be reliably measured (Glaser, 1969; Studt, 1972; Stanley, 1976). However, with the exception of the California Community Treatment Project, incorporation of this variable into the design of parole supervision effectiveness research has been lacking. Waller (1974) and others have noted the critical importance of parole officer discretion in determining success rates of parolee groups, yet few researchers have focused on this potential contaminant.[6] Neithercutt and Gottfredson suggested that "agency orientation" is another factor that must be considered, and Martinson (1975) documented a method for measuring this orientation, yet this factor has not been routinely considered in this body of work.

This listing of potential confounding and contaminating factors that affect the quality of our knowledge on the effectiveness of parole supervision could be extensive, but the essential question remains. On the basis of what we currently know, can rational public policy choices be made regarding the abolition or retention of parole supervision?

Should We Experiment Further?

In many public policy decisions, there is an important alternative to choice between dichotomous positions. In the choice between retention or abolition of parole supervision, the third alternative may be most appropriate given the limitations of our knowledge. The third alternative is, of course, to decide not to decide, at least for a while. In order for this alternative to be considered a rational response to the policy dilemma, the hiatus created must be both limited and purposive. If further research and experimentation on parole supervision holds promise for discovery of more useful and less equivocal answers to the question of supervision effectiveness, the decision not to decide pending the outcome of further research represents a rational choice under conditions of uncertainty.

Is further research likely to produce such answers? For von Hirsch and Hanrahan, the answer is, it depends. Their position on the abolition or retention of parole supervision depends primarily on the moral position taken regarding appropriate punishment, and only secondarily on the demonstration of the utility of community supervision (and the inherent revocation threat) in reducing recidivism.[7]

Stanley's (1976) position on the need for further experimentation is confusing. In a section headed "An End to Policing," his assessment of the evidence to date leads him to conclude that:

> [T]he alternative is plain: abolish supervision of the releasee. Don't visit his job or his home or his tavern; don't make him come into the office or write in. Leave him alone, except for making help available (1976: 190).

However, earlier Stanley concludes that "to assess the effectiveness of the policing and assistance functions of parole officers, additional controlled studies are needed" (1976:180).

How would such a research program be conducted? From the previous discussion of the many factors that may affect the effectiveness of parole supervision, it is clear that this research enterprise would be a considerable undertaking. Moreover, to provide better answers than those currently available, such research would have to simultaneously consider, at minimum, the four elements of parole supervision discussed above.

While complex and demanding, the type of research needed could be carried out under the auspices of a receptive jurisdiction. It would require that the paroling authority conduct standard release reviews for a large sample of inmates approximately one year prematurely.[8] From this pool, and using standard parole release criteria, inmates would be selected as "candidates" for "premature" early release. From the pool of qualified candidates, assignment to early release/no early release groups would be made on a random basis. Those assigned to the premature early release status would be discharged immediately to one of four parole supervision groups reflecting the dual supervision elements of assistance and control. These groups would be provided either: (1) standard parole supervision; (2) voluntary assistance only; (3) surveillance only; or (4) neither assistance nor surveillance. Those not selected for premature early release would be released at the appropriate early release point *to similar caseload groups.* Non-candidates would be released through standard alternative release mechanisms. In jurisdictions such as New York with a conditional release procedure the conditional releasees would be discharged to similar randomly assigned caseload groupings.

Several assumptions would have to be maintained to secure the integrity of the research design. First, any prerelease planning efforts by the correctional or parole authority must be equivalent for the groups. The length of the supervision period (i.e., time at risk of supervision) must also be equivalent, necessitating legislative approval in some instances. Caseload sizes in each of the supervision modes must be equivalent in order to control for caseload size effects. Finally, the problem of equivalent "opportunities to fail" for the supervised and non-supervised groups must be addressed. Equivalence in this regard would require the suspension of parole revocation based solely on technical violations during the study period for *all* releasees.

Of course the principal limitation of the proposed design is that in many states (New York is an example) *eligibility* for first release does not obtain until the inmate had served the minimum term (minus any credits for pretrial incarceration time). In jurisdictions where the paroling authority is statutorily constrained from releasing inmates prior to expiration of the judicially-imposed minimum, the "premature early release" component of the design may face constitutional obstacles. Such problems would be minimized in the case of jurisdictions wherein the sentencing structure empowers judges to set only maximum terms, with the paroling authority empowered to establish minimum terms (and thus eligibility).

In the absence of statutory authority to establish minimum periods of imprisonment, the design could be approximated by standard procedures for setting groups to equivalence through statistical control of *a priori* risk, and the supervision phase of the design could be carried out within the authority of the parole board to set the terms and conditions of parole.[9] In order to provide more information on the effectiveness of the supervision elements, the random assignment to the four community supervision statuses is the critical element of the design. As Waller notes, an "interesting omission in contemporary research is the lack of comparisons between new treatments and no treatment at all" (1974:12). Commenting on the several caseload size variation studies conducted during the 1960's, Waller observed that "few studies...compare men released under varying degrees of parole supervision with those released without parole.... 'Minimum' supervision, contrary to popularly held ideas, is still supervision" (1974:12). Since Waller's observations in 1974, the only significant exception to this assessment has been the Sacks and Logan studies of a single class of felons in Connecticut. In addition to the dearth of research on *no* supervision, little work has focused on the *components* of parole supervision. As Waller reports, "rarely have analyses been carried out to see whether any particular component of intensive supervision was in any way related to outcome" (1974:198).

The research design discussed above is an extension of the two-group model suggested by Stanley (1976). Stanley's design would incorporate only the "standard parole" and "voluntary assistance only" caseload groups. The four-group design allows for additional variation in the subgroups to be independently assessed. For example, intensive employment counseling, job development and referral can be contrasted with individual therapy interventions for personal, marital or family problems. Similarly, within the surveillance only group, discrete intensity levels of supervision could be employed, or subgroups could be differentiated on the basis of dominant surveillance technologies.

Conclusion: The Immediate Policy Choice

The dilemma of the utilitarian policy maker is aptly described by Sacks and Logan as "what to do when you don't know what to do." The policy question of abolition or retention of parole supervision requires sharp focus on the *functions* served by parole supervision and the *effectiveness* of parole supervision in serving those functions. If the principal functions of parole supervision are community protection and reintegrative assistance to offenders, the policy question reduces to whether parole supervision, as currently organized and administered, is the most effective vehicle for achieving those goals. An ancillary question that flows from the previous inquiry is whether parole supervision can be *made* more effective in serving those ends.

The research to date provides a pessimistic answer to the first question. The evidence that parole supervision is effective in reducing (or even delaying) recidivism among released offenders is weak and contradictory, fundamentally questioning the utility of post-institutional community supervision as a deterrence mechanism. Alternative models for organizing the surveillance function, involving use of existing community-based law enforcement resources or emergent technological innovations, come quickly to mind. For example, statutory provisions requiring that local law enforcement officials be notified of the impending release of some classes of offenders could serve as the basis for legislation that would transfer supervision of parolees from parole agencies to police departments. Moreover, experimental applications of two-way electronic tracking of offenders via implanted transceivers have been reported for some time. Alternative mechanisms for the delivery of reintegrative assistance services—either through other public sector service delivery systems or through the private sector—are also available as the "privatization" of correctional services develops.

Adoption of a position in favor of continued research and experimentation on parole supervision implies a willingness to investigate ways to improve the *existing* parole supervision apparatus. Cost-related arguments cannot decide the issue because whether the abolition of parole supervision would be more or less expensive (measured in financial terms or by social costs of increased recidivism) depends entirely on what replaces parole supervision if it is eliminated. A government-funded but private sector administered reintegrative assistance network of agencies and services may be more or less expensive than the present parole field agency. Similarly, if the elimination of the surveillance function of parole results in the need to invest more in local police services to maintain community protection, economic savings accrued as a result of the elimination of parole supervision will be quickly eaten up by increased police expenditures.

The chief benefit of deciding not to decide until further research can be undertaken on the question of the effectiveness of parole supervision is that, unlike the abolition or retention positions, the alternative does not close out any options for the policymaker. A limited time extension of the mechanism coupled with a mandate for innovative research and experimentation holds potential that new alternatives will emerge from the research. These alternatives may range from new organizational structures for post-release community supervision to new conceptualizations of the appropriate clients for the system.[10]

In sum, public policymakers might impose a "sunset" restriction on parole supervision, given the pessimistic assessment of the effectiveness of parole supervision in reducing recidivism provided by the research literature. The sunset provision could be accompanied by a mandate for the conduct of an independently administered program of experimentation and research that would build upon the foundation of the earlier studies and provide additional answers to the questions that have not been explored previously. Lest expectations about the ability of this research agenda to provide unequivocal answers become inflated, the boundaries of the program should be developed in conjunction with the policymakers who will be the consumers of these research products.

It is important to recognize that the sunset provision with the accompanying research mandate is not a mechanism for avoiding policy choices. It represents neither "business as usual" nor radical change. Rather, since comparatively little research has focused on the community supervision component of the parole function, keeping the jury out until better evidence can be assembled represents a cautious and rational approach to policy decisions.

Endnotes

[1]Although the issues and questions raised in this chapter are framed in the context of parole, it is clear that these concerns apply to probation as well. (See Banks,

Siler and Rardin, 1977). However, the historical origins of probation differ from parole, and disenchantment with the effectiveness of probation supervision has not reached the level of that of parole. Moreover, while this discussion focuses exclusively on adult offenders, a recent report by Jackson (1983) indicates that very similar findings obtain on the efficacy of parole supervision with youthful offenders.

[2]A distinguishing feature of this research — diversity in the selection of criteria of "failure" — can be noted here. For this reason, the criterion employed is noted for each study.

[3]Note that the use of a conviction criterion would treat technical violations of the rules of parole as "success" cases. This is an often used compromise which does not eliminate all of the problems associated with comparing supervised and non-supervised groups, but at least creates groups that are at approximately equal risk of failing.

[4]A direct test of the relative importance of the various elements of parole supervision was not made.

[5]In later studies of this genre, recognition that the time involvement required for the supervision of each client is not constant across the caseload led to the incorporation of "workload units" into the distribution of the caseloads. These workload units were generally derived on the basis of offender risk scores.

[6]Compare, for example, the voluminous body of research focusing on the variation in release decisionmaking by parole boards, with the dearth of empirical work on the exercise of discretion by parole officers in regard to the revocation decision. The work of Takagi (1969) is the most obvious exception.

[7]"The answer depends on the moral issue... whether parole supervision can be squared with the requirements of justice, even if it were made to work" (von Hirsch and Hanrahan, 1979:64). Under a strict desert-based model of justice the problem of parole supervision is not *per se* objectionable, but the additional punishment inherent in revocation for violation of the rules of parole is repugnant. That is, additional prison time imposed on one offender as a result of revocation amounts to additional punishment for the original offense. To the extent that this additional sanction violates the principle of commensurate desert, secondary sanctions cannot be squared with a desert-based model. If the sanctions attached to revocation were limited so that time owed as a result of revocation represented only a minor deviation from the original term, and if it could be shown that such sanctions were effective in reducing recidivism, von Hirsch and Hanrahan would have less difficulty accepting continued supervision with revocation under a modified desert model.

[8]Obviously, early release cannot be ethically withheld from inmates who are otherwise qualified at the time of the first statutory review. To ameliorate this concern the experimental groups are derived from inmates whose first parole eligibility is at least one year away.

[9]It must be stressed here that the ability of current social science research methods to predict *a priori* risk of recidivism among offenders is far from perfect. The lack of "fit" achieved by these statistical models in predicting recidivism has several serious consequences that are often overlooked. To the extent that variation in post-release outcome is left unexplained by these models, to speak of "controlling"

the selection effect overstates the case. At best, partial control is achieved, but control in the classical experimental sense of the term is not.

[10]For example, Sacks and Logan comment on the fact that the *need* for parole intervention is seen as uniformly distributed among released inmates. Alternative models might focus on *selective parole* for particular offender groups, just as notions of selective incapacitation of high rate criminal offenders have gained currency in recent years. This approach coincides with Palmer's (1983) "differential intervention" position, and frankly acknowledges that parole supervision may not only fail to help some offenders, but actually hinder their reintegration.

References

Banks, J., T. Siler and R.L. Rardin. (1977). Past and present findings on intensive adult probation. *Federal Probation* 41:20-25.

Carter, R.M. and L.T. Wilkins. (Eds.) (1975). *Probation, Parole and Community Corrections.* Second Edition. New York: John Wiley and Sons.

Citizens' Inquiry on Parole and Criminal Justice, Inc. (1975). *Prison Without Walls: Report on New York Parole.* New York: Praeger.

Dawson, R. (1969). *Sentencing.* Boston: Little-Brown.

Duffee, D. and B. Duffee. (1981). Studying the needs of offenders in prerelease centers. *Journal of Research in Crime and Delinquency* 18(2):232-253.

Flanagan, T. (1982a). Explaining the parole decision: the effect of alternate conceptualizations on analyses of decisionmaking. In N. Parisi (Ed.) *Coping with Imprisonment.* Beverly Hills, CA: Sage.

Flanagan, T. (1982b). Risk and the timing of recidivism in three cohorts of prison releasees. *Criminal Justice Review* 7(2):34-45.

Glaser, D. (1969). *The Effectiveness of a Prison and Parole System.* Abridged Edition. Indianapolis: Bobbs-Merrill.

Gottfredson, D. (1975). Some positive changes in the parole process. Paper presented to the annual meeting of the American Society of Criminology, Tucson, Arizona, November.

Gottfredson, M.; S. Mitchell-Herzfeld and T. Flanagan. (1982). Another look at the effectiveness of parole supervision. *Journal of Research in Crime and Delinquency* 18(2):277-298.

Hussey, F. and S. Lagoy. (1983) The determinate sentence and its impact on parole. *Criminal Law Bulletin* 19(2):101-130.

Jackson, P. (1983). Some effects of parole supervision on recidivism. *British Journal of Criminology* 23(1):17-34.

Krajick, K. (1983). Abolishing parole: an idea whose time has passed. *Corrections Magazine* 9(3):32-40.

Lerner, M. (1977). The effectiveness of a definite sentence parole program. *Criminology* 15(2):211-224.

Lipton, D.; R. Martinson and J. Wilks (1975). *The Effectiveness of Correctional Treatment.* New York: Praeger.

Martinson, R. (1975). A static-descriptive model of field supervision. *Criminology* 13(1):3-20.

Martinson, R. and J. Wilks. (1977). Save parole supervision. *Federal Probation* 41(3):23-27.

Neithercutt, M. and D. Gottfredson. (1973). Caseload size variation and difference in probation and parole performance. Washington, D.C.: Federal Judicial Center. Reprinted in W. Amos and C. Newman, (Eds.) (1975). *Parole*. New York: Federal Legal Publications.

Nuttall, C.P. and associates. (1977). *Parole in England and Wales*. Home Office Research Studies No. 38. London: Her Majesty's Stationery Office.

Palmer, T. (1983). The "effectiveness" issue today: an overview. *Federal Probation* XX(X):3-10.

Sacks, H. and C. Logan. (1979). *Does Parole Make a Difference?* Storrs, CT: University of Connecticut Law School Press.

Sacks, H. and C. Logan. (1980). *Parole: Crime Prevention or Crime Postponement?* Storrs, CT.: University of Connecticut Law School Press.

Stanley, D. (1976). *Prisoners Among Us: The Problem of Parole*. Washington, D.C.: The Brookings Institution.

Star, D. (1978) *Summary Parole: A Six and Twelve Month Follow-up*. Research Report No. 60. Sacramento: California Department of Corrections.

Studt, E. (1972). *Surveillance and Service in Parole*. Los Angeles: UCLA Institute of Government and Public Affairs. Reprinted 1978 by National Institute of Corrections, U.S. Department of Justice.

Takagi, P. (1969). The effects of parole agents' judgments on recidivism rates. *Psychiatry* 32:192-199.

von Hirsch, A. and K. Hanrahan. (1979). *The Question of Parole*. Cambridge, MA.: Ballinger.

Waller, I. (1974). *Men Released from Prison*. Toronto: University of Toronto Press.

Wilson, R. (1977). Supervision (the other parole) also attacked. *Corrections Magazine* 3(3):56-59.

The Organization and Effectiveness of Community Corrections

Harry E. Allen
San Jose State University

Overview

This article defines community corrections and identifies the major components of this portion of the criminal justice system. The general goals and organization of community corrections are detailed, along with an assessment of what is believed currently known about the effectiveness of community programs. We close with a sobering challenge, a review of the wisdom of the policy of community corrections in light of developments in the general area of corrections in the last decade. We begin with the historical development of the current scene.

Introduction

Like ancient Gaul, the history of corrections in the United States can be divided into three parts or eras, presented in more detail earlier. Known as the reform, clinical and reintegration eras, each has its unique assumptions about the nature of offenders and what American society should do in response. In brief, correctional history represents a series of 90 degree turns, the most recent one to reintegration.

Reform (1790-1930).

The reform era began concretely in 1790 and rapidly expanded until 1930, when the Great Depression, impact of the developing social sciences, Freudian psychology, and philosophical debates brought about its over-due demise. Unfortunately, some of the untoward consequences of this era linger on, hampering community corrections. One example is the over-reliance on imprisonment as a response to crime. What did this era represent?

The reform era was a period of moralistic reform, predicated on making offenders change through serving long sentences, the use of corporal punishment (a practice recently resurrected in proposed policy: Newman, 1983), hard labor, and repentance. This era of the penitentiary and the reformatory found corrections attempting to imprint community goals, values and standards through rigorous schedules and disciplines. We incarcerated to make inmates better citizens, so they would repent, see the errors of their ways, and behave as non-offenders did.

Correctional administrators were expected to earn profits for the State through use of free inmate labor, and were retained in that role if escapes and prison disturbances were few and profits large. Reform was the philosophical goal of corrections, but profits were their objective. Inmates and parolees had no rights, and parole officers were frequently law enforcement officers. There was no farewell to arms in these earlier years, from which were to emerge parole, probation, halfway houses, volunteers in corrections, and many other innovations as alternatives to the counterproductive prison.

The Clinical Years (1930-1967).

In 1930, the Federal Bureau of Prisons was established and a brilliant professional administrator appointed as its first Director: Sanford Bates. In the next decade, while the labor unions nailed the coffin lid down on prison industry through repressive legislation on the national scene, Bates introduced diagnosis, classification, group and individual therapy programs, and educational and vocational training into Federal prisons, from which they were quickly adopted by state prisons. The era placed low emphasis on community safety; instead, high emphasis was placed on treating the offender, using treatment professionals, isolation in a therapeutic environment, and the "medical model" of corrections. Obviously, the underlying cause of the crime was not seen as a moral one, as offenders did not choose to be evil. It was "sickness," unattained potentials, maladjustment, lack of education, unresolved conflicts, and other factors usually traceable to early childhood. We promised to make the client ("patient") well through rehabilitation, and considerable strides were made in the name of treatment, along with some interesting legal problems involving "tinkering with the mental processes."

We should never have promised a "hospital" (Conrad, 1975), for our correctional technology was still underdeveloped. Worse still, we were asking the wrong questions about the nature of crime and its "cure." Raising false hopes, we created a split between treatment and custody staffs that has yet to be bridged. We permitted, even encouraged, widespread discretion by sentencing judges, parole boards and parole officers and, above all else, failed to recognize that law violators must be forced to deal with underlying problems in their own communities; the offenders' communities have responsibilities to meet the challenge of crime on their own grounds.

Reintegration (1967 - ?).

The third era emerged from sobering events: the assasination of a President, a presidential candidate, and a major civil rights leader. In 1965, then President Lyndon Johnson appointed a blue-ribbon Committee, charged with developing a blue-print for meeting the challenge of crime in a free society (President's Commission, 1967). We mark the birth of the reintegration era at the year Johnson's Committee issued its major reports: 1967.

Reintegration was then recognized as the *process* (sometimes painfully slow) of *enabling offenders—whatever the causes of their illegal behaviors—to utilize existing community resources to gradually change their behaviors until they are meaningfully integrated into their local communities.* The correctional objective became to create realistic alternatives in the community of the offender so he or she would develop a satisfactory lifestyle, tolerable to the community and not dependent on illegal behavior. This would require using diverse community resources; where these were not available, correctional personnel were to encourage their development, as change agents or advocates. As the National Advisory Commission (1973: 1:2) noted about the former eras:

Corrections and the Criminal Justice System

The pressures for change in the American correctional system today are building so fast that even the most complacent are finding them impossible to ignore. The pressures come not only from prisoners but also from the press, the courts, the rest of the criminal justice system, and even practicing correctional personnel.

During the past decade, conditions in several prison systems have been found by the courts to constitute cruel and unusual punishment in violation of the Constitution. In its 1971-72 term, the U.S. Supreme Court decided eight cases directly affecting offenders, and in each of them the offender's contention prevailed.

The riots and other disturbances that continue to occur in the Nation's prisons and jails confirm the feeling of thoughtful citizens that such institutions contribute little to the national effort to reduce crime. Some maintain that time spent in prisons is in fact counterproductive.

It is clear that a dramatic realignment of correctional methods is called for. It is essential to abate use of institutions. Meanwhile much can be done to eliminate the worse effects of the institution—its crippling idleness, anonymous brutality, and destructive impact. Insofar as the institution has to be relied on, it must be small enough, so located, and so operated that it can relate to the problems offenders pose for themselves and the community.

These changes must not be made out of sympathy for the criminal or disregard of the threat of crime to society. They must be made precisely because that threat is too serious to be countered by ineffective methods.

Many arguments for correctional programs that deal with offenders in the community—probation, parole, and others—meet the test of common sense on their own merits. Such arguments are greatly strengthened by the failing record of prisons, reformatories, and the like. The megainstitution, holding more than a thousand adult inmates, has been built in larger number and variety in this country than anywhere else in the world. Large institutions for young offenders have also proliferated here. In such surroundings, inmates become faceless people living out routine and meaningless lives. And where institutions are racially skewed and filled with a disproportionate number of ill-educated and vocationally inept persons, they magnify tensions already existing in our society.

The failure of major institutions to reduce crime is incontestable. Recidivism rates are notoriously high. Institutions do succeed in punishing, but they do not deter. They protect the community, but that protection is only temporary. They relieve the community of responsibility by removing the offender, but they make successful reintegration into the community unlikely. They change the committed offender, but the change is more likely to be negative than positive.

It is no surprise that institutions have not been successful in reducing crime. The mystery is that they have not contributed even more to increasing crime. Correctional history has demonstrated clearly that tinkering with the system by changing specific program areas without attention to the larger problems can achieve only incidental and haphazard improvement. Today's practitioners are forced to use the means of an older time. And dissatisfaction with correctional programs is related to the permanence of yesterday's institutions. We are saddled with the physical remains of last century's prisons and with an ideological legacy that has implicitly accepted the objectives of isolation, control and punishment, as evidenced by correctional operations, policies and programs.

Corrections must seek ways to become more attuned to its role of reducing criminal behavior. Changing correction's role from one of merely housing society's rejects to one of sharing responsibility for their reintegration requires a major commitment on the part of correctional personnel and the rest of the criminal justice system.

Behind these clear imperatives lies the achievable principle of a much greater selectivity and sophistication in the use of crime control and correctional methods. These great powers should be reserved for controlling persons who seriously threaten others. They should not be applied to the nuisances, the troublesome, and the rejected who now clutter our prisons and reformatories and fill our jails and youth detention facilities.

The criminal justice system should become the agency of last resort for social problems. The institution should be the last resort for correctional problems.

Thus the thrust of corrections and the goals and missions of its agencies and personnel underwent sharp change in less than two decades, shifting from a medical model approach of seeking cures for clients' illnesses in the antiseptic and isolated "hospital wards" of the clinical prisons, to the new correctional objective of stressing reintegration in a community setting.

Reintegration demands changes in probation and parole practices: a team approach, pooled caseloads, service brokerage, referral services, job placement development, and in-community officer activism to develop needed programs to retain offenders in the community. It is in this period from which the greatest expansion of community corrections emerged, not only in terms of what probation and parole professionals were expected to do, but also in pretrial and partial-release programs. Using start-up funds available from the impacts of President Johnson's Committee and following certain decisions by the U.S. Supreme Court, a variety of diverse community corrections programs emerged or were resuscitated: diversion, prosecutorial diversion, youth service bureaus, halfway houses, week-end detention, shock probation and shock parole, community work-orders, work and educational furlough, restitution, probation subsidies, statewide community correctional plans and schemes, group and foster-home services for juveniles, and diversion of status offenders from the juvenile court, to name a few. In less than 20 years, no correctional system in the free world underwent such rapid and major changes and upheavals. It is in this light that we ask the important question that Livy did two millenia ago: "Where are we going ("quo vadis")?".

The Current Correctional Scene

To explain the context of the current era, we should first define community corrections as *those programs focusing on the correction of offenders which attempt to minimize penetration of the offender into the correctional process, in which offenders either spend at least part of their time in the community or have the opportunity for extensive interactions with the community and which involve community resources in the correctional process* (Seiter and Allen, 1985:3).

Serving Sentences

The reader should have begun to sense, from the suggestive list of community corrections programs above, that most offenders serve some or all of their sentences in the community, rather than in the prison. There are many reasons for this, including the exhorbitant costs of prisons, the inhumaneness of most prisons and the untoward consequences that result from long-term imprisonment, and the evidence on effectiveness. In brief, community corrections programs are believed to be more humane, less expensive, and at least as effective as institutional corrections. (We will reserve this topic for later discussion.)

Information on the sentence dispositions of offenders can be seen in Table 1, which deals with adult offenders in prison and the community. As the start of each year from 1981 through 1983, there were almost three times as many offenders on probation than in prisons, and persons under parole supervision were more than half the number in prisons. Only 22 out of 100 offenders were incarcerated; the other 78 were serving their sentences in the community, under one or more components of community corrections. The latter would include, *inter alia:*

1. deferred prosectuion;
2. probation without adjudication;
3. probation;
4. halfway houses;
5. community treatment centers;
6. restitution programs;
7. drug and narcotic abuse treatment programs (such as Methadone Maintenance programs);
8. community service orders;
9. week-end detention;
10. parole; and
11. numerous variations of these basic programs.

Another striking conclusion available from the data in Table 1 is that all correctional components seem to be growing rapidly. Actually, the size of the total community supervision population has grown steadily since 1979, and most of this growth has occurred in the probation population, while the size of the parole population has increased more slowly. Since 1979, the adult probation population has grown by more than 265,000 cases—a 25 percent increase, while the parole population has risen by more than 26,000—a 12 percent figure (U.S. Department of Justice, 1982b).

Table 1
Adult Offenders in Community-Based Corrections and Imprisoned: 1981-1983

Year	On Probation	Imprisoned	On Parole	Total
1981	1,118,097	369,388	220,438	1,707,923
1982	1,225,934	414,362	225,539	1,866,176
1983	1,335,359	431,929*	243,880	2,011,068

*As of July 1, 1983.

The other major incarceration component in America is the jail, sometimes referred to as the "cloacal region" of the criminal justice system, for jails are the neglected component of the system, suffering from a wide range of maladies that include benign neglect, chronic underfunding, personnel shortage and undertraining, rapid population turnover, and classic neglect by most political leaders. The U.S. Department of Justice conducted national jail surveys in 1972, 1978, and 1982; the results can be found in Table 2 (U.S. Department of Justice, 1983a). Jails in 1982 held one inmate for every two in prison, but it should be remembered that, in 1982, 60 per cent of the jail inmates were unconvicted.

Table 2

Jail Populations
1972, 1978, 1982

Year	Population*
1972	141,600
1978	158,000
1982	207,853

*As of February of these years.

Such data serve many uses but, for our purposes, they clearly demonstrate that most offenders are in community-based correctional programs. The goals of each program may vary from component to component and obviously differ across projects (such as halfway houses) within a component. Yet there are five basic goals of community corrections:

1. Provide services for reintegration of offenders;
2. Control risk and lessen future criminal behavior;
3. Develop correctional services within a community;
4. Strengthen the ability of a community to accept responsibility for dealing with community problems and provide or marshall resources to attain this goal; and
5. Control prison populations.

Organizational Structure

With the rapid implementation, expansion, revitalization and acceptance of community corrections in the last two decades, we would suspect a major organization would have provided direction and coordination to forge community corrections into a unified portion of the criminal justice system. Unfortunately, this has not been the case. Instead, numerous local leaders, innovators, organizations, mass media representatives, concerned citizens and even ex-offenders have rather spontaneously created a patchwork pattern of community corrections, sometimes despite determined opposition. Arguments abound on such questions as whether probation should be located in a state executive office or in a county judicial unit, or whether the probation component should be merged into the parole unit. Fortunately, there are sufficient similarities to permit generalizations.

County Probation

Probation is usually perceived to be a county component. It is by far the most widely used form of community supervision and has traditionally been granted by the courts as an alternative disposition to a jail or prison sentence, usually in conjunction with a suspended sentence. The overall probation population includes both misdemeanants and felons, who probably otherwise would be in prison. At year end of 1982, in 22 of the 28 states that separated their probationers into misdemeanants and felons, more than half were convicted felons.

It should be noted that, although the judiciary continue to impose this sanction as a less expensive and less severe alternative sentence to incarceration, most courts have the authority to link a period of probation to a term of incarceration, and have increasingly been doing so. The four major combinations of probation and incarceration include:

1. *split sentence,* where the sentencing court specifies a specific period of incarceration to be followed by a period of probation under supervision (as in the Federal Court system);
2. *modification of sentence,* permitting the original sentencing court to reconsider the offender's prison or jail sentence within a limited time and change the sentence to probation;
3. *shock probation,* a program in which the incarcerated felon is released after a period of confinement (the "shock") and resentenced to probation (available in 14 states); and
4. *intermittent incarceration,* a program in which an offender on probation may spend nights or weekends in jail (U.S. Department of Justice, 1983b).

The combination of probation with incarceration (punishment) is philosophically contradictory and may represent the judiciary's efforts to balance the community corrections requirements with the strident demands for punishment from justice system conservatives (Reckless and Allen, 1979; Vito, 1983).

State Parole

Parole is generally seen as a state program (although some larger counties have parole from jail programs). As the second major form of community supervision, parole always follows release from an institution, usually from a prison. About three out of four inmates exiting from prisons are released onto parole supervision; the other 25 percent are released to the community unconditionally.

Prisoners enter parole status through one of two ways: (1) discretionary release, following a parole board decision and currently available in all but 9 states; or (2) mandatory release, occurring at expiration of maximum sentence (minus any good time or earned time credits subtracted from the maximum term). In the latter, the parole board has not released the offenders. Mandatory releasees also include offenders paroled under determinate sentencing statutes that provide for release to parole at a prescribed or "determined" date. In reality, parole supervision is not much influenced by whether an inmate is paroled by a parole board or by mandatory release.

Currently, there are nine states, generally referred to as the "determinate sentencing" states, whose parole boards no longer have discretionary releasing power. These include California, Colorado, Connecticut, Illinois, Indiana, Maine, Minnesota, New Mexico, and North Carolina. Parole *supervision* was also abolished in Maine (1976) and Connecticut (1981). The question of how well releasees are reintegrated in the absence of parole supervision remains unanswered. In 1982, Connecticut reported an ex-prisoner recidivism rate (reincarcerated for a new offense) of 23 percent, moderately low; the corresponding rate for Maine was 48 percent, the second highest in the nation (American Correctional Association, 1983: xxii).

Private Residential Corrections.

Residential correctional facilities, such as halfway houses, group homes, work-release centers, and community reintegration centers, are predominately seen as in the private sector. This is somewhat misleading, as many state parole supervision agencies have created state-managed residential centers that are comparable to those in the private sector.

Residential correctional programs have a long if not well documented and evaluated history and can be traced back to the dedicated work of Maude Booth, prior to the turn of the century. Their period of greatest growth has been in the last 15 years, and their national impacts on community corrections have been assessed. Based on a review of some 55 evaluations of halfway houses and a survey of over 150 individual programs, Allen *et al* (1978) described the development and operations of halfway houses. Their conclusions were that such facilities provided effective assistance in locating employment and are as effective (and less expensive) as other community release alternatives and prison in preventing criminal behavior.

Funding Issues

Regardless of the organizational location of the community corrections component, funding is an area critical to the effectiveness of a program. All community corrections programs suffer from being funded from a variety of often unreliable sources. For example, private sector corrections programs may depend on contracts with local and state units of government, third-party payments (such as state parole supervision agencies reimbursing a halfway house for services provided parolees by paying a "per diem" fee), fund-raising efforts by program leaders from within the private sector, residents' per diem charges or in-kind work, federal training contracts, or gifts. Such funding is unpredictable and goal attainment in some situations may have been delayed for this basic reason.

Even state agencies are not immune from the fiscal impacts private sector community corrections must face. In California, in part due to the inability of that State's legislature to deal with demands for local tax relief, a citizens' tax revolt ("Proposition 13") led to a Constitutional amendment that rolled property tax rates back to levels prevailing in 1975. In the ensuing fiscal constraints, one in four probation officer positions disappeared. Sentencing judges were generally correct in their assessment of the inability of a markedly reduced probation staff to handle greatly expanded caseloads. Commitments increased to California prisons as a result, and California must now open a 400-bed facility each month just to keep pace with commitments (Bancroft, 1983).

Statewide Systems

Three states have established correctional policies that address many of the financial issues identified above, using State resources to encourage counties to develop more comprehensive, flexible alternatives to commitment to prison, and to bolster community corrections. These leaders are California, Minnesota, and Oregon.

In 1965, California enacted the first identifiable package of community corrections legislation: the California probation subsidy. The assumption was that probation represented a more effective, less costly and safer correctional alternative than incarceration in state prison. To receive probation subsidy money, a county would have to reduce its number of prison commitments from historical commitment rates, improve its local probation services, and provide resources for probationers. While the crime rates did not go down and the prison commitment rates later soared due to inmigration and Proposition 13 effects, a newer County Justice Subvention Program was designed to (1) provide grants to counties to develop and improve local correctional systems, particularly for juveniles and nonserious adult offenders; (2) create a county advisory board charged with the task of developing a comprehensive community corrections program; and (3) reduce commitments to prison. The program has not yet been extensively evaluated and is beset by demands by local law enforcement administrators to use Subvention money to build jails, previously forbidden under the probation subsidy program.

Minnesota's Community Corrections Act (CCA) was created in 1973, building on earlier successes in local probation services. Among its purposes are (1) to transfer to local units of government responsibility for correctional services for non-serious offenders, (2) reduce commitments to juvenile training schools and state prisons, and (3) promote comprehensive correctional planning at the state level. This innovative program represents perhaps the best example of involvement of local communities in corrections, and spells out responsibilities of both counties and state departments of correction. Using a charge-back feature, the Minnesota Department of Correction reduces the subsidy to participating counties for committing offenders to prison who have sentences of less than five years—a strong disincentive to commitment. The per-day and per-term costs of community corrections in Minnesota are far less than those of Minnesota state prisons, indicating that community corrections can develop and maintain effective community corrections (Nelson et al, 1978).

The Oregon counterpart to the Minnesota CCA was enacted in 1977, and provides subsidies to participating counties. The latter must create a community corrections advisory board, develop and submit an approved comprehensive community corrections plan, and develop a network of sentencing alternatives that would provide treatment for all but the truly dangerous offenders. There is also a charge-back feature ("negative subsidy") for commitment of the least dangerous offenders by participating counties ($4000 per each Class C offender committed from a participating county must accompany the commitment papers).

The net impact of efforts to develop a statewide community corrections system, when viewed from the evidence of the California, Minnesota and Oregon experiences, is the realization that, given a mix of incentives, structure, leadership and advice, counties and states can develop meaningful reintegration programs that will reduce commitments and strengthen community corrections.

Effectiveness

The data on community corrections programs and the overall assumptions underlying community corrections in general are mixed. Some have claimed that "nothing works" (Martinson, 1974) or that parole is ineffective and should be abolished (Citizens' Inquiry on Parole and Criminal Justice, 1975; Fogel, 1975). Others want to abolish probation and institute corporal punishment (Newman, 1983), and still others wax enthusiastic over the alleged benefits of the death penalty (van den Haag and Conrad, 1983).

When weighed in entirety, absent the rhetoric and ideology of ascerbic debate, the evidence of effectiveness of community corrections would lead a reasonable person to conclude that community corrections is no less effective as imprisonment, is considerably less expensive, has markedly less criminogenic impact on clients, and is more humane and reintegrative than over-reliance on incarceration in penal institutions or jails (Seiter and Allen, 1976).

Lest one take undue comfort in this evaluative conclusion, there are four warning signals on the horizon, questions for which answers must be eventually sought. These trends can best be stated as tentative assumptions deserving our evaluative attention.

1. There is some evidence that, as community corrections programs and opportunities expand, a "net-widening" effect occurs, drawing into correction programs and control those who would not have been the attention of corrections but for the existence of available programs. Perhaps this is best seen in prosecutorial diversion, which permits prosecutors to divert sometimes unwilling and legally innocent clients into a treatment program in exchange for non-prosecution of an unfounded and unprovable charge. Another possible example is diversion of the status offender from juvenile courts into unwelcomed treatment. Not legally delinquent, the juvenile may be compelled to participate in a coercive program in lieu of the alternative of formal processing and probation or even placement in a training institution. The alternative policy may well be benevolent nonintervention!

2. Funding shifts, retrenchments, reallocations and recessions bode particularly ill for the private sector of community corrections. States should establish priorities and statewide systems that would encourage involvements of the private sector, which has less personnel strictures, attracts more highly motivated innovators, locates funds from private sources, serves to educate the general public, and can provide leadership for particular projects. (These groups may, in only a few decades, provide probation presentence investigations and supervision, build our jails, run our prisons, and reintegrate our offenders!)

3. In tax shortfall situations and inadequate public resource allocations, there is a tendency to underallocate resources to community corrections, particularly probation. Not only does underallocation pose serious threats to prison population size and safety in the community, it also has the potential for initiating a "domino-effect" when offenders are released: prisons are criminogenic institutions.

4. Finally, there is some evidence that elected officials are unwilling to make the necessary hard decisions on community corrections. The easiest escape from conflicting demands is to "fund-out" all resources to meet higher priority needs (police protection, fire, mandated school programs, cost-sharing welfare programs, and so on) and then plead the politician's pledge: "We gave the most we

could to those who vote and need and regret we are unable to honor your request due to fiscal restraints.'' Those seeking a concrete example of the pledge in action are encouraged to tour your local jail.

Community Corrections as a Policy

For the first time since the mid-1970s, the crime rate in the United States (1983) dropped from the year before. This unexpected benefit defied conventional wisdom about crime trends and causes. Yet the one single factor about which criminological wisdom seems safest is that, in the United States, when there is a "baby boom" (sharp rise in the birth rate), crime and delinquency will increase in 16 years and then remain uncomfortably high for at least a decade—longer if selective migration of the disadvantaged were to occur. Our most recently noticed baby-boom was immediately after World War II (1945-54) and our prisons have never been fuller. We have tens of thousands of prison cells under construction in many states; once built, they will probably remain full or at capacity.

In the 1990s, our next baby boom should be upon us, as the children of the World War II population explosion reach the high crime rate ages of 16-29. What will corrections be like in 1995?

If community corrections were not implemented nationwide, or CCAs developed in most states, we will most likely find corrections in the same position as currently, with some untoward discomfort. First, while the current commitment rate to prisons is approximately 154 per 100,000 population, by 1995 there should be 196/100,000 population, or at least 575,000 inmates. A straight-line projection would be 1.2 million people in prison, housed at a cost of $42,000 per inmate, living in prison cells that would cost $112,000 to construct. The per capita criminal justice cost would be $306/year, and the rate of recidivism would be approximately what it is now. In short, we would not have less crime, more safety, less fear, or less recidivism. Prisons temporarily incapacitate, provide specific deterrence for the instant inmate, punish, and create hostility, anger and the yearning for revenge. Prisons do not make society safer, and politicians and academicians who argue to the contrary do a gross disservice to the very citizens they so glibly deceive.

If community corrections follows the reintegration model and is implemented into a coherent integrated and unified system providing the range of services necessary for the gradual integration of offenders into acceptable community lifestyles, we will still have prisons, but they will be treated as a scarce resource; we will know that prisons may temporarily incapacitate, punish and generate further crime. Social scientists have difficulty proving the good that prisons do but have consensus on the harmful effects.

In 1995, there will be a general consensus that community corrections programs are no less effective than prisons, are more humane, less costly, and more desirable. By that date, it is conceivable that we will have recognized the wisdom of developing a community's resources so offenders can resolve their problems in the community and the community will cease denial of its role in giving rise to criminal acts, so easily accomplished when commitment to prison removes the evidence.

By 1995, statewide community corrections planning should be so widespread that states without a CCA will be the exception. What will have caused this shift? There are four major factors that will have coalesced to induce adoption of reintegrative community corrections.

1. The futility of mass incapacitation will be realized, and selective incapacitation of our most dangerous offenders should be the norm.
2. The operating costs of prisons will more than double, as will the costs of constructing prison cells.
3. On-going evaluations of community corrections programs will provide further evidence of cost-effectiveness.
4. The public's demand for accountability in corrections will lead to program evaluation and informed decision-making by correctional administrators and politicians.

Thus we end with a note of optimism. Reintegration as the philosophical basis for a correctional system is less than two decades old. Giant strides have been made in developing community programs, innovative practices, trained and experienced personnel, and knowledge dissemination. Research and evaluation studies are on-going, and policy implications are becoming even more evident. We cannot afford the punitive approach, and have an articulated (if not yet unified or consolidated) series of alternatives from which to choose. We will choose reintegration over the corrupt and ineffective route of imprisonment. Community-based corrections is the next wave in our correctional history.

References

Allen, Harry E. *et al. Halfway Houses* (Washington, D.C.: U.S. Government Printing Office, 1978).

American Correctional Association. *Directory* (College Park, Maryland: ACA, 1983): xxii.

Bancroft, Ann. "San Quentin to Get New Warden, Reform," *San Francisco Chronicle* (November 2, 1983): 6.

Citizens' Inquiry on Parole and Criminal Justice. *Prisons Without Walls* (New York: Praeger, 1975).

Conrad, John P. "We Should Never Have Promised a Hospital," *Federal Probation* 39 (1975): 3-9.

Fogel, David. *We Are the Living Proof: The Justice Model for Corrections* (Cincinnati: Anderson, 1976).

Martinson, Robert. "What Works? — Questions and Answers About Prison Reform," *The Public Interest* (1974): 22-54.

National Advisory Commission on Criminal Justice Standards and Goals, *Corrections* (Washington, D.C.: U.S. Government Printing Office, 1973): 1-2.

Nelson, E. Kim; Ohmart, Howard; and Harlow, Nora. *Promising Strategies in Probation and Parole* (Washington, D.C.: U.S. Government Printing Office, 1976).

Newman, Graeme. *Just and Painful: A Case for the Corporal Punishment of Offenders* (New York: Macmillan, 1983).

President's Commission on Law Enforcement and Administration of Justice. *The Challenge of Crime in a Free Society* (Washington, D.C.: U.S. Government Printing Office, 1967).

Reckless, Walter C. and Allen, Harry E. "Development of a National Crime Policy: The Impact of Politics on Crime in America," in Edward Sagarin, (ed.), *Criminology: New Concerns* (Beverly Hills, CA: Sage, 1979): 129-138.

Seiter, Richard P. and Allen, Harry E. "The Effectiveness of Halfway Houses: A Reappraisal of a Reappraisal," *Chitty's Law Journal* (1976): 196-200.

_____, *Community-Based Corrections* (New York: Holt, 1985).

United States Department of Justice, Bureau of Justice Statistics. *Jail Inmates: 1982* (Washington, D.C.: Department of Justice, 1983a).

_____, *Probation and Parole, 1982* (Washington, D.C.: Department of Justice, 1983b).

van den Haag, Ernest and Conrad, John P. *The Death Penalty in America: A Debate* (New York: Plenum, 1983).

Vito, Gennaro I. "The Politics of Crime Control: Implications of Reagan Administration Pronouncements on Crime," *Journal of Contemporary Criminal Justice* 2 (1983): 1-7.